DEFINING AMERICAN PSYCHOLOGY

Defining American Psychology

The Correspondence between Adolf Meyer and Edward Bradford Titchener

edited by Ruth Leys and Rand B. Evans

THE JOHNS HOPKINS UNIVERSITY PRESS BALTIMORE AND LONDON

Printed in the United States of America

The Johns Hopkins University Press
701 West 40th Street
Baltimore, Maryland 21211
The Johns Hopkins Press Ltd., London

The paper used in this publication meets the minimum requirements of American National Standard for Information Sciences—Permanence of Paper for Printed Library Materials, ANSI Z39.48-1984.

Library of Congress Catalog Card Number 89-33535
ISBN 0-8018-3865-7

Library of Congress Cataloging in Publication data will be found on the last printed page of this book.

The photograph of Adolf Meyer on page ii is from the Adolf Meyer Papers, The Alan Mason Chesney Medical Archives, The Johns Hopkins Medical Institutions. The photograph of Edward Bradford Titchener on page iii is from the private collection of Rand B. Evans.

Contents

Preface

The correspondence between Adolf Meyer (1866–1950) and Edward Bradford Titchener (1867–1927) constitutes one of the most important, perhaps the most important, hitherto unpublished intellectual exchanges in the history of American psychology. Focusing as it does almost exclusively on basic epistemological and methodological problems, the correspondence throws fascinating light on the formative years of psychology as a discipline and on its complex ties to psychiatry, medicine, and allied fields. No other body of writings so clearly epitomizes the conflicts and tensions inherent in American psychological thought at the beginning of this century.

This edition of the correspondence between Meyer and Titchener concludes an undertaking begun more than twenty years ago. In 1969, in connection with a projected biography of Titchener, Rand Evans visited the Cornell University Archives in the Olin Library, Cornell University, where Titchener's papers had recently been opened for research. The collection had been donated to Cornell by Titchener's children and had been supplemented by further correspondence from university officials and from Titchener's former students. At the time of Evans's first visit, the papers had been organized but not completely catalogued. In surveying the collection, Evans came across Meyer's 1918 letters to Titchener. These letters stood out not only numerically but because of their intense concentration on systematic issues. A reference in one of them indicated the existence of an earlier, equally significant series of letters from Meyer written in 1909, only three of which were found in the Titchener Papers. Microfilm copies were made of all Meyer's letters in the Titchener Papers. Unfortunately, Titchener did not make carbon copies of his own letters until the 1920s, so at the time of Evans's visit to Cornell, Titchener's side of the exchange with Meyer remained unknown.

In 1971, Evans reviewed the Adolf Meyer Papers in the Welch Medical Library at the Johns Hopkins University. Meyer's papers had been housed in the Welch Library since 1963 but had not been intensively consulted, except by Eunice Winters, Meyer's editor and biographer. The collection was uncatalogued and in disarray. However, by sheer luck Titchener's 1909 and 1918 letters to Meyer and carbons of Meyer's 1909 and 1918 letters to Titchener (plus one original) were found grouped together in several file folders and were Xeroxed. The Adolf Meyer Papers were closed in 1973 when the collection was placed in storage elsewhere for lack of space in the Welch Library. Unfortunately, at about that time an undetermined number of letters and documents was mislayed or destroyed, including apparently most of Titchener's letters and many of Meyer's carbons.

In 1975, Ruth Leys was appointed by the Johns Hopkins University to sort, organize, and index Meyer's papers. At this time, Eunice Winters restored to the collection numerous letters and documents that she had borrowed. Titchener's letters to Meyer were not recovered, but Evans made available copies of his Xeroxes to complete the collection. In 1980, the Adolf Meyer Papers, now catalogued and organized, were deposited in the Alan M. Chesney Medical Archives of the Johns Hopkins Medical Institutions for use by scholars. Subsequently, in 1983, a box containing thirteen originals of Titchener's letters to Meyer, four drafts of Meyer's letters in his own hand, and sixteen carbon copies of Meyer's letters to Titchener was found in the historical collection of the Institute of the History of Medicine at Johns Hopkins by the librarian of the collection; the box also contained typed copies (of unknown origin) of most of the remaining exchanges between the two men. These materials were added to the Adolf Meyer Papers.

In the process of organizing Meyer's papers and preparing articles and a projected book on Meyer, Leys was also impressed with the interest and importance of the Meyer-Titchener correspondence. In 1984, Leys and Evans decided to collaborate on an edition of the exchange.

The present edition is based entirely on Titchener's and Meyer's original letters where these exist or on Xerox copies of the originals made by Evans in 1971 before they disappeared. Of a total of twenty-five Meyer letters, nineteen are in the Titchener Papers in the Cornell University Archives. Five (5M, 7M, 8M, 12M, and 17M) now exist only in Xeroxes of carbons in the Meyer Papers and in typed copies. In addition, internal evidence in 47M, Meyer's letter of December 22, 1918, indicates that 46M (November 12, 1918) was never sent. It now exists only in the Xerox copy made by Evans in 1971 from the original typescript in the Meyer Papers, now presumed lost, and in a carbon copy. Since it is an important letter in which Meyer gives a final summary of his position in response to Titchener's last restatement of his own credo, it has been reproduced here.

All twenty-two of Titchener's letters to Meyer are presently in the Adolf Meyer Papers in the Alan Mason Chesney Medical Archives. As indicated above, thirteen originals have survived. Nine letters—2T, 4T, 6T, 9T, 10T, 11T, 13T, 16T, and 18T—exist only in Xerox copies made by Evans in 1971 from originals now presumed lost, copies that have accordingly been used for this edition, and in typed copies.

Meyer and Titchener also briefly exchanged letters in 1905 and again in 1921–22. Their correspondence is located in the Titchener and Meyer Papers at Cornell University and Johns Hopkins, respectively. These letters are obviously not part of the primary exchanges of 1909 and 1918. They are not significant for the discussion and are not included in this edition.

A tabulation of the letters included in this edition is provided in the Appendix.

Fortunately, almost all the letters on both sides of the correspondence were typed. Neither Titchener nor Meyer had particularly readable handwriting. Only a few postcards and Meyer's last note to Titchener are handwritten. Both Meyer and Titchener occasionally made minor handwritten corrections and emendations in their letters, and these have been indicated in the text.

To facilitate a reading of this challenging and rewarding correspondence, we have prepared essays designed to throw light on the careers of the two men and on the conceptual issues at stake in their exchange. The interpretations presented in these essays reflect our independent judgments of the meaning and significance of the debate; thus we have not felt it necessary or appropriate to arrive at a consensus on points where we disagree.

Acknowledgments

We are indebted to the following friends and colleagues for variously providing useful comments on our essays, helping us locate items, assisting in the conduct of library research, and providing us with valuable editorial assistance: Jonathan Crewe, Donald Fleming, Michael Fried, Alfred Fuchs, Sander L. Gilman, Werner Hamacher, Gary Hatfield, Mary Henle, Herbert Kessler, Nancy McCall, Kevin Pask, Joan Scott, Michael Sokal, Nancy Stepan, and Katherine Verdery.

We also wish to thank the Department of Manuscripts and University Archives, Cornell University Libraries and the Alan M. Chesney Medical Archives of the Johns Hopkins Medical Institutions for permission to reproduce the Titchener and Meyer letters in their collections.

The initial organization and annotation of the correspondence was made possible by National Science Foundation Grant SES-8319882 to Rand Evans.

Note on the Text

In the present edition, textual matters have been kept to a minimum. Our editorial policy has been to identify proper names, books, articles, and events but to refrain from clarifying points of interpretation. The reader will find detailed discussions of the issues covered in the correspondence in our introductory essays.

In general, we have tampered very little with the correspondence. All of Titchener's letters were sent from Ithaca, New York. Meyer's 1909 letters were sent from the Pathological Institute, Ward's Island, New York (although Meyer was appointed professor of psychiatry at Johns Hopkins University in 1908, he did not move to Baltimore until 1910); his 1918 letters were sent from Baltimore, Maryland. We have not felt it necessary to indicate the address on each letter. Dates have been standardized, but the various salutations and valedictions used by the authors in the course of their correspondence have been preserved as an index of the fluctuating relations between the two men. Minor punctuation errors such as the occasional failure to close a bracket or a quotation mark have been silently corrected; none was deemed to be of psychological importance or interest. The use of quotation marks has been standardized according to American practice, but slight inconsistencies and variations in punctuation have been retained for flavor, as have abbreviations. Most important, we have deliberately preserved Titchener's English spelling, about which he had strong feelings. Thus, in a letter to McKeen Cattell, Titchener vigorously protested Cattell's editorial corrections of Titchener's manuscript. Insisting on the right to retain his English spelling and punctuation, he objected: "How can you expect people to write decently when you put their treasures through a mangle and turn them out all machine-made products?"[1] The placement of diagrams and postscripts has also been indicated as faithfully as possible. In one letter, the name of a patient's relative has been abbreviated in the interest of confidentiality.

We have used a system of numbering the letters devised by William McGuire for his edition of *The Freud/Jung Letters: The Correspondence Between Sigmund Freud and C. G. Jung* (Princeton, N.J.: Princeton University Press, 1974). As explained in the preface, the total number of items in the exchange is forty-seven: twenty-five from Meyer, twenty-two from Titchener.

1. Titchener to Cattell, 29 November, 1904, The J. McKeen Cattell Papers, Library of Congress.

DEFINING AMERICAN PSYCHOLOGY

The Scientific and Psychological Positions of E. B. Titchener

Rand B. Evans

Edward Bradford Titchener (1867–1927) is known to historians of the behavioral and social sciences more as an historical character than for his ideas.[1] Stories of his lecturing to his classes in Oxford academic robes, his cheerful dogmatism, his penchant for cigars, his colorful formality, his exclusion of women from his Experimentalists meetings, his paternalistic treatment of students (even of those long since graduated), his tendency to take offense, his proclamation of the "uselessness" of his psychology—these habits and putative traits have become part of the standard lore on Titchener.[2] Exaggeration and oversimplification of the man and his ideas in both oral tradition and published histories have left us with little more than a caricature of someone who was, in fact, highly complex.[3] The publication of the correspondence between Titchener and Adolf Meyer gives the scholar an opportunity to examine in detail Titchener's thought on psychology and science and to see him in his role of defender of psychology as a fundamental science. The letters also give us a chance to look at the subtlety of his ideas and the difficulties of interpreting them.

The two sets of correspondence of 1909 and 1918 provide us with a view of Titchener and Adolf Meyer at different points in their careers and in the development of psychology as an academic and professional discipline. When the correspondence began, Titchener was at the peak of his career. Although William James was still alive in 1909, he had long since turned his back on the rigors of laboratory psychology for the comfort of the method of philosophical reflection. It was Titchener and his group at Cornell who epitomized experimental introspective psychology. Because of its prominence and identifiability, it is easy to forget that Titchener's structuralist school never dominated American psychology, at least in terms of numbers. It was the American functionalists, whether at Chicago or at Columbia or unaligned, and represented in this correspondence by Adolf Meyer, who were numerically in the majority. Yet Titchener and his followers eclipsed most of the other experimental psychologists of their time, many of whom made significant contributions but who had no particular system or organized following by which they could be easily classified and remembered. Some recent writers, in attempting to renovate the historical record, have gone to the opposite extreme, underestimating Titchener's importance.[4] Titchener's contribution and that of his followers to the psychology of their day were far greater than their numbers would suggest.

Titchener fully understood the advantage held by an organized minority in the midst of an unorganized majority. At the time of Titchener's death, E. G. Boring called Titchener a "cardinal point" in the systematic psychology of his day. "The clear cut opposition between behaviorism and its allies, on the one hand, and something else, on the other, remains clear only when the opposition is between behaviorism and Titchener, mental tests and Titchener, or applied psychology and Titchener."[5] Within five years of Titchener's death, however, Edna Heidbreder called his system a "gallant and enlightening failure."[6] Titchener might have agreed with her assessment since he held that theories and systems are inevitably failures because they must continually change and grow or become overtaken by new data and the theories and systems which are based on them.

If this is true, one might ask why we should be concerned about Titchener and his system, aside from historical curiosity. In fact, the details of Titchener's system *are* of less significance to us today than the conceptual principles on which they were based. For example, Titchener's views on the nature of observation are more important than the specifics of how sensations combine into perceptions. It is in Titchener's efforts to establish psychology as a scientific discipline and to make the laboratory the center of the psychological enterprise that we find most of his direct and lasting influence on psychology. He was not alone in these efforts, of course, and his positions were often extreme. However, of all the figures in the early days of the "new psychology" in America, Titchener stands out in his steadfast devotion to these goals and to their acceptance in the American psychological scene.

Titchener's systematic notions as well as his positions on psychology as a laboratory science were based on an elaborate and interrelated set of principles, and nowhere can one find a better exposition of them than in his correspondence with Adolf Meyer. Much of the value of the Titchener-Meyer letters is that they deal with fundamental questions including not only the status of systematic psychology but also the definition of psychology and its place in the world of science and life. It is these larger and more fundamental issues that should concern us since they cut to the heart of the psychological enterprise, past, present, and future.

The purpose of this essay is to introduce Titchener to the reader and to discuss in capsule form some of the fundamental principles on which his thought, as expressed in this correspondence, is based. Meyer's life and a detailed discussion of the issues in the correspondence will be included in Ruth Leys's essays which follow.

Titchener's Life and Career

In 1909, when Titchener entered into this correspondence, he was 42 years old and had been in the United States for 17 years. He was born in 1867 in Chichester, an old market town in Sussex, England. He came from a well-to-do family of the merchant and professional class. His grandfather, Edward, was a barrister in Chichester who lived in a magnificent late Renaissance house designed, it was said, by Christopher Wren. However, Titchener's father, John, was not successful and was able to support his family only marginally, moving from job to job. He died when Titchener was 13. Years before that, however, Titchener had been sent to live with his grandfather. There he learned the values and ways of the English upper middle class and what it meant to be an "English gentleman." He would never lose his identification as an English gentleman and the social code that went with it. The death of his grandfather and other economic misfortunes decimated the family fortune and put Titchener largely on his own for the funding of his education.

Titchener's earliest education was at the hands of a tutor. He then attended the Prebendal School in Chichester, the local Anglican cathedral school, and later, because of his abilities, he was sent on scholarship to Malvern College, a boys' public school. At Malvern, Titchener enrolled in the classic curriculum. Although he was initially withdrawn and bookish, Titchener grew in confidence and became more socially confident. Academically, he was perhaps the best student in the school during his time there, winning continuing scholarships that funded his stay and which finally gained him a scholarship to Brasenose College, Oxford.

Titchener was one of the top students at Brasenose and obtained a coveted "double first" on his examinations. He remained in the classic curriculum and was tutored by Walter Pater, one of the most polished prose writers of the nineteenth century. Titchener's education was steeped in the classics. In philosophy, he was particularly influenced by the British empiricists, especially David Hume.

Rather late in his career at Oxford, Titchener discovered the new biology of Charles Darwin and Thomas Huxley. He became a follower of Huxley and of the philosophical wing of the Darwinian movement led by Herbert Spencer. At one time, he considered himself a disciple of Spencer, and it seems likely that it was as a result of reading Spencer that Titchener became interested in psychology. Initially, Titchener was drawn to a comparative animal psychology, one that emphasized a comparison of mental attributes. In the 1880s, comparative psychology was still quite underdeveloped, and Titchener's main contact with it was through George John Romanes, whose work was primarily anecdotal. Even in those early days, Titchener was drawn to systemization. He was put off by the unsystematic nature of Romanes and the other comparative psychologists of his time and swung over to the other end of the spectrum, to a strictly human psychology and the systematic approach of Wilhelm Wundt. Since he had very little scientific training, Titchener was urged not to go to Wundt's laboratory in Leipzig directly after graduation from Oxford. Instead, he remained an extra year at Oxford, working in the physiological laboratory of John Scott Burdon-Sanderson. For Titchener, the year with Burdon-Sanderson was an intensive introduction to the physiological substrate and to the fine points of the experimental method. In 1890, after his year of experimental physiology, Titchener went to Leipzig to study with Wundt.

In the early 1890s, when Titchener was at Leipzig, Wundt was at the height of his power and influence. In those days, Wundt's laboratory at Leipzig was *the* place to be for psychologists interested in the new experimental psychology. With Titchener's interests in systematic psychology, he could not have picked a better time to work with Wundt, whose lectures tended to anticipate the content of his books considerably and who was in the midst of formulating his revision of the third edition of his *Grundzüge der physiologischen Psychologie*

(Principles of Physiological Psychology). In the resulting fourth edition, Wundt departed from the approach in his earlier editions in which he catalogued the known facts of psychology and moved toward a more systematic structure on which such facts could be summarized. At Leipzig, Titchener took all of Wundt's courses and also those by Oswald Külpe, Wundt's *Dozent*. He also took courses in physiology and microscopy in other institutes at Leipzig. Titchener seems to have been personally close to Wundt and his family during his two years at Leipzig. He went with them to their Hartz Mountain retreat during at least one long Christmas holiday and was a frequent guest in their home. There were strains in the relationship, however, although perhaps only at the professional level. Titchener found Wundt too inflexible and uncompromising. He even considered leaving him to work with a "lesser figure" like Hermann Ebbinghaus, but nothing came of it.

One source of Titchener's dissatisfaction with Wundt appears to have had its basis in Titchener's positivistic leanings and Wundt's rejection of positivistic notions. Although it is an oversimplification to call Titchener simply a follower of Mach, there were aspects of Mach's thought which would influence Titchener for the remainder of his career. I will discuss in more detail the influence of Mach's ideas later in this essay.

After gaining his doctorate from Wundt in 1892, Titchener hoped to return to England, preferably to Oxford, for a life of research and teaching. Unfortunately, England, and particularly Oxford, were not ready for experimental psychology. There was also the possibility of a position at Francis Galton's Kensington Laboratory in London. From his student days at Oxford, Titchener had known Francis Galton quite well and had maintained a correspondence with him, even to the point of working on a system of fingerprint analyses for him. However, this possibility disappeared when Galton's laboratory closed before Titchener's graduation.

The year before Titchener graduated from Leipzig, his classmate Frank Angell, had gone to Cornell and taken up a position in psychology there. Before the year was out, however, Angell accepted a position at the new Stanford University in California for the fall of 1892 and suggested Titchener as his replacement at Cornell. The offer was made, and Titchener, who had no other options, accepted. He came to Cornell in 1892, planning to stay only a couple of years until something opened up in England. Instead, he continued there for the remaining 35 years of his life. Because of these events, Titchener never achieved his two youthful goals: to become an Oxford don and to be a Fellow of the Royal Society.

At Cornell, as was typical at the time, Titchener taught in the psychology curriculum of the Department of Philosophy in the Sage School of Philosophy. In 1895, only three years after joining the faculty, Titchener was granted tenure and became head of the new Department of Psychology. In 1895, Titchener joined E. C. Sanford and G. Stanley Hall as coeditor of the *American Journal of Psychology*. Soon, Titchener controlled a full third of the pages of the *Journal* and was able to provide a ready outlet for the publications of his students and others with similar experimental and systematic leanings. In his articles and textbooks issued in the 1890s, Titchener consistently upheld the role of experimental introspective psychology as the way of the future in opposition to the then largely nonexperimental psychologies of function exemplified by George Trumbull Ladd, John Dewey, and William James.

Titchener found American psychology to be a morass of conflicting points of view, dominated by a "watered-down Cartesianism." It seemed to him muddle at its worst. To the degree to which there was a central core to American psychology at all, it was found in William James's recently published *Principles of Psychology* (1890). James's *Principles* represented a great step forward for American psychology since it legitimated the secular study of mental life. Prior to James's book, most psychologies in America were written by ministers or by those with a religious bent. Even George Trumbull Ladd, in his *Elements of Physiological Psychology* (1887) saw the need to identify mind finally with a "real unit-being," a soul.[7] James, by contrast, had produced a thoroughly naturalistic approach to mind. Although not rejecting the concept of soul, he ruled it out as a subject matter for an empirical psychology. While representing a significant advance, James's psychology, in Titchener's view, was hardly systematic by comparison with European writers such as Wilhelm Wundt and Franz Brentano. James's psychology was also a psychology of mental function, the preexperimental "descriptive" psychology Titchener rejected as "muddle." Titchener sought to introduce Americans to a thoroughgoing structural psychology, using experimental, introspective methods to study the normal, adult, human mind.[8]

To do this, Titchener felt the need to expose Americans to the new experimental psychology of Germany. In the 1890s there was very little of the German literature available in English translation, so

Titchener published English translations of Wundt's *Lectures on Human and Animal Psychology* and Külpe's *Outline of Psychology* for use by students in undergraduate psychology courses. Titchener attempted in vain to translate Wundt's more substantial *Grundzüge der physiologischen Psychologie.* Unfortunately, as fast as Titchener managed a translation of one edition, Wundt produced a new one. In 1896, Titchener published his own version of the new psychology in his *An Outline of Psychology.* After three revisions, the book was completely rewritten and published in part in 1909 and in its entirety in 1910 as *A Textbook of Psychology.*

By the turn of the century, Titchener had become a major figure in American psychology. His *An Outline of Psychology* was a standard textbook in the introductory courses around the country. Between 1901 and 1905, he published his *Experimental Psychology* in four volumes. Commonly known simply as "Titchener's Manuals," this set of books perhaps did more to promote careful laboratory instruction in psychology programs than any other single publication. Two of the four volumes in the set, the larger two, were written for the use of instructors who did not themselves have training in laboratory work. Generations of psychologists cut their experimental teeth on these books. Even in departments where the content of Titchener's psychology was rejected, his *Experimental Psychology* was the standard text in the experimental course.

In 1904, Titchener founded the Experimentalists, an informal group of psychologists, primarily drawn from the eastern United States, which met annually to discuss developments in experimental psychology. While individual members might have rankled at times at Titchener's domination of the group, most of the members, particularly those of the generation younger than Titchener, accepted him as a given and even appreciated his kindly autocracy.[9]

The year 1909, when his correspondence with Meyer began, was a banner year for Titchener. His *A Textbook of Psychology* was completed, and the first half was ready to appear. The entire volume appeared the following year. He had recently released two books that were based on successful lecture tours: *The Elementary Psychology of the Thought Processes* and *Feeling and Attention.* He was the heir apparent to the presidency of the International Congress of Psychology that was being planned to meet in America in 1913,[10] and he was the primary experimental psychologist invited to participate in the Vicennial Lectures at Clark University. It was at this conference that Sigmund Freud and Carl Jung were introduced to the American audience and at which Titchener was given the task of representing the interests of experimental psychology. In addition, Titchener's attendance at the conference had another purpose: he was being considered for the headship of the Department of Psychology at Clark University, a position that he would be offered but which he would decline.[11] It was a time in Titchener's life when all the possibilities lay open before him.

During the next decade, Titchener continued to lead the introspectionistic experimental psychologists. He was offered but refused headships in psychology at Harvard and for a second time at Clark. During the period 1909 through 1918, he produced perhaps his best doctoral students, certainly some of his most famous, including Edwin G. Boring, John Paul Nafe, and Karl M. Dallenbach. His writing, although not as prolific as during the first decade of the century, included a briefer introductory textbook, *A Beginner's Psychology*, published in 1915. The "large system" he had talked about for several years was still not begun. Titchener began writing chapters for the prolegomena to that large system during the time of his 1918 correspondence with Meyer, however, and one can see similarities between Titchener's arguments in the correspondence and those in the prolegomena.

The structure of Titchener's systematic psychology changed during the decade between 1909 and 1918. He began to move away from a strict adherence to elements and attributes and more toward a multidimensional approach. It would be the twenties before that approach was well developed, and except for student theses and a couple of notes published by Titchener, the new thrust of his psychology went unreported.[12]

After the First World War and for the remaining years of his career, Titchener seemed to lose his commanding position at the focus of the American psychological scene. The number of his publications dropped off significantly primarily because of the time required to be sole editor of the *American Journal of Psychology*. He was still acknowledged and recognized as the leader of structuralism, but by the time of his death in 1927, his system was treated more as a landmark for systematic comparison than as a source of current issues. After Titchener's death, structuralism faded from the scene.

This is not to say that Titchener's influence on psychology died with him. This issue will be discussed at the end of this essay.

Titchener and Positivism

Part of the success of Titchener's psychology was in the promotion of positive science in American psychology. His positive science was influenced by Ernst Mach and Richard Avenarius but must not be considered identical to either. It was at Leipzig that Titchener was introduced to the ideas of the German physicist Ernst Mach and philosopher of science Richard Avenarius. Several recent writers, including this author, have emphasized the influence of Ernst Mach's positivism on Titchener.[13] Titchener's notions of positive science did not originate with Mach, however, nor with Auguste Comte. Frank Angell tell us that Titchener was thought of at Leipzig as being allied with the English associationists.[14] Titchener described his own position in his *Outline of Psychology* (1896) as "that of the traditional English psychology."[15] Much of Titchener's "positivism" is easily identifiable with the thought of Francis Bacon and particularly with that of David Hume. There also appear to be significant influences on Titchener's ideas from the positivistic aspects in the thought of James Mill, John Stuart Mill, and Herbert Spencer. Mach and Avenarius, after all, did not invent positivism nor did Auguste Comte, who named it. In one form or the other, positivism had been around since the early days of the Renaissance and is evident in most thoroughgoing empiricisms. Mach, himself did not use the term to represent his own position.[16] John Stuart Mill, Herbert Spencer, and Thomas Huxley specifically rejected identification of their views as positivistic,[17] objecting to Comte's positivism.[18]

This is not to deny, however, that Avenarius and particularly Mach influenced Titchener's thought and certainly his vocabulary. My point is that Titchener was a thoroughgoing empiricist in the tradition of Hume long before he was introduced to the thought of Avenarius or Mach. He was prepared for German positivism by his Humean background, which is at the root of much of the positivism of Comte and Mach as well. I would contend that Mach acted to incite a crystallization of Titchener's own views rather than giving him views to mimic.

I am making this digression because present-day writers have done with Titchener much as those commentators of the last century did with Mill, Spencer, and Huxley. The fact that Titchener shared some of the views of Mach and Avenarius does not mean that he carried all the baggage that goes with the term "Machian positivist." In the same way, just because Titchener made use of some of the concepts of British empiricists, particularly David Hume, does not mean that he accepted the range of their ideas. Titchener was seeking his own way and rejected far more of the ideas of the "English school" and of Mach and Avenarius than he accepted. Such labels are a convenient shorthand and have short-term heuristic value, but in the long run, particularly for complex thinkers such as Titchener, such labels are counterproductive. Titchener served no master but himself, and he constructed his scientific and psychological position by selecting ideas that fit his own scheme of thought when he encountered them from a wide range of writers. Mach and Avenarius were two such sources of many.

Titchener encountered Mach's thought through the *The Analysis of Sensations* which made its first appearance in 1885 but which Titchener probably did not come upon until 1891. It was probably at the *Stammtisch*, the reserved mealtime table around which Titchener, Oswald Külpe, and other graduate students and *Dozents* from the Psychological and Physiological Institutes at the University of Leipzig met to discuss issues that would have been heresy in the laboratory, that Mach's notions came up for discussion. Richard Avenarius's *Kritik der reinen Erfahrung* which appeared in two volumes, one in 1888 and one in 1890, would have been quite new then and may have been the pathway to Mach, since he and Mach were talking about similar things. It was from Avenarius that Titchener got many of his notions of experience as being logically dependent on versus independent of the organism. In general, however, Titchener seems to have followed Mach more than Avenarius.

It is difficult to know the immediate influences of Avenarius and Mach on Titchener. A congenial idea, once encountered, would often gestate in Titchener for years before reaching expression in his lectures or writings. I would argue that Mach's positivistic notions most influenced Titchener during the first decade of the twentieth century, peaking with the publication of Titchener's *A Textbook of Psychology* and with the first exchange of letters with Adolf Meyer. By the time of the second exchange a decade later, Titchener appears to have believed that he had transcended much of positivism. He even attacked Meyer because of *his* positivistic positions, although the aspects of positivism Titchener rejected in Meyer were the very aspects he had rejected in Mach and Avenarius, particularly those of a teleological nature.

It is relatively safe to conclude, however, that one early influence of Mach on Titchener had to do with the definition of elements and attributes. Külpe and Titchener stood with Mach in opposition to Wundt in saying that time (duration) and space (extent) were directly observable aspects of sensations and were not, as Wundt believed, derived from inferences of qualities or intensities. It is a fundamental precept of positivism that the data of experience speak for themselves and that inferences are of a lesser significance. This apparently small divergence had great systematic significance. For Wundt to bring space and time into his system, it was necessary to call on accessory concepts such as unconscious inference and the doctrine of creative synthesis. Bringing space and time into their psychologies as directly observable attributes of sensation, just as with qualities and intensities, allowed Külpe and Titchener to build their systems on direct observables rather than on inferences. Although Külpe eventually dropped his positivistic approach, his *Grundriss der Psychologie* (1893) is the epitome of a positivistic approach to introspective psychology.[19] Titchener felt that he[20] had played a significant part in the conceptualization of that book through his discussions with Külpe at Leipzig while the book was being blocked out. Külpe's *Grundriss* was the first of the "German classics" Titchener translated into English for the use of his students even before producing his own *An Outline of Psychology*, which was based on a similar plan. Titchener, like Külpe, moved to reduce all of psychological data to direct sense-experience and made use not only of Wundt's attributes of quality and intensity and Külpe's duration and extent but also added clearness or attensity to his list of attributes for sensations. This allowed Titchener to disregard Wundt's doctrine of apperception with its volitional and functional overtones. In carrying all this out, Titchener went beyond Mach and stripped his version of Wundtian psychology of its active and functional aspects, making his system much more passive and Humean than the voluntarism of Wundt or the teleological tendencies of Mach would have allowed.

Another significant influence of Mach on Titchener was a relativistic view of scientific description. Külpe had used "point of view" as early as 1893, but Titchener employed it only much later in his *A Textbook of Psychology* (1909, 1910). Titchener's use of point of view and the relativistic view it creates are highly significant not only in his formulation of psychology but also in his view of the relationship of the sciences. Titchener's position is described in some detail later in this essay.

Beyond the topics of scientific observation and description, however, there is little that Titchener accepted from Mach. He particularly rejected the utilitarian and teleological aspects of Mach's economy of thought, for instance, just as he rejected the utilitarian and inferential notions of the British associationists.

During the last decade of his life, which includes the second exchange of letters with Meyer, Titchener seems to have made a significant shift in his thought. He appears to have deserted the classic positivistic and sensationalistic notion that the facts of experience are "nakedly found" in the sense-data. In his letter to Meyer of May 25, 1918 (36T), Titchener identifies Meyer with classical positivism and himself with a position far more Baconian than Machian, in which relativism seems exchanged for truth that is found after excluding biasing *idola*:

> Doesn't our great difference amount to this:—
>
> That you regard things, situations, objects, as literally "given," and therefore "found" by the investigating mind, just as they are, just as they lie: so that the mind aforesaid may bring to bear upon them whatever methods of research it regards as profitable for theory or practice; whereas I (so to say) run the "objects" and the "investigating mind" together, in such wise that for me nothing is literally given and nothing therefore is nakedly found; but in every case the *object* dealt with is a function of the *method* which deals with it? . . .
>
> So your first question is: Here are such-and-such data; how can I best treat them? And my first question is: Here are such-and-such data; how must they already have been treated to appear such-and such?
>
> Where you, for instance, find naked facts, waiting to be treated, I may find (as has happened in our correspondence) very-much-worked-over affairs bearing all the ear-marks of common-sense interpretation upon them,—nothing naked at all, but something very definitely clothed. (36T)

Titchener's concept of point of view has taken him beyond the positivism of Mach's *Analysis of Sensations* but not beyond relativism. A "fact" of experience is no longer a "given" but is something embedded in the point of view in which it has been viewed. Careful identification of and consistency in the observational point of view are necessary to identify the matrix in which the fact is embedded. Relativism has not been discarded by Titchener, however. For him, the fact of experience is not absolute; it exists only in terms of that matrix. Sensation, in Titchener's later view, has reality only in the context of the introspective psychological point of view. It is "true" for this point of view only.

Titchener began to move away from the use of elements and attributes in his system and toward dimensions of experience in a more phenomenological orientation. Long after this correspondence was completed, Titchener seemed to be moving even farther into a qualitative, descriptive type of psychology, closer in some ways to the views of Carl Stumpf and David Katz than to those of Wundt. These developments did not receive public exposition since Titchener never completed his large system, which is apparently where he was to spring his new system on the psychological public.[20]

In 1929, two years after his death, the chapters he had completed were gathered together by H. P. Weld and published as *Systematic Psychology: Prolegomena*.[21] Two chapters had previously appeared as articles in the *American Journal of Psychology*. As the term "prolegomena" suggests, the book was not the system itself but only a conceptual introduction to it. Aside from it as well as the initial chapters of his introductory textbook, *A Textbook of Psychology*, a few journal articles, and to a much lesser degree, the initial chapters of his *A Beginner's Psychology*, there is surprisingly little in print on Titchener's conception of psychology. The correspondence between Titchener and Meyer is the most complete exposition of Titchener's views on psychology as science and on the definition of psychology. To foster a better understanding of his positions as expressed there, the following discussion is offered.

Titchener's Conceptual Bases

Point of View

If there is a single term that epitomizes Titchener's approach as expressed in this correspondence, not only to psychology but to science and knowledge in general, it is point of view. Point of view is the particular observational or attitudinal perspective an individual takes concerning the world of existence. Under the influence of Ernst Mach, Titchener approached knowledge in a relativistic way.[22] Extending Mach's notion, Titchener believed that there is only one existential universe but that it may be observed in a multitude of ways, depending on the point of view taken by the observer. No one of these points of view is necessarily truer than another. For correct understanding of the existential universe, Titchener believed it was essential for the observer to specify the particular point of view being taken and to follow that point of view consistently. Titchener believed that the subject matter of a discipline is produced by means of observations made through a particular point of view. To mix the point of view within a given observation would produce subject matters made up of incompatible or at best inconsistent contents. The result of such an uncritical mix he called "muddle," which he believed to be perhaps the greatest threat of all to systematic understanding.

One aspect of this relativistic view is Titchener's critical view of science. According to Titchener, there are three primary, alternative points of view within the the "world of experience": common sense, science, and technology. The world of experience deals with events that can be experienced, as contrasted with the "world of faith," which deals with the hopes and beliefs beyond experience.

Titchener represented science as neither the first nor the most pervasive point of view held by mankind. There is first the primitive point of view, which Titchener preferred to call "common sense." This is the view that has been held by most humans throughout history just as it is today. It is practical and has survival value. The attitude taken by this point of view is personal and interested. The object of common sense, then, is value, the good or evil that derives from objects, events, and beliefs as they affect the individual or the group with which the individual identifies. The goal of the commonsense individual is utilization, to derive values for one's own benefit. Everyone holds to this commonsense point of view most of the time, and all but a few hold to it exclusively. It is the "natural" point of view with which we all live and which has reference not only to the world of experience but also to the world of faith.

According to Titchener, the scientific point of view is almost the mirror image of that of common sense. He held that science is as artificial a point of view as common sense is a natural one. Science has facts as its object and is founded only in the world of experience. For Titchener, a fact is what something *is*, not what it *is for*. Scientific description for psychology involves an accurate representation of some experience or process, the "is." Common sense involves the "is for," the value of the object or process. To illustrate: if a group of people is shown a common stapler and asked "What is it?" the most common response will be "a stapler." If asked "What is a stapler?" the response will usually be "It is a machine that attaches papers together." Titchener held that such a response was typical of the common sense point of view since it dealt with value, what the object is for rather than facts, what it is. Scientific description includes an analysis of the materials that make up the stapler and the configuration of such materials. If properly done, these facts should be sufficient for someone to fabricate a stapler without knowing what it is used for. Physically, the stapler is the same for both common sense and scientific observers, but the nature of the descriptions made by these observers is very different because of their differing attitudes. From Titchener's perspective, the attitude of the scientist is impersonal and disinterested; that is, the scientist must hold himself aloof from the process under study and attempt an impersonal investigation. Although the notion of science as value-free has been under heavy attack in recent years, it was a central part of the positivistic position adopted by Titchener, who understood that the separation of value from science is difficult but held it essential.

According to Titchener, a third point of view exists, one that is intermediate between common sense and science, and is that of technology. The object of technology is the value derived from facts; but these fact-values, as Titchener called them, are different from the values of common sense. This is because common sense values can be derived from a number of sources not necessarily based on facts—beliefs, fears, hopes, and the like. The fact-values of technology are values derived from facts, usually scientific. The facts of science are based on observation, on the world of experience. The technological point of view is like that of common sense, however, in that its attitude is also personal and interested. Also, like common sense, technology seeks to utilize the values derived from facts for good or evil. Technology is closer to common sense than it is to science but differs from common sense in that its fact-values are based on scientific facts and on observables.

As Titchener shows, these three points of view represent different perspectives on the same existential universe. "Existential" here means "as it appears in experience." To a scientist, a pattern of rock strata tells a story of earth history, of the creatures that lived there, and the way species developed. To the technologist, the same strata give a hint as to the probability of mineral deposits that could be profitably extracted. To the common sense person, these strata could indicate the likelihood of a cave or ledge to serve as protection against the weather or as a fortification from attack.

In Titchener's conception of science, which he calls the critical view of science, these three points of view are not in opposition to one another but are merely different ways of looking at the common universe of existence. Everyone holds the common sense point of view most of the time, but a few individuals are able to spend part of their daily lives in the technological point of view. Still fewer spend part of their day in the scientific point of view. It is also possible for one individual to occupy all three points of view during the same day but not at the same time. The crux of this aspect of Titchener's relativism is that there are different ways of looking at the world, and these ways will determine what is observed. That difference is acceptable as long as the different points of view are not mixed together uncritically. This is why Titchener was so adamant about keeping pure (scientific) psychology separate from applied (technological) psychology. Applied psychology uses the facts of scientific psychology but has as different a point of view from scientific psychology as civil engineering has from theoretical physics or agriculture from theoretical biology. Titchener believed that the model of separation of applied from theoretical sciences found in physics and biology should also hold for psychology. To Titchener, there can only be one science: either a position is scientific or it is something else. Neither is there such a thing as applied science: either it is science or technology or some axiology or system of values. Meyer was unable to understand this position.

The Fundamental Sciences

Although for Titchener there is only one science, there may be many scientific disciplines. Just as science is separated from common sense and technology by differing points of view, so within science are the scientific disciplines separated from one another by their points of view. Following this logic, Titchener held, for instance, that physics describes the same universe as does psychology but describes it as logically independent of the nervous system (the experiencing individual). This difference in the observational point of view leads classical physics to describe as vibrations and radiations what psychology describes as pitches and hues. The difference is not in the universe observed but in the point of view taken by the observer. Since subject matter is determined by point of view, there can be as many disciplinary subject matters as there are discriminable points of view.

In Titchener's view, however, there are three fundamentally different scientific points of view: physics, biology, and psychology. Physics, as demonstrated above, takes the position of analyzing the universe with man left out, that is, describing the universe logically independent of the organism or experiencing individual. A wavelength of 600 nm exists whether or not there is an organism or experiencing individual. The experience, red, however, exists only for the experiencing individual and is dependent on an organic system, the central nervous system. Biology and in particular, physiology, describe the universe in terms of the functions of the organism itself regardless of whether the physical stimulus (physics) produces an experience (psychology). Just as in the case of the distinctions among science, common sense, and technology, it is not important which point of view the individual takes as long as it is defined and consistently held throughout the scientific analysis.

Titchener considered the task of science to be twofold: description and explanation. In the tradition of Sir Isaac Newton, Titchener defined description as the analysis of the whole into its further unanalyzable components. In Titchener's usage, explanation is not in terms of cause and effect but in terms of covariation. For instance, the explanation of a described psychological process is found in the biological process that parallels it. This does not prove that the biological "causes" the psychological or the reverse but only that the two events, one psychological and one biological covary, that is, change together.

In this same view, psychology observes the universe and describes it in terms of the orthodox classification of experiences: sensations, images, and feelings. Psychological description is logically dependent on the nervous system so that if psychology explains at all, it explains in terms of the nervous system or in other words, in biological terms. In Titchener's scheme, each of the fundamental sciences describes at one level and explains at the level of the immediately more basic science.

Biology describes, that is, analyzes, this same universe in terms of living systems, reproduction, circulation, digestion, nervous, and so forth. It then explains in the terms of physical description, specifically in terms of the compounds of carbon, hydrogen, oxygen, and nitrogen, the life elements.

Physics, since it views the universe with the organism left out, that is, logically independent of the organism, describes the universe in terms of elements, the elements of the periodic table. Physics then explains those described observations in terms of the interrelation of mass, space, and time.

This much of Titchener's view is derived and expanded from

Avenarius. Thus, when psychologists explain their scientific data (descriptions) in terms of the nervous system (biology), Titchener would consider them still acting as psychologists. When, however, psychologists begin working on the nervous system for its own sake, descriptively, he would say they are no longer working as psychologists but as biologists in the subdiscipline of neurophysiology. Titchener did not object to individuals switching descriptive levels, as long as they understood that their point of view had shifted as well and that their neurophysiological descriptions were not to be mixed together uncritically with their psychological descriptions as though they were equivalent.

It was just this sort of mixture to which Titchener objected in Meyer's formulations. For instance, when Meyer argues that psychology should make the "adjustive reaction" its unit of analysis, Titchener rejects Meyer's proposal from experimental, introspective psychology not only because Meyer's unit is teleological, and thus to Titchener less than scientific, but also because:

> the term is borrowed from a definite science, from biology, and therefore cannot pass muster as the "unit and prototype" for work in a separate science, written from another point of view, namely, psychology. Biology cannot legislate to psychology, any more than it can legislate to physics or ethics. But within biology the biologist can do as he pleases; and if psychopathology finds biology's proximate terms useful, so much the better for psychopathology. I have no quarrel. (4T)

Titchener "has no quarrel" because he believes that for psychology to take over a unit such as adjustive reaction as its unit of analysis, it must function as a biological discipline and not as a psychological one. He holds that introspection is the unique and fundamental method of psychology. "Introspection is valid only in psychology," he concludes, therefore excluding from psychological the adjustive reaction and disciplines, such as Meyer's psychobiology, that would use it from psychological muster.

The Subdisciplines

Continuing to follow the logic of his system, Titchener divided each of the fundamental scientific disciplines into a number of subdisciplines in psychology, each of which was determined by its particular point of view. Titchener distinguished several such subdisciplines including physiological psychology, psychophysics, experimental introspective psychology, and anthropological psychology. Each looks at the same existential universe but describes it differently, thus creating different subject matters. Titchener held that each discipline and subdiscipline must state explicitly its particular point of view and must stick to it. A fact for one point of view is not the same as for another. Inconsistency in this matter would lead, he warned, to a confused and muddled subject matter.

Experimental versus Other Psychologies

Titchener carried through on this matter of definition of point of view to a fault. The very narrowness of which he was accused, even by psychologists of his own day, was quite intentional and was part of his attempt to carve out a definable species of the genus psychology to call his own and to specify its subject matter precisely.

It is a widely held belief that Titchener was opposed to all the forms of psychology except his own; this is not wholly accurate. Titchener actively promoted animal psychology, for instance. He was largely responsible for the Macmillan Company's publication of Margaret Washburn's *Animal Mind* and Robert M. Yerkes's *Dancing Mouse*. He was deeply interested in anthropological psychology, the psychology of primitive peoples, and even seriously considered adding an anthropologist to the faculty of his department at Cornell. In Titchener's view, these psychologies were not, however, part of experimental introspective psychology, his own special area of study. Titchener was involved in the systematic, introspective study of psychology making use of data obtained by means of the experimental method. He made it very clear that his textbooks were a survey of that particular subdiscipline. He mentioned the other subdisciplines but urged the student who was interested in them to find published treatments elsewhere. Where Titchener fought against the other subdisciplines was when they attempted to deal with the subject matter he had demarcated as experimental, introspective psychology without recognizing the particular point of view such a subject matter requires. It was muddle Titchener was combating and not other brands of psychology. This battle had been easy enough in the 1890s; comparative, developmental, and abnormal psychology did not make much use of experimental techniques in those days. Even functional psychology, the psychology of William James and George Trumbull Ladd, had been easily relegated to a psychological subdivision parallel to experimental psychology because its data were not derived experimentally. The transition from functional psychology to functionalism, particularly that wrought by James Rowland Angell

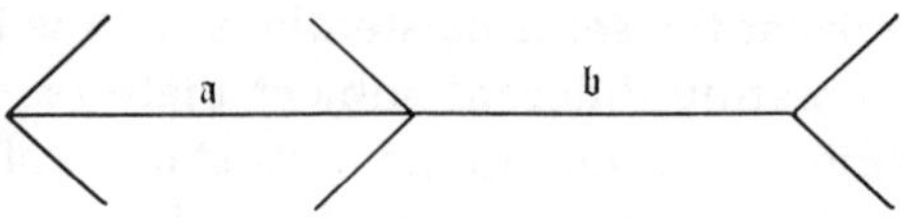

Figure 1. Müller-Lyer Illusion

at Chicago during the first decade of the twentieth century, made matters more difficult for Titchener, however. Chicago functionalism was also experimental and, while Meyer's approach was far from identical with any functionalist psychology, he *was* attempting to carry over a form of functionalism into his psychobiology. Thus, Meyer, in seeking his definition of psychology, was challenging Titchener at his own doorstep.

Titchener's view of the place of the laboratory in experimental psychology will be discussed later in this essay.

Stimulus Error

One result of the uncritical mixture of points of view is what Titchener called the stimulus error, encountered when a psychologist mixes together his knowledge about the physical stimulus with the experience "produced" by that stimulus. An example Titchener liked to use was that of the Müller-Lyer illusion. Shown the two lines in Figure 1, how should we describe them? To Titchener, the psychological description would be "two visual extents with *a* longer than *b*." The commonsense observer, if he knows something about the physics of the Müller-Lyer illusion, however, might describe it as "two lines that look unequal but which are really equal." Titchener would say that physically, the lines are equal; psychologically, they are not. By mixing the physical with the psychological standpoints, the result is muddle, neither consistently physical nor psychological.[23]

Psychophysical Parallelism

Another significant aspect of Titchener's relativistic notion of observation is found in his version of psychophysical parallelism. Titchener adhered to the doctrine of psychophysical parallelism over against the commonsense view of mind-body interactionism. He says:

> Our own position has been that mind and body, the subject-matter of psychology and the subject-matter of physiology, are simply two aspects of the same world of experience. They cannot influence each other, because they are not separate and independent things.

> For the same reason, however, wherever the two aspects appear, any change that occurs in the one will be accompanied by a corresponding change in the other.[24]

He handles the matter of mind-body relationship, following Avenarius, in terms of dependent versus independent experience.[25]

> If we look at the whole experience under its independent aspect, we find that certain physical events, certain stimuli, affect the body; they set up in the body, and especially in the nervous system, certain physical changes; these changes cause the secretion of tears. This is an exhaustive account of the experience, considered as independent of the experiencing person. If we look at the experience under its dependent aspect, we find that our consciousness has been invaded by grief or remorse or some kindred emotion. The two sets of events, physical and mental, are parallel, but they do not interfere with each other.[26]

These are points of view that make up the relational equation in Titchener's psychological science: one physical or biological and the other psychological.

I should point out that later in his career, including the latter period of this correspondence, Titchener came to question whether psychology needed explanation. He was moving decidedly toward a form of dimensional description, dropping elements away and emphasizing attributive dimensions. He clearly viewed description as psychology's primary task. Explanation, because it was in physiological terms anyway, might be best left to physiologists.

Because of these later shifts, he came to see the mind-body problem and the doctrine of psychophysical parallelism largely transcended.[27]

Meaning

It was Titchener's determination to keep the observational point of view consistent, avoiding a mixture of perspectives, that led him to exclude meaning from psychological description.[28] In this, Titchener diverged from his English empirical and associational background. To Titchener, psychological description involved that which is directly observed—sensations, images, and feelings—and not inferences made from them. Titchener tells us:

> We can observe only what is observable; and we cannot observe any product of logical abstraction. We cannot, therefore observe relation, though we can observe content-processes that are given in

> relation. We cannot either observe change, though we can observe changing content-processes for so long a time as attention, under the observational Aufgabe, may be maintained. We cannot observe causation, though we can observe content-processes that are definitely conditioned. And so it is in other cases. Psychological description can deal only with content-processes under their empirically distinguishable attributes.[29]

Titchener exhorts the psychological observer to describe what the experience is and not the meanings derived from it. For instance, if the observer places a finger in a glass of water, a Titchenerian would describe directly the pressure and coolness; those are the elementary sensations produced in that experimental condition, although images such as feelings of pleasantness or unpleasantness accruing to the sensations may be called up as well. However, according to Titchener, the observer who reports "wetness" is not describing the experience or the content-process but rather the meaning of the experience. Nevertheless, Titchener does accept that it is possible to do a psychological study of the psychological constituents of meaning. Meaning can be studied psychologically by studying the content-processes, usually kinesthetic or verbal images, that carry the meaning. To Titchener, meaning, psychologically speaking, is produced by a pattern of content-processes that form a context for another content-process. Titchener's position was that the meaning of an experience should not be confused with the experience itself nor should the two be mixed together uncritically.

Titchener's position on meaning is perhaps his most original contribution to psychology. It also played a major role in this correspondence. We might do well to consider in some detail just what meaning was to Titchener. In his *Textbook*, Titchener tells us:

> No sensation means; a sensation simply goes on in various attributive ways, intensively, clearly, spatially, and so forth. All perceptions mean; they go on, also, in various attributive ways; but they go on meaningly. What then, psychologically, is meaning?[30]

Meaning, to Titchener, was psychologically always context. He held that one mental process is the meaning of another mental process if it is the context of that mental process. By context, Titchener means "the mental process which accrues to the given process through the situation in which the organism finds itself."[31]

> Originally, the situation is physical, external; and, originally, meaning is kinaesthesis; the organism faces the situation by some bodily

> attitude, and the characteristic sensations which the attitude arouses give meaning to the process which stands at the conscious focus, are psychologically the meaning of that process. For ourselves, the situation may be either external or internal, either physical or mental, either a group of adequate stimuli or a constellation of ideas; image has now supervened upon sensation, and meaning can be carried in imaginal terms.[32]

By "situation" here, Titchener is referring to a form of *Aufgabe*, a task or problem "that is normal to the particular organism," that is, one which is familiar to the organism. Situation, externally regarded, "is a collocation of stimuli; but it becomes a situation only if the organism is prepared for selective reaction upon that collocation."[33] Titchener tells us that "any sensory or imaginal process whatsoever is able . . . to carry the meaning of any other."[34]

Somewhat later, Titchener pointed out that meaning may also be carried "unconsciously," that is, physiologically:

> There is . . . a further stage: a stage in which *meaning is carried not by any sort of sensation or image, but simply and solely by physiological processes*, by some set or disposition of the brain. When the practised reader skims a number of pages in quick succession; when the musician renders a composition in the prescribed key; when an accomplished linguist shifts from one language to another as he turns to his right or left hand neighbour at a dinner table; in cases of this kind there need be no discoverable context; the stimuli press the button and the brain, prepared by constant practice in the past, now does the rest. The experiences *mean*, positively enough; the "sense" of the pages is grasped, as the eye hurries over the lines; the three flats on the staff set the player's hand and eye for the key of E[flat]; the question put in French is suitably answered in the same language; everything takes place *as if* there were a fringe of images that gave meaning to the bare perception; and yet imaginal fringe and kinaesthetic setting may be conspicuous only by their absence. Of course, there *has been* context; one does not learn French and German, or transpose on the piano, by gift of ready-made nervous system. . . . The point is, however, that an habitual and often-repeated context does, presently, lapse altogether; the nucleus is not always supplemented; the nervous system can now do, by a set or disposition that has no mental correlate what it used to do by processes that had as accompaniment the sensations or images of the context.[35]

The situation, then, is the context, the fringe or background that gives meaning to the experience at the focus or foreground. It can be a transitory collection of sensations or it can be what was later called "set." As the context changes, so does the meaning that accrues to the foreground. A swastika will have a very different meaning to someone who has just been reading a history of Nazi Germany than it will to someone who has just read an article on Hindu symbolism. The content-process, the "object," remains the same, but its context has changed and with it the meaning it carries.

How then does the context mean? I interpret Titchener to say that the context does not mean as long as it remains context. If we shift our attention from the foreground to the context, what was previously context now becomes foreground. It can then mean if it is brought together with another context. Is this infinite regress? I believe he would answer "no." Meaning is produced through the relationship of an experience at the focus of attention (foreground) with an experience at the margin of attention (context). One does not go farther back than context. If one shifts attention to the context, one is dealing with a different equation, even if the previous foreground becomes the new context.

Titchener holds that one may study meaning psychologically but only in terms of content-processes. What he opposes is mistaking meanings for content-processes and their uncritical mixing as though they were equivalent experiences. It is for this reason that in this correspondence, Titchener repeatedly attempts to get Meyer to define his terms. Once the terms have been sufficiently defined, it would not be difficult to separate out which are content-processes and which are meanings.

This distinction between the description of content-processes and meanings was at the heart of the long, unresolved imageless thought controversy between Titchener and Oswald Külpe. Külpe's *Bewusstseinslage*, the vague experience unanalyzable as image or sensation, was, to Titchener, a product of meaning experiences uncritically mixed with the experiences of thought.[36]

Titchener's Definition of Psychology

Psychology as System versus Psychology as Data of Experience

Logic and inference *do* have a place in Titchener's system. Titchener makes a distinction between "science as observation" and "science as system." Science as observation deals with the description of the existential universe from a particular point of view resulting in a particular subject matter, the facts of experience. Science as system is a different enterprise, involving the construction of a logical arrangement of those facts so as to understand their relationships. Science as system, then, is made up of facts plus logic. In Titchener's thinking, the system of psychology is the inevitable end result of observational psychology just as in the general case, science is the result of observation. If the data are coherent and from a consistent point of view, the resulting system also will be coherent. If the data are muddled, the system will be inconsistent and incoherent.

The experimental method in science is to Titchener a plan for an observation. It is usually made up of some situation defined in terms of a physical stimulus. The observation, the introspective report in Titchenerian psychology, is made up only of experiences, content-processes without reference to the physics or the biology. It is when the observations are completed and the relationship between the physical stimulus and the introspective observation is made by the experimenter that the scientific meaning of the observation becomes evident. The relationship is brought together by the experimenter, however, not by the observer. The danger of the stimulus error is that the observer takes the point of view of both the observer and the experimenter. The experiment is the first stage in the systemization of the facts of experience. In the same way, explanation of a psychological process is carried out by the experimenter. The explanation for a sensory experience is in terms of the physiology, but in the course of introspection, the observer should not be thinking about the nature of the neurophysiology, only about the experiences at hand.

Although the observational and systematic aspects of psychology are related, they are not the same in Titchener's view. There are, for instance, systematic concepts that are abstractions based on observations rather than being directly observable themselves. Titchener's use of elements is of this sort. The element of sensation, for instance, is not directly observable. Certainly, an individual sensation may be described in terms of certain attributes: quality, intensity, duration, and so forth. Sensation itself, however, is a systematic term based on abstraction from observing many individual sensations through their observable attributes and does not necessarily have an immediate observational reality itself. The systematic concept of sensation is based on observation and logic. An individual sensation is based on direct observation. Much of the difficulties surrounding an understanding of Titchener's psychology may be traced to a confusion of the difference between the observable and the systematic.

What, then, is psychology for Titchener? As has already been shown, observational psychology differs from systematic psychology. In the same way, Titchener uses the term "psychology" in both a general or broad meaning and in a special or narrow meaning. He was very careful about terms but he assumed that once he defined a term, the reader would understand his meaning of it, and from then on it would require no repetition. Because of this assumption, Titchener had a tendency to truncate, to give a shorthand for a conditionalized term since he had already informed the reader that psychology was to be used in a given sense throughout that publication. Making matters even more complicated, the meaning of a term might be conditionalized across the course of a book through a process of gradual modification. Misunderstandings appear to have occurred because readers in Titchener's day, as in our own, had a tendency to read only the section of a book that concerned them or that part including the topic with which they were dealing at the moment rather than reading the book as a whole. Just as with the writings of William James and Wilhelm Wundt, taking Titchener piecemeal is a dangerous thing to do. The loss of context will almost assure misunderstanding.

The following example may demonstrate the difficulty of understanding what Titchener meant by psychology. In the early pages of his *An Outline of Psychology*, he defines psychology as "the science of mental processes."[37] He then carefully defines "science," "mental," and "processes." Later in the same chapter, he talks about the subdivisions of psychology. He explains that the definition of psychology as the science of mental processes "may be termed general psychology" and that it includes "many special branches of psychological enquiry with which we shall not be directly concerned in this book."[38] He then goes ahead and mentions briefly animal psychology, social psychology, child psychology, and mental pathology, but he warns the reader that he will not be dealing with those subdisciplines in his book. The psychology which Titchener treats in detail is that of "normal, adult, human, individual psychology."[39] Having said that, Titchener assumes that whenever he uses the term psychology in the future, the reader will assume that he is using it in that narrow sense. When talking about psychology in its broader meaning or in one of its special divisions, he will use the phrase "general psychology" or "psychology in the broad sense" or one of the special divisional names. Sometimes he will use the phrase "psychology in its narrower meaning" to stand for his own position when he is discussing several subdisciplines together. In general, however, he assumes his readers know how he is using the term. Often they do not. For this reason, many writers have believed that Titchener rejected the branches of psychology outside normal, adult, human, individual psychology. He did not; he merely chose to write about what he considered to be the psychological core and leave the specialty areas to others. Titchener's commentary, then, assumed his narrow meaning of psychology, although his words have often been used as though they pertained to psychology in its broader sense. This may sound like so much semantic game playing, but it is on such things that conceptual arguments hinge.

Another distinction already mentioned which Titchener made was among experimental psychology, physiological psychology and psychophysics. Experimental psychology, Titchener calls his own. He tells us that experimental psychology "insists that the psychological method of introspection . . . shall be employed under 'experimental' conditions; that is, under conditions which reduce the possibility of mistakes to a minimum, and which enable one enquirer to test or check the work of another by exactly repeating it for himself."[40] Titchener's psychology was descriptive rather than explanatory, and as such, it was primarily qualitative rather than quantitative. He sought to describe experience, not measure it. "Physiological psychology," Titchener says, is wider than experimental psychology in that it "demands a detailed knowledge of certain parts of physiology" (the physiology of the central nervous system and of the sense organs attached to it) and that it is narrower "in that it employs no methods of investigation except those which are followed in the physiological laboratory."[41] Physiological psychology runs parallel to experimental psychology but derives its data in a different way and directs its interest toward the bodily processes themselves rather than toward the experiences that covary with them. Titchener defines psychophysics as "the science of the relation of mind to body." The psychophysicist uses the data from experimental psychology and from anatomy and physiology to bring the mental and bodily facts into connection, "to discover the *laws* of the connection." Again, psychophysics studies problems similar to those of experimental psychology, but from a different point of view. G. T. Fechner defined psychophysics as "an exact science of the functional relation or relations of dependency between body and mind."[42] Basically, what psychophysics does is to measure the relationship between physical stimuli and mental processes and then infers lawful processes in the body that mediate the two. Fechner's law is basically a measurement of the operation of mediate processes, not of psychological processes themselves, as Titchener would define them. When Titchener uses the term psychology, he presupposes its use as experimental, introspective psychology and not as physiological psychology or psychophysics.

So, in general, Titchener used psychology in his writing to stand for the science of the mental processes of normal, adult, human, individuals as obtained through introspective analysis under experimental control. When he says that a given psychological position is not psychology, this is the psychology that it is not.

Just as observational psychology was designated by a variety of terms, so was systematic psychology. In his "The Postulates of a Structural Psychology," Titchener differentiated several systematic approaches to psychology, each roughly analogous to divisions in the biological sciences.[43] First was a structural psychology which Titchener saw as a parallel to morphology. Structural psychology was experimental psychology. Titchener tells us:

> The primary aim of the experimental psychologist has been to analyze the structure of mind; to ravel out the elemental processes from the tangle of consciousness, or (if we may change the metaphor) to isolate the constituents in the given conscious formation. His task is a vivisection but a vivisection which shall yield structural, not functional results. He tries to discover, first of all, what is there and in what quantity, not what it is there for.

This was the position Titchener took as his own and which he held as prior to the other systematic approaches.

The second systematic approach was that of functional psychology. Rather than dealing with the analysis of experience into its constituent parts, functional psychology is "the collective name for a system of functions of the psychophysical organism." Titchener identified this functional psychology with the older, descriptive psychology, by which he meant the philosophical psychology of the nineteenth century. The same objects of study may be dealt with differently in the structural and functional systems. Titchener uses the example of the association of ideas.

> The phrase "association of ideas," e.g., may denote either the structural complex, the associated sensation group, or the functional process of recognition and recall, the associating of formation to formation. In the former sense it is morphological material, in the latter it belongs to what I must name . . . physiological psychology.

Just as experimental psychology is to a large extent concerned with problems of structure, so is descriptive psychology, ancient and modern, chiefly occupied with problems of function.

> Memory, recognition, imagination, conception, judgment, attention, apperception, volition, and a host of verbal nouns, wider or narrower in denotation, connote, in the discussion of descriptive psychology, functions of the total organism. That their underlying processes are psychical in character is, so to speak, an accident; for all practical purposes they stand upon the same level as digestion and locomotion, secretion and excretion. The organism remembers, wills, judges, recognizes, etc., and is assisted in its life-struggle by remembering and willing. Such functions are, however, rightly included in mental science, inasmuch as they constitute in sum, the actual, working mind of the individual man. They are not functions of the body, but functions of the organism, and they may—nay, they must—be examined by the methods and under the regulative principles of a mental physiology.

Titchener held that it was essential to have a psychology of structure before there could be a viable psychology of function. Titchener saw as early as his *An Outline of Psychology* that there was a danger in the study of function leading structure:

> When we have found a function, we are tempted to translate the function off-hand into terms of structure. We are likely unless we are extremely careful, to invent a structure to carry the function. . . . All sorts of imaginary processes have been foisted upon the structure of mind by the neglect of psychologists to keep the two enquiries, the anatomical and the functional, distinct.[44]

Titchener considered functional psychologies to be little more than a passing fashion, a thrust of post-Darwinian enthusiasm into the psychological realm, "when evolution seemed to answer all the riddles of the universe,"[45] and "nourished on analogies drawn from a loose and popular biology." He considered it "a parasite, and the parasite of an organism doomed to extinction."[46]

Titchener blocks out other systematic approaches to psychology:

ontogenetic psychology, the psychology of individual childhood and adolescence; taxonomic psychology, a psychology of individual differences, the functional psychology of the collective mind, or a social psychology; and a phylogenetic psychology. It is the distinction between experimental, structural psychology and descriptive, functional psychology that most concerned Titchener in the 1890s, however, since the psychologies of William James, John Dewey, and James Rowland Angell fell into the functional category and were the major competitors to his own experimental, structural psychology. By the second edition of his *An Outline of Psychology*, published in 1899, Titchener formally distinguished between structural and functional psychology using psychology for the structural approach.

The distinction between these two positions is significant in the correspondence between Titchener and Meyer, since Meyer argues from a form of this same functionally oriented psychology.

Psychology and the Laboratory

Titchener believed that central to his psychological enterprise was the laboratory. While there were other sources of data for psychological system making, the laboratory with its control of observation was paramount. To forward the cause of the laboratory, Titchener published his *Experimental Psychology*. Its four volumes, issued between 1901 and 1905, were inestimably influential in the development of laboratory psychology. They became standard manuals for laboratory practice and were widely used long after Titchener's death in 1927. Titchener was not the only American psychologist in the 1890s pressing for experimental psychology, of course, but it was his influence that was most widely felt. While most of his doctoral students finally wandered away from his structural system, they stayed close to the ideal of the laboratory as the center of the psychological enterprise, in both research and teaching. The impact of his four volume *Experimental Psychology* cannot be overestimated, nor should it be underestimated. Generations of psychologists used the student manuals, and generations of teachers of psychology used the instructor's manuals that made up the set. Even psychologists such as John B. Watson, who would reject virtually every content of Titchener's system and introspective methodology, felt the need to express his debt to Titchener for the instruction he received through those volumes. "I did not know a great deal of experimental psychology," Watson wrote, "until your Instructor's

Manual (Qualitative) fell into my hands."[47] Even today, the manuals remain the most complete capsulation of early experimental psychology ever carried out. It is not overstating matters to say that Titchener was largely responsible for the shift in American psychology from the use of the philosophical method of reflection to that of controlled experiments in the laboratory. He was certainly responsible for the establishment of the laboratory course in experimental psychology as a basic part of every psychologist's undergraduate education.

Titchener also argued for psychology as an experimental, laboratory science in his *Textbook*. In the section entitled "Method of Psychology," Titchener discussed experimentation as it pertains to the concepts of observation and introspection. "Observation," according to Titchener, is at the basis of all science, particularly experimental science, and "implies two things: attention to the phenomena, and record of the phenomena; that is, clear and vivid experience, and an account of the experience in words or formulas."[48] To get this "clear and vivid experience" and accurate report, science makes use of the the experiment.

> An experiment is an observation that can be repeated, isolated and varied. The more frequently you can *repeat* an observation, the more likely are you to see clearly what is there and to describe accurately what you have seen. The more strictly you can *isolate* an observation, the easier does your task of observation become, and the less danger is there of your being led astray by irrelevant circumstances, or of placing emphasis on the wrong point. The more widely you can *vary* an observation, the more clearly will the uniformity of experience stand out, and the better is your chance of discovering laws. All experimental appliances, all laboratories and instruments, are provided and devised with this one end in view: that the student shall be able to repeat, isolate and vary his observations.[49]

Observation in psychology and observation in physics are more similar than different. The former is called introspection; the latter is called inspection. Titchener held that there was practically no difference between the two methods of observation, only the point of view taken. Titchener cites a simple example. Suppose the chord c-e-g is struck. You are asked to say how many tones it contains. "You may repeat this observation; you may isolate it, by working in a quiet room; you may vary it, by having the chord struck at different parts of the scale, in different octaves." The method is the same as would be used by a physicist counting the swings of a pendulum or taking readings from a galvanometer scale. "There is a difference in subject matter: the . . . tones are dependent, not independent experiences: but the method is essentially the same."

That the laboratory was central to Titchener's structural psychology is clear. While there were other approaches, such as the method of analogy, it was the laboratory that Titchener felt held open the way for a true science of psychology. Even in 1910, Titchener viewed the functional psychologies as still too immature in their methodology and perspective to reach the level of laboratory science. Titchener's confidence in the use of the experimental method, which for him was experimental introspection, was unbounded. At the conclusion of his *Textbook*, he writes to his reader that:

> if he decides to throw in his lot with the experimentalists of the human laboratory, he may be assured that he could not join their society at a more favourable time. The experimental method, having conquered the whole domain of nature and of life, is pressing forward to the highest reaches of mind, to thought itself. It needs no gift of prophecy to foretell that the first half of this century will mark an epoch in the history of scientific psychology.[50]

Titchener's Goals for Psychology

Having seen some of the concepts on which Titchener's thinking was based, we can perhaps better understand his goals for psychology. He had many, but three appear to have been primary. First was the promotion of a systematic psychology of the structural type; second, making psychology synonymous with experimental, laboratory-oriented pursuits; and third, establishing psychology as one of the three fundamental sciences along with physics and biology. The first of these, the establishment and promotion of a systematic psychological position, is how most psychologists know Titchener, through his structuralism. It was clearly how Titchener wanted to be remembered. In the long run, however, probably his most significant contribution was the second goal, establishing once and for all the laboratory as the fundamental source of data in psychology. It was the third goal, however, that of making psychology a fundamental, basic science, coordinate with physics and biology, by which Titchener sought to cut out a permanent niche for psychology in the world of science and, at the same time, set a framework in which psychology as he defined it would always have a place. Had

Titchener succeeded in his three goals, psychology would necessarily have developed very differently that it did. The assumption of his definition of psychology vis-à-vis biology and physics would have relegated behaviorism and psychobiology directly into the biological disciplines. Much of the discussion in this correspondence treats this important issue of psychology as a fundamental science.

The Correspondence

All this material has been by way of introduction to the correspondence between Titchener and Meyer. Titchener made a statement at the Clark University Vicennial meeting in 1909 that the ideas of psychoanalysis were not new at all but were outdated adaptations of association theory. This was the proximal stimulus for Meyer's initiation of the first grouping of their correspondence. The paper on appetite by Edwin Boring and Amy Luce from Titchener's laboratory was the stimulus for the second.[51] Meyer apparently had hopes of establishing a definition of psychology that would encompass Titchener's psychological views as well as those of Freud and Jung and even Meyer's own psychobiology. That Meyer and Titchener failed in this attempt should not surprise us. No such synthesis has ever been successful. Their attempt, however, gives us great insight into their psychological positions and the issues of psychology and psychiatry of their time. It also has something to say about modern psychological thought, in particular modern cognitive psychology, and the question of psychology's place in the world of science as well.

Titchener's views on the nature of science, on psychology as science, and his views on psychological concepts are all related. He had a penchant for intellectual and conceptual consistency, a characteristic that made him a good systematist, allowing him to link every systematic component with every other component and to develop his system against the backdrop of an explicit philosophy of science. Titchener also assumed and expected the same from his colleagues and competitors, but was usually disappointed. This disappointment sometimes led Titchener to underestimate both the value and the potential impact of those movements and ideas in which he found little or no logical underpinning. This was certainly the case with his attitudes toward the behaviorism of John B. Watson, Freud's psychoanalysis, and Adolf Meyer's psychobiology as well.

That Meyer and Titchener failed to find a common ground

should not surprise psychologists. Psychology then as now seems to have no middle ground. Even had such a middle ground been found, the history of psychology would probably have remained unchanged. Both Titchener and Meyer represented, at least in terms of psychology, dead ends. The next generation of psychologists would be concerned with problems other than those considered by Titchener or Meyer. J. B. Watson's behavioral revolt was aimed at least as much against functionalist approaches to psychological problems as against those of the structuralists. Meyer's psychobiology would have little in common with the psychobiology that would emerge later. Meyer, for all his pronouncements in this correspondence, would have only the most peripheral influence on psychology.

Titchener's influence in psychology persisted long after the demise of his systematic formulations. I have already alluded to his influence on making the laboratory the center of the psychological enterprise. That was certainly his greatest and longest-lived contribution to psychology.

Titchener's elementistic model, although he later went beyond it, was a strong influence on J. B. Watson's own formulations. Watson was much taken with the elegance of Titchener's systematic structure, and dismissed the wholistic model of Chicago functionalism for an elementistic approach. Watson's efforts were not so much at dropping concepts such as sensation, feeling, memory, and so forth from behaviorism but in finding behaviorally measurable equivalents. While it is easy to overestimate the connection, the logic of Watson's elaboration of complex behaviors from simple muscle twitches is clearly in imitation of Titchener's earlier elementistic system.

Another influence of Titchener on subsequent psychological formulations is in his later search for dimensions of experience, an approach that permeated the Cornell department during the last ten years of Titchener's life and for years afterward. E. G. Boring's attempt to physicalize Titchener in his *Physical Dimensions of Consciousness* are directly traceable to Titchener's ideas.[52] Through Boring, attempts by his student S. S. Stevens to find scalar dimensions for sensory experience can be indirectly linked to Titchener's dimensional approach.

So, who won the battle of the letters? Perhaps the answer is neither Titchener or Meyer and yet both: neither, because both of their psychological traditions were gradually coming to an end in psychology. Within fifteen years neither structuralism nor functionalism would be a major contender in the psychological arena.

The issues raised in the correspondence were never resolved. Many of Titchener and Meyer's deliberations of issues, however, can be of real importance in present-day discussions on the crisis of modern psychology. Psychology, which has been wandering for more than a decade, under attack for the barrenness of its research, has been searching for an alternative to behavior theory. Cognitive psychology, which has arisen largely in response to that search, has yet to prove whether it represents a new way for psychology or another dead end. It is perhaps cognitive psychology, more than any other aspect of present-day psychology, that can benefit from these discussions. The problems encountered and disputed by Titchener and Meyer have relevance to modern cognitive psychology. Just as with Meyer's psychobiology, one question facing cognitive psychology has to do with whether it is to be a psychological discipline or an intrusion into psychology of the amalgam called cognitive science. Does it matter? Well, that, of course, is the issue, and it was just one of the issues addressed by Titchener and Meyer in this correspondence.

Notes

1. I wish to thank Dr. Mary Henle for her review of this introduction and her recommendations for improvements.

2. E. G. Boring has probably done more than anyone to create and perpetuate the "standard" image of Titchener. See, for instance his *Psychologist at Large* (New York: Basic Books, 1961), 22–29; idem, "Edward Bradford Titchener: 1867–1927," *American Journal of Psychology*, 38 (1927): 489–506; idem, "Boring on Titchener," in *A History of Cornell*, ed. Morris Bishop (Ithaca: Cornell University Press, 1962); idem, *A History of Experimental Psychology*, 2d ed. (New York: Appleton-Century-Crofts, 1950), 410–20.

3. A particularly unfortunate result of historical oversimplification and stereotyping has been Margaret Rossiter's treatment of Titchener in her *Women Scientists in America: Struggles and Strategies to 1940* (Baltimore: Johns Hopkins University Press, 1982). She takes the fact that Titchener excluded women from his Experimentalists and infers from it that Titchener was a misogynist who actively attempted to exclude women from psychology. This caricature has been repeated in several other publications since, citing Rossiter as authority. Nothing could be more wrong. It *is* a fact that Titchener excluded women from the Experimentalists. Titchener held the paternalistic belief that women would object to smoke-filled rooms and frank discussion. He created the Experimentalists along the lines of an English men's club. That is a fact and is no more defensible in present-day terms than any other male-only club; but this is the sole evidence brought against Titchener. Rossiter does not point out that Titchener produced more women Ph.D.'s than any other male psychologist of his day, both in absolute number and in proportion to males. Almost half of his Ph.D.'s were women. She also does not discuss the fact that Titchener actively promoted his

female doctorate students just as he did the males and that he felt professional disappointment whenever one chose marriage over a career. She also does not mention that Titchener hired the first woman instructor at Cornell. This he did over the objection of his dean since there were male candidates available. Titchener was staunchly in favor of every woman having sufficient education to have an independent career should she choose it or personal circumstances require it.

It is certainly true that women were excluded from many areas of science, and it is probably true that exclusion from the Experimentalists may have been to the disadvantage of women graduate students. I say may have been, since the far larger and more influential American Psychological Association had women members. Still, to make an argument that would cast Titchener in the role of a misogynist, attempting to defeminize psychology is simply not supportable based on the evidence.

4. A. L. Blumenthal, "Shaping a Tradition: Experimentalism Begins," in *Points of View in the Modern History of Psychology*, ed. Claude Buxton (New York: Academic Press, 1985), 71–74.

5. Boring, "Edward Bradford Titchener, 1867–1927," 489.

6. Edna Heidbreder, *Seven Psychologies* (New York: Appleton-Century-Crofts, 1932), 151.

7. G. T. Ladd, *Elements of Physiological Psychology* (New York: Charles Scribner's Sons, 1889), 688.

8. E. B. Titchener, "The Postulates of a Structural Psychology," *Philosophical Review*, 7 (1898): 449–65; idem, "Structural and Functional Psychology," *Philosophical Review* 8 (1899): 290–99.

9. E. G. Boring, "Titchener's Experimentalists," *Journal of the History of the Behavioral Sciences* 3 (1967): 315–25.

10. R. B. Evans and F. J. D. Scott, "The 1913 International Congress of Psychology: The American Congress That Wasn't," *American Psychologist* 33 (1978): 711–23.

11. Rand B. Evans and William A. Koelsch, "Psychoanalysis Arrives in America: The 1909 Psychology Conference at Clark University," *American Psychologist* 40 (1985): 942–48.

12. R. B. Evans, "E. B. Titchener and His Lost System," *Journal of the History of the Behavioral Sciences* 8 (1972): 168–80.

13. Ibid.; Kurt Danziger, "The Positivist Repudiation of Wundt," *Journal of the History of the Behavioral Sciences* 15 (1979): 205–30.

14. Frank Angell, "Titchener at Leipzig," *Journal of General Psychology* 1 (1927): 197.

15. E. B. Titchener, *An Outline of Psychology* (New York: Macmillan, 1896), vi.

16. J. Bradley, *Mach's Philosophy of Science* (London: Athlone Press, 1971), 206. Mach uses the term in response to Max Planck's reference to his views as positivistic in an article published posthumously.

17. Herbert Spencer writes the following: "The disciples of M. Comte think that I am much indebted to him; and so I am, but in a way widely unlike that which they mean. Save in the adoption of his word 'altruism,' . . . and in the adoption of his word 'sociology,' . . . the only indebtedness I recognize is the

indebtedness of antagonism. My pronounced opposition to his views led me to develop some of my own views." Herbert Spencer, *An Autobiography* (New York: D. Appleton and Co., 1904), 1: 517–18.

18. Thomas Huxley, "The Scientific Aspects of Positivism," in Huxley, *Lay Sermons, Addresses, and Reviews* (New York: D. Appleton and Co., 1874) 150.

19. Külpe concluded that "Mach's philosophy rests upon an entirely unsafe and insecure foundation, in so far as it finds its support solely in sense-data, in immediate experience, and in that which is given in consciousness." He adds that "even psychology is not feasible as a pure science of consciousness." Oswald Külpe, *The Philosophy of the Present in Germany*, trans. Maud Lyall Patrick and G. T. W. Patrick (London: George Allen and Co., 1913), 57.

20. Some of these changes and some ideas as to their origins may be found in Evans, "E. B. Titchener and His Lost System."

21. E. B. Titchener, *Systematic Psychology: Prolegomena*, ed. H. P. Weld (New York: Macmillan, 1929).

22. Ernst Mach, *Die Analyse der Empfindungen und das Verhaeltniss des Physischen zum Psychischen* (Jena: Gustav Fischer, 1885).

23. Titchener may have set a standard too high even for himself. See Mary Henle, "'Did Titchener Commit the Stimulus Error?' The Problem of Meaning in Structural Psychology," *Journal of the History of the Behavioral Sciences* 7 (1971): 279–82.

24. E. B. Titchener, *A Textbook of Psychology* (New York: Macmillan, 1910), 13.

25. Ernst Mach, *The Analysis of Sensations*, trans. C. M. Williams (1906; New York: Dover Publications, 1959), 51.

26. Titchener, *Textbook*, 14.

27. Evans, "E. B. Titchener and His Lost System," 168–80.

28. For a discussion of the background of Titchener's positions on meaning, see R. B. Evans, "The Origins of Titchener's Doctrine of Meaning," *Journal of the History of the Behavioral Sciences* 11 (1975): 334–41.

29. Titchener, "The Schema of Introspection," *American Journal of Psychology* 23 (1912): 498.

30. Titchener, *Textbook*, 367.

31. Ibid.

32. Ibid.

33. Idem, *Lectures on the Experimental Psychology of the Thought-Processes* (New York: Macmillan, 1909), 175 fn.

34. Idem,, *A Beginner's Psychology* (New York: Macmillan, 1915), 120–21. (Underlining has been deleted.)

35. Ibid.

36. See idem., *Thought-Processes*; For a position sympathetic to Külpe, see George Humphrey, *Thinking: An Introduction to Its Experimental Psychology* (1951; New York: John Wiley and Sons, 1963), 106–131. For an alternate view on Titchener's problems with meaning, see Henle, "Did Titchener Commit the Stimulus Error?"

37. Titchener, *Outline*, 4–5.

38. Ibid., 17.

39. Ibid.

40. Ibid., 19.

41. Ibid., 20.

42. G. T. Fechner, *Elemente der Psychophysik*, in *Experimental Psychology: Instructor's Manual, Quantitative*, trans. E. B. Titchener (New York: Macmillan, 1905), xxii.

43. Titchener,"The Postulates of a Structural Psychology."

44. Idem, *An Outline of Psychology*, 2d ed. (New York: Macmillan 1899), 23.

45. Idem, *Systematic Psychology*, 253.

46. Ibid., 254.

47. Watson to Titchener, 14 December 1908, The E. B. Titchener Papers, Cornell University Archives.

48. Titchener, *Textbook*, 20.

49. Ibid., 20.

50. Ibid., 552.

51. E. G. Boring and Amy Luce, "The Psychological Basis of Appetite," *American Journal of Psychology* 28 (1917): 443–53.

52. E. G. Boring, *The Physical Dimensions of Consciousness* (New York: Century Co., 1933).

Adolf Meyer: A Biographical Note

Ruth Leys

No greater power to change our minds about the problems of psychiatry has been at work in the interior of the psychiatric profession in America than the personality of Adolf Meyer. . . . I shall designate him as a ferment, an enzyme, a catalyzer. I don't know that we could abide two of him. But in our present status we must be glad there was one of him.

With this back-handed compliment, the president of the American Psychiatric Association, E. E. Southard paid tribute in 1919 to a man who had already dominated American psychiatry for more than twenty years and who would continue to exert a crucial influence on his colleagues until his death in 1950. Meyer's approach in psychiatry was part of a movement that, toward the end of the nineteenth century, aimed to provide a naturalistic explanation of mental disease. As such, it reflected a more general tendency in late nineteenth-century American and European science toward bringing all of nature, including the mind, under natural law. However, Meyer resisted the widespread tendency to rely on exclusively organic interpretations of mental illness. Rejecting the dualism of mind and body on which such an organic approach depended, Meyer emphasized instead the interlocking of structure and function in the development of mental disease. For Meyer, psychiatry became the study of the behavior of each individual in his or her total environment. Accordingly, he directed American psychiatry away from classification, the description of symptoms, and the study of brain lesions toward the study of the "personality." Meyer's dynamic, "psychobiological" approach shared certain features with contemporary trends in European psychiatry, in particular with psychoanalysis. At the same time, because of its close links with the concepts of functionalism, pragmatism, pluralism, and common sense associated with Charles S. Peirce, William James, and John Dewey, Meyer's psychobiology may be regarded as a distinctively American achievement.

Meyer's links with his age were many and close, which is to say that any overall assessment of the significance of his contribution to American psychiatry will be partly a function of our assessment of the Progressive Era, a period that for some time now has been the object of intense scrutiny on the part of scholars in a number of related fields. Traditional accounts of the treatment and care of the mentally ill have seen in the rise of the asylum and the attendant emergence of psychiatry as a professional discipline evidence of a more enlightened treatment of the dependent and deviant. From this perspective, failures in the institutional care of the mentally ill have been viewed as transitory, and Meyer's psychobiological theories have been hailed as a major contribution in a continuous movement to humanize the treatment of the mental patient.

Since the 1960s, however, this liberal interpretation has been challenged by historians and others who have developed a more skeptical account of the function of mental institutions and the motives of psychiatric reformers. According to this revisionist, sometimes Marxist, sometimes Foucaultian approach, mental asylums are instruments for the disciplining and surveillance of dependent and unproductive populations, and psychiatric reformers are at best naive agents of social control. From this point of view, Meyer's liberal, dynamic psychiatry is seen as having provided the ideological rationale for a major reconstruction of the American mental health movement designed to extend the control of elites over American sociocultural institutions.[1] Not that this kind of revisionist (or "oppositional") history is necessarily destined to have the last word: the debate is not over, and we are likely to see increasingly complex and sophisticated interpretations of the medical and social reform movements in this period.[2] The correspondence between Meyer and Edward Bradford Titchener provides materials of central importance to this ongoing process of reevaluation.

Adolf Meyer was born in 1866 in a small village in the canton of Zurich.[3] The son of a liberal Zwinglian minister, he chose medicine over theology. After studying at the University of Zurich and completing his state medical examination in 1890, he spent a year studying in England, Scotland, and Paris with Hughlings Jackson, Jean-Martin Charcot, and others. Like his contemporary Sigmund Freud, with whose psychoanalytic theories Meyer's psychiatric ideas would initially be linked in the early years of this century, Meyer first turned his attention to the nervous system, completing his doctoral dissertation on the structure of the reptile forebrain under August Forel in 1892. Disappointed in his ambitions for a research career in Switzerland, Meyer emigrated in 1892 to the United States where he soon found a position as pathologist at the Illinois Eastern Hospital for the Insane at Kankakee, a public asylum about fifty miles south of Chicago.

Eunice Winters has observed that Meyer "came to Kankakee frankly to get brain material; he left it two and a half years later with a professional commitment to the hospitalized patient."[4] Dominated by political patronage, cut off from contact with a medical center and from university research opportunities, the state institution at Kankakee presented the twenty-six-year-old Meyer with a challenge and an opportunity—one that with characteristic determination he immediately seized. When he arrived at Kankakee, he subsequently recalled, "I found the medical staff . . . hopelessly sunk into routine and perfectly satisfied with it. With six and later eight physicians to 2,200 patients, there was many an excuse, and even sufficient reason why the medical work and records should not have been kept up to the necessary standards":

> A bewildering multiplicity of cases stared me in the face. It would have been the easiest thing for me to settle into the traditions—I had to make autopsies at random on cases without any decent clinical observation, and examinations of urine and sputum of patients whom I did not know, and for physicians who merely filed the reports—I had a chance to take to some legitimate efforts of doing something more ambitious, making slides or working out some special autopsy cases. But whenever I tried to collect my results, I saw no safe clinical and general medical foundation to put my findings on. This was discouraging. In publications grown on such ground our literature abounds. They are difficult to assimilate, fragmentary and homeless, devoid of any suggestion of their belonging to a harmonious whole. Why should they be increased in number?[5]

Committed to reforming the American asylum system by introducing modern, European clinical methods and laboratory procedures, Meyer, at Kankakee and subsequently at the Worcester Lunatic Hospital in Massachusetts, to which he moved in 1895, introduced a number of innovations that would influence asylum practice throughout the United States. Chief among them was Meyer's insistence on something approaching the modern staff conference, at which, for the first time, the patient was interviewed in the presence of the assembled asylum staff, with a stenographer present to take down the physician's dictated observations. Meyer also emphasized the standardization of the case history and its transformation into a systematic, comprehensive record of all the mental and physical facts deemed relevant to the case; and he established internships based on competitive examinations. Meyer was not alone in urging reform at this time, but because of his energy and drive he would play a critical role in determining the shape of the institutional reorganizations that followed.[6]

It was at Kankakee, too, that Meyer began to lecture to the staff on neurology and mental diseases, to read carefully the neuropsychiatric literature, and to challenge the German-inspired premises and assumptions on which that literature was based. He later observed:

> To the son of a Swiss Zwinglian minister and nephew of a medical practitioner, the problem of the nature of man, of mind and body and of their integration, was not a mere abstract problem. . . . The early helps that happened to be available in my father's library were in the direction of the rigid psychophysical trend of German science, as laid down in the works of two leaders who had both for a time been professors at the University of Zürich—Lange, the historian and critic of materialism, whose book gave me valuable historical foundations, but no working solution; and Wundt, Lange's successor. . . . Somehow both Lange and Wundt's essays had failed me in my quest for a satisfactory understanding of life and psyche.[7]

Several influences were particularly important in helping Meyer break away from the rigid dualism of mind and body on which both Friedrich Albert Lange's work and Wilhelm Wundt's psychophysical researches were based. Those influences included the British empiricists, especially James Mill and Thomas Henry Huxley, from whom Meyer obtained a broader, more biological approach to the human individual but whose dualism of mind and body, free of interaction, he rejected; the Boston neurologist Morton Prince, friend of William James, who in a provocative neo-Kantian critique of the English neurologist Hughlings Jackson's concept of mind-body concomitance, insisted on the dynamic effectiveness of the mind; and hypnotism, which, through the investigations of Charcot, Hippolyte Bernheim, Freud, Forel, James, Prince, Boris Sidis, and many others in Europe and the United States, attracted the fascinated attention of scientists and the lay public alike.[8] Meyer practiced hypnotism briefly on his arrival in America, and although characteristically he took a conservative stand on its more popular manifestations he followed closely the debates between the rival schools. Hypnotism and suggestion contributed to the breakdown of mind-body dualism by convincing Meyer of the causal efficacy of the mind in psychiatric cases.

These developments encouraged Meyer to attack classical neurology and fashionable hereditarian ideas associated with the theory of degeneration. As he began to impose himself as the leader of the advanced guard in American psychiatry, he started to criticize contemporary enthusiasm for theories of cortical localization and the attempt to build psychiatry entirely on the basis of hypothetical lesions in the brain. From the outset Meyer opposed the tendency to reduce psychology to neurology by substituting physiological for psychological explanations—a point that would later be at issue between himself and Titchener.

Meyer's insistence on the necessity of subordinating neurology to the study of the actual, individual patient was powerfully reinforced by his exposure, in the mid-1890s, to the work of the German psychiatrist Emil Kraepelin (1856–1926). In 1896, in the fifth edition of his influential textbook, *Psychiatrie: Ein Lehrbuch für Studirende und Aerzte,* Kraepelin, in a radical break with the past, drew a distinction between two fundamentally different psychotic disease processes: dementia praecox, which according to him led progressively and invariably to deterioration; and manic-depressive insanity, a disease unit which he described as combining simple and recurrent melancholia with mania but which did not terminate in deterioration. Meyer at once welcomed the clarification brought about by Kraepelin's departure from tradition and was among the first to introduce the new classification into the American asylum system.[9]

However, it was not so much Kraepelin's diagnostic contribution that Meyer valued—from the start he expressed doubts about Kraepelin as a diagnostic guide. Rather, Meyer credited Kraepelin with two fundamental developments. First, Kraepelin gave renewed impetus to clinical observation in psychiatry by maintaining the necessity of studying the life events of the individual chronologically, in terms of the eventual outcome of the disease. He thus implicitly lent support to a *historical* investigation of the human subject. Second, by suggesting that mental disorders were specific disease processes of specific origin and prognosis, Kraepelin opened the door to an "experimental" approach in psychiatry by suggesting the possibility of modifying the course of events in each case. That is, Meyer credited Kraepelin with foregrounding the *experiment* as the fundamental technique for bringing the study of the psychiatric patient into the domain of the empirical sciences.[10]

But Meyer soon departed from Kraepelin's doctrines in certain crucial respects. In particular, Meyer moved away from Kraepelin's fatalistic concept of the disease process as having an organic origin and a fixed result. Instead, he emphasized the role of life experiences in the etiology of mental disease. As a result, he broadened the scope of psychiatry to include the personal, psychological, and social experiences influencing the patient and introduced a more dynamic and optimistic attitude toward the possibility of preventing and curing mental disease. Thus, as Christine Mary Shea has rightly remarked, behind each of Kraepelin's "symptom clusters" Meyer recognized "dynamic forces driving the patient into illness."[11] "It was not one factor which Meyer considered important," his student Sir David K. Henderson has stated, "but all the factors, sexual, social, and environmental, which must always be considered in relation to the life of the individual. The total personality in his environmental setting. It was this comprehensive viewpoint which constituted so great a departure from the formal, descriptive methods which had preceded it."[12]

In developing a life-history or historical approach to the psychiatric patient Meyer was also decisively indebted to the ideas of William James and the related theories of the newly emerging Chicago school of functionalism. As Danziger has observed, James's innovative proposal was that "psychology should stop pretending that what it studied were entities like the associations between ideas or mental faculties like intelligence. Such creations . . . were never given in experience, and it was experience that psychology would have to learn to start with if it was to be a science."[13] By appealing to experience James implicitly contravened the view that mind and body were radically distinct entities and hence were incapable of interaction. Thus in spite of the psychophysical dualism provisionally adopted in his widely read *Principles of Psychology* (1890), James continually undermined dualism by showing that common sense, the facts demonstrated by hypnotism and suggestion, and Darwin's theory of evolution all proved that the mind had causal agency and had evolved for a purpose. The chief purpose of the mind, James suggested, was to select from among the myriad sensations impinging on the organism those most needed for survival in order to help it adjust efficiently to the environment on the model of organic adaptation. In short, James embraced an evolutionary, teleological psychology according to which the function of the mind was to enable the individual to pursue specific interests and achieve specific goals.

As a result of James's functional approach to mental experience, the unit of psychological investigation was no longer held by his followers to be the abstract mental elements of the association school but rather the *situation,* defined as that which combined the human organism and its environment in one analytic scheme and in relation to which neither the organism nor the environment could be considered separately or independently. Psychology studied the mind in use, James and the functionalists maintained, in the ordinary, practical situations of everyday life. Even science itself was a product of specific human situations: its truths were neither impersonal nor absolute but were always relative to specific human interests and specific human needs. Utilitarian, concrete, and incomplete, scientific knowledge, like consciousness itself, subserved particular human purposes and goals.

Declaring that his ambition was to establish a specifically American psychiatry based on the principles of James, Dewey, and other members of the Chicago school—with many of whom he was personally acquainted—Meyer, in a series of pioneering articles published between 1897 and 1909, extended James's and Dewey's ideas to psychopathology by evolving a functional or what he characterized as a "psychobiological" approach to mental disease.[14] The years after 1902, when he moved from the Worcester Lunatic Hospital to take up a position as director of the Pathological Institute of the New York State hospital system, were especially productive in this regard. Married in 1902 to Mary Potter Brooks, Meyer used his apartment as the setting for regular dinners with Dewey, James Harvey Robinson, and other progressives.[15]

Under Meyer's leadership, the Pathological Institute was reorganized so as to serve as a research and training center for the entire state asylum system. Convinced by James's and Dewey's attack on Cartesian dualism, Meyer came to treat the reactions of each person to the environment as units of a dynamic psychology that denied a radical separation between function and structure. Within this functional paradigm, Meyer made use of the concept of habit as formulated by Peirce and James and elaborated by Dewey to bridge the organic and psychical aspects of the individual. He argued that the cumulative effect of early faulty habit patterns was to produce abnormal or "inefficient" behavior in later life. In effect, Meyer interpreted mental illness as essentially caused by problems of living. The mentally ill person was viewed not simply as an individual composed of a number of separate organs, each of which was liable to structural disease, but as a unit of social organization whose harmonious relationship to the social-physical environment had been disrupted or destroyed.

Moreover, Meyer suggested that each individual was capable of reacting to a broad range of environmental situations with only a small number of responses or "reaction types." "Every individual is capable of reacting to a very great variety of situations by a limited number of reaction types," he wrote.[16] A strong typological emphasis therefore characterized Meyer's psychiatric thought, even as he also sought to stress each individual's uniqueness or "spontaneity."[17] As Meyer's ideas evolved, he increasingly stressed those small deviations from the norm which, if detected early, might be prevented from developing into more serious conditions in later life. As a consequence, he broadened the categories of mental illness to include an array of cases that did not fit traditional asylum classifications.

Meyer also applied his ideas to more serious deviations from the norm. In particular, he extended his psychobiological approach to the study of dementia praecox, or schizophrenia, as Eugen Bleuler renamed it in 1911. On the basis of his functional theories, Meyer suggested that some individuals responded to stressful situations with a "schizophrenic reaction" because they had developed habitually inadequate ways of adjusting to the environment. He thereby inaugurated a search for the specific dynamic factors that led to the schizophrenic reaction and introduced a practical emphasis on the possibility of preventing the disease by the timely adjustment of life habits. Meyer's conviction that schizophrenia was not always the inexorably deteriorating disease process that Kraepelin had taken it to be corresponded to certain analogous ideas being developed at roughly the same time by Bleuler, Carl Jung, and the staff of the famous Burghölzli mental hospital in Zürich. As a result of Meyer's dynamic approach to schizophrenia, American psychiatrists experienced a new wave of therapeutic optimism in their treatment of this formidable disease.[18]

These developments coincided with the rise of the psychoanalytic movement. At first glance, Meyer's psychobiology appeared to share certain characteristics with the Freudian school. Both represented a reaction against the somaticism of the previous generation in favor of a more dynamic approach to the individual. Both sought to understand the psychological causes of mental disease. Both were products of (and in turn, contributed to) the psychotherapy movement, which focused attention on the causal role of psychological factors in psychiatry; and both were influenced by the late nineteenth-century interest in childhood and sexuality that set the stage for a new, genetic psychology of the self. Meyer recognized these similarities and played a leading role in the warm reception given psychoanalysis in the United States during the first decade of this century. But he also confronted psychoanalysis with the demand that it reformulate its theoretical concepts in functional terms so that they could meet the same critical standards of empirical verification that were in force in the other natural sciences. Jung's well-known word-association experiments impressed Meyer precisely in this regard, because they helped specify empirically and concretely the dynamic factors at work in mental life and thus served to operationalize the rather mysterious concepts with which he and the Freudians worked. In short, Meyer viewed Jung's tests as an important step toward objectivity in psychopathology and as a valuable contribution to the functional program of extending the experimental method to areas previously considered inaccessible to science.[19]

By 1909, the year he began his correspondence with Titchener, Meyer had emerged as the leader of American psychiatry. He had also laid down the essential features of his psychobiological program; the years that followed saw the consolidation of his approach rather than the introduction of new ideas. With his appointment in 1908 as first professor of psychiatry at Hopkins and director of the Henry Phipps Psychiatric Clinic, a position he held until his retirement in 1941 at the age of seventy-five, he acquired a powerful institutional base from which to promulgate his views. Meyer's numerous activities during his long career are reflected in the more than 250 articles and reviews that were collected together in four volumes after his death in 1950 (he never managed to complete the book on which he worked intermittently for many years). In spite of the infelicities of Meyer's prose, these volumes are an invaluable resource, not only for their wealth of information about the growth of American psychiatry at the beginning of this century but also for Meyer's often astute historical reflections on the developments in which he took part.[20]

The first volume, on neurology, is of interest above all for Meyer's "segmental-suprasegmental" concept, first enunciated in 1898, according to which the nervous system had evolved ever-higher layers or "levels" of organization, each of which had its distinct functions that united the various organs into a whole. As the seat of the higher psychobiological functions, including symbolization, the suprasegmental level, or forebrain, represented the great advance in neural organization that had taken place with human evolution.[21] Intended to serve as the foundation of his psychobiological theories, Meyer's segmental-suprasegmental concept embodied a novel method of understanding the central nervous system. "Meyer's functional approach to the study and analysis of the nervous system was a radical departure from the traditional inert cumbersome descriptions that were primarily concerned with form," a student of Meyer has recalled. "It was the custom to divide the nervous system into brain and cord, and to subdivide each into morphological units. Meyer broke completely with this practice. He regarded the nervous system as a series of transverse functional segments (not necessarily metameric) which worked together as an organ of the personality." For Meyer, the same author has noted, "psychiatry and neurology, with its anatomic correlate, have always been closely interrelated. This attitude reflected the prime principle of his psychobiological concept that mind and body occupy no separate compartments in the biological framework of the individual; that both work together in terms of the whole; and that the end product of this integration is the personality."[22] As this remark suggests, Meyer's conceptualization of the nervous system as a series of levels, each a new structure with distinct functions, was indebted not only to Hughlings Jackson's concept of functional levels but also to Charles Sherrington's concept of the "integrative" function of the nervous system.[23] In spite of his commitment to a dynamic psychiatry, Meyer all his life remained deeply drawn to normal and comparative neuroanatomy, as his characterization of these as his "pet fields" suggests [30M], and indeed made several important contributions to the neurological-neuroanatomical literature.

The higher psychobiological functions associated with the forebrain are the topic of the second volume of Meyer's collected papers, devoted to psychiatry. Here are to be found Meyer's influential reports on the condition of American psychiatry in the 1890s; his recommendations for the organization of medical work at Kankakee, Worcester, New York, and Baltimore; his earliest psychobiological formulations; his pioneering articles on dementia praecox and the prepsychotic schizophrenic personality type; and his many articles on psychopathology charting his relations to the work of contemporaries such as James, Dewey, John B. Watson, Prince, Hugo Münsterberg, William McDougall, Freud, and others.

In reading through this volume one is bound to be struck by Meyer's repeated appeals to the objective and factual in psychiatry. "[N]ow that the North Pole and the South Pole have come so close to being properly discovered, man has at last taken courage to study his own kind."[24] Meyer's remark has been quoted by Alexander Leighton as typical for at least two reasons: "First, its apparent indirectness and mild sarcasm are a subtle means of bringing together a number of ideas which are increasingly revealed the more one examines the statement. Second, he frequently used this reference to polar exploration as a means of introducing his belief that the study of man could be carried out on a scientific basis."[25] As Meyer well understood, "the formulation as to what is science depends to some extent on what we consider *facts*."[26] "Anything the presence or absence of which as a factor in a formulated situation makes a difference" was his definition, an experimental conception that found characteristic expression in the following statement:

> The fundamental principle of the non-dogmatic attitude is the adherence to a series of non-prejudicial queries which hold for all events worthy of inquiry:
> 1. What is the fact in question? . . .
> 2. What does the event or fact lead to, or how does it react to tests?
> 3. What are the conditions for its existence or course?
> 4. How can it be influenced, and what is our attitude to the event?[27]

But these questions were not as nonprejudicial as Meyer liked to believe. Rather, they expressed a positivist strain within Meyer's pragmatic psychology which aligned his approach more closely than he realized with Titchener's program, a positivist strain instrumental to Meyer's effort to establish psychiatry as a medical science.

In the essay that follows I explore this important aspect of Meyer's thought and consider as well its implications for Meyer's attitude toward psychoanalysis. It is worth noting in this connection that after World War I, especially in response to the growing popularity of psychoanalysis in the lay world, Meyer became more outspoken in his criticism of Freud. He acknowledged Freud's role in promoting a dynamic view of the personality but rejected what he considered to be Freud's pessimistic emphasis on the claims of unconscious sexual instincts and on the inevitability of repression in civilized society:

> As part of an ingenious and remarkably fertile theory of psychology, itself to my mind the product of a one-sided generalization of certain pathological disorders, repression has been made a one-sided explanation of all possible normal common sense facts. . . . The most remarkable evil effects are laid at the door of various so-called repressions in the sex life. . . . The overconfidence in the existence, and especially the necessity of satisfying so-called "instinct," more than any other fact, has led to giving modern psychology the impress of the existence of quasi-immutable and obligatory demands, patterned, without further discrimination, after the facts prevailing in the hunger and food instinct.[28]

In the light of Freud's complex understanding of the relation of the neuroses to the sexual drives, one might dispute Meyer's equation of Freud's concept of infantile sexuality with hunger. But perhaps even more interesting is Meyer's implicit assumption that the individual is able to face his or her own deficiencies and deploy his or her own resources—a view that, translated into therapy, stresses the patient's more or less conscious insights as against the Freudian emphasis on the rôle of unconscious conflict and the necessity and difficulty of acknowledging the demands of repressed desire.[29] Thus, although Meyer tried to engage in a dialogue with psychoanalysis, he increasingly represented his own psychobiological methods as offering a more pluralistic and optimistic approach to the individual, one more in tune with the democratic trends of American society. The result was that through his influence he contributed significantly to that shift within the psychoanalytic movement itself—from depth to surface, unconscious to conscious, libido to personality—associated with the ego-psychology revisions of the neo-Freudian school.

The second volume of Meyer's collected papers also allows us to assess Meyer's response to behaviorism. Meyer was not a behaviorist in the sense of its founder, John B. Watson; but as a functional psychologist with close ties to Watson at Johns Hopkins between 1908 and 1920, Meyer initially shared many of his colleague's intellectual assumptions. Both men began their careers under the influence of the Chicago school of functionalism, with its goal of determining objectively the biological, adaptive functions of the mind. Both shared a commitment to making psychology an empirical science and hence to introducing public, objective observations in the field. Both were convinced that the methods of psychology could not be restricted to introspection, as Titchener believed, but had to be expanded to include the observations of others. Both, therefore, believed that animal psychology could make a significant contribution to the study of human behavior. On the basis of these shared assumptions, Meyer and Watson began a quasi-collaboration in 1908, when they both joined the faculty of Johns Hopkins.

Nevertheless, as I indicate in my ensuing essay, their collaboration could not survive Watson's radical behaviorist turn in 1913. Behaviorism laid down the path that a major wing of American academic psychology would follow up to the present day (although there are signs that its influence is rapidly waning); but it posed a serious challenge to those who, like Meyer, were confronted in their daily work with practical questions involving the mental experience of disturbed patients. It was not that Meyer objected to Watson's emphasis on the importance of studying human behavior objectively, or even to Watson's attempt to explain behavior in reflex terms. But he strongly disapproved of the dogma of exclusive salvation that Watson preached. Thus Meyer opposed Watson's radical elimination of mind from psychology and insisted instead on the importance of including the patient's subjective experiences, in the form of the life story, among the "positive" data of the field.

Watson's many popular articles and books, together with his success in applying his behaviorist principles to the field of advertising, combined to make him one of the most authoritative spokesmen for the "new" psychology in the 1920s. Nevertheless, his assumption that behaviorism would completely eclipse Meyer's functional psychobiology proved to be overconfident. It is true that, for reasons I shall suggest, Meyer's ambition to devise a method that would adjudicate between competing explanations in the field was philosophically incoherent and was, in that sense, destined to fail. However, throughout Meyer's lifetime (and, to some extent, down to the present day), the aspiration to do full justice to the best insights of disparate approaches and to integrate explanations drawn from the realms of the physical and the mental continued to motivate a significant portion of the psychiatric profession, for whom Meyer remained an important guide.

It was in his capacity as a teacher that Meyer exerted his greatest influence. As clinical director of the Worcester State Hospital, he was responsible for training a large number of junior staff, many of whom went on to become leaders of American psychiatry. Subsequently, through his directorship of the New York Pathological Institute and especially through his long tenure at Hopkins, Meyer influenced generations of psychiatrists, who spread his ideas not only throughout the United States but to Europe, South America, and Japan.[30] The third volume of Meyer's collected papers document this aspect of his career. Especially important in this regard are his articles on the method of examination, his plans for instructing medical students in the study of the personality, and his description of the life chart.

Included in this volume are also materials documenting Meyer's role in the movement to establish standards for training and certification in the field. As Gerald Grob has shown, that movement, which began unofficially at the turn of the century but which became organized only in the 1920s, was as much an attempt to expel nonmedical personnel from psychiatry as it was an effort to improve psychiatric education. Involving a number of competing organizations, its tangled history reflected the strong internal rivalries that governed relations among psychiatrists, neurologists, psychoanalysts, and other groups. The movement culminated in 1934 with the founding of the American Board of Psychiatry and Neurology; Meyer chaired the organizational meeting of the board and served on its first examination.[31]

While the existence of the board helped secure greater legitimacy for psychiatry as a field, it did not fulfill Meyer's hopes that it would resolve sectarian disputes. The uneasy relationship between psychiatry and neurology, for example, was reflected in the decision of the board to establish separate qualifications and examinations in those specialties. Moreover, throughout the 1930s psychoanalysis made headway as an independent profession, owing in part to the existence of a large, affluent middle class and the fee-for-service tradition of medical practice. From another perspective, as Grob has emphasized, the success of the board, limited as it was, had the double consequence of helping psychiatry achieve a closer integration with general medicine and thereby a greater degree of professional legitimacy, but of doing so at the expense of shifting the locus of practice away from the large mental hospitals to child-guidance clinics and private practice. In short, one unexpected outcome of the reform movement in American psychiatry, with which Meyer was so closely associated, was the regrettable social and medical marginalization of the chronically ill, institutionalized patient.

Finally, Meyer played an important role in what became known in the United States as the mental hygiene movement, a role that is documented in the fourth volume of his collected papers. The movement itself had many aspects, but roughly we can say that it reflected a vast increase in the scope of psychiatric authority as psychiatry expanded into extramural and community settings such as the family, the school, and the prison. This is an aspect of Meyer's career that surfaces only tangentially in his correspondence with Titchener, although it is consistent with the arguments put forward there. Thus Meyer was instrumental in helping establish the National Committee of Mental Hygiene, an organization founded by Clifford Beers, whose classic autobiographical account, published in 1908, of his experiences as a mental patient helped provide the momentum for a broad program of asylum reform in the United States.[32] Through his involvement with the national committee, Meyer helped determine the direction of the mental hygiene movement in two decisive ways. First, he redirected the movement away from its initial concern with the institutional care of the insane to include a broad range of disorders not traditionally part of the psychiatric domain. Second, he helped ensure that psychiatric professionals would control the mental hygiene movement by insisting that only medically trained personnel, not lay people, had the expertise to place the study of human conduct on a scientific footing.

Meyer's psychobiological model of human nature was fundamental to the mental hygiene movement. Reacting against traditional rationalist interpretations of human behavior, Meyer paid less attention to the role of ideas in determining conduct than to the contribution of feelings and emotions. Borrowing from the culture-personality constructs of the Chicago functionalists, particularly the work of Charles Horton Cooley and George Herbert Mead, Meyer emphasized the ways in which the emotional beliefs of individuals were shaped or conditioned by the different groups to which they belonged. His work also bore a close relationship to the ideas of the sociologist, W. I. Thomas, whose writings, as Leighton has observed, paralleled Meyer's in many striking respects.[33] Through Meyer's influence, psychiatrists increasingly stressed the role of the family, school, peers, workplace, and community—in short, the social environment—in the socialization of the individual. The parent-child relationship was deemed of primary importance in this regard. Through the repeated interactions between parent and child, the latter was seen as internalizing the norms and values of the family and as building up those emotional attitudes and predispositions that constituted his or her personality. Largely as a result of Meyer's influence, genetic explanations of social deviancy gave way to a dynamic explanation of human behavior based on the contribution of emotional and instinctual experiences. Out of this development emerged the influential child-guidance and parent-education movement of the 1920s.

In attempting to explain why Meyer is studied so little today, commentators have focused on a variety of factors. These factors include the notorious obscurity of Meyer's writings, which are poorly organized and lack literary appeal; his inability to systematize and, in particular, to define developmental stages with anything like the concreteness and explanatory power of Freud—one reason that even his most devoted students often turned to psychoanalysis; and—from the perspective of recent advances in our understanding of the chemistry of the brain—the failure of his environmental, psychobiological approach to elucidate the mechanism of schizophrenia and other major mental diseases. At the same time, these commentators acknowledge, the decline in Meyer's influence is only apparent, for he so profoundly imposed upon the entire profession his conception of the problems of the field that what had seemed innovative to psychiatrists such as Southard in 1919 has now become, for better or worse, a virtual truism of mainstream American psychiatric practice.[34] Yet, exactly how this process of incorporation occurred still remains to be described. My purpose in this biographical note has not been to assess the overall significance of Meyer's achievement. Rather, it has been to set the stage for the close analysis of the Meyer-Titchener correspondence that follows, on the assumption that until we have an enhanced appreciation of the intellectual, institutional, and professional issues at stake in Meyer's psychobiological program any such effort of assessment will be premature.

Notes

Epigraph: E. E. Southard, "Cross Sections of Mental Hygiene, 1844, 1869, 1894," *American Journal of Insanity* 76 (1919): 107.

1. In a large literature, see especially Michel Foucault, *Madness and Civilization: A History of Insanity in the Age of Reason,* trans. Richard Howard (New York: Pantheon Books, 1965); idem, *Discipline and Punish: The Birth of the Prison,* trans. Alan Sheridan (New York: Pantheon Books, 1977); David J. Rothman, *The Discovery of the Asylum: Social Order and Disorder in the New Republic* (Boston: Little, Brown, and Co., 1971); idem, *Conscience and Convenience: The Asylum and Its Alternatives in Progressive America* (Boston: Little,

Brown and Co., 1980); Gerald N. Grob, *The State and the Mentally Ill: A History of Worcester State Hospital in Massachusetts, 1830–1920* (Chapel Hill: University of North Carolina Press, 1966); idem, *Mental Illness and American Society, 1875–1940* (Princeton: Princeton University Press, 1983); Richard W. Fox, *So Far Disordered in Mind: Insanity in California 1870–1930* (Berkeley and Los Angeles: University of California Press, 1978); Andrew Scull, ed., *Madhouses, Mad-Doctors, and Madmen: The Social History of Psychiatry in the Victorian Era* (Philadelphia: University of Pennsylvania Press, 1981); Martin J. Wiener, ed., "Humanitarianism or Control"? A Symposium on Aspects of Nineteenth-Century Social Reform in Britain and America," *Rice University Studies* 67 (1981): 1–84.

2. For example, the recent work of Walter Benn Michaels on a series of American texts and cruxes of the late nineteenth- and early twentieth-centuries challenges a number of the assumptions and oppositional terms which have structured much of the debate over the Progressive Era thus far. Walter Benn Michaels, *The Gold Standard and the Logic of Naturalism. American Literature at the Turn of the Century* (Berkeley and Los Angeles: University of California Press, 1987).

3. For general accounts of Meyer's life and thought, see Gerald N. Grob, "Adolf Meyer on American Psychiatry in 1895," *American Journal of Psychiatry* 119 (1963): 135–42; idem, *The State and the Mentally Ill*, chap. 8; idem, *Mental Illness and American Society, 1875–1940*, 112–18; Gerald Klerman, "The Psychobiology of Affective States: The Legacy of Adolf Meyer," in *Research in the Psychobiology of Human Behavior*, ed. Eugene Meyer III and Joseph V. Brady (Baltimore: Johns Hopkins University Press, 1979), 115–31; Theodore Lidz, "Adolf Meyer and the Development of American Psychiatry," *American Journal of Psychiatry* 123 (1966–67): 320–32; Alfred Lief, ed., *The Commonsense Psychiatry of Adolf Meyer: Fifty-two Selected Papers, Edited, with Biographical Narrative* (New York: McGraw-Hill, 1948).

4. Eunice E. Winters, "Adolf Meyer's Two and a Half Years at Kankakee," *Bulletin of the History of Medicine* 40 (1966): 441.

5. Meyer, "Aims and Plans of the Pathological Institute for the New York State Hospitals" (1902), in *The Collected Papers of Adolf Meyer*, ed. Eunice E. Winters, 4 vols. (Baltimore: Johns Hopkins Press, 1950–52), 2:93 (hereafter cited as *CP*).

6. For the history of the late nineteenth-century reform movement in American psychiatry, see especially Barbara Sicherman, "The Quest for Mental Health in America, 1880–1917" (Ph.D. diss., Columbia University, 1967); Christine Mary Shea, "The Ideology of Mental Health and the Therapeutic Liberal State: The American Mental Hygiene Movement, 1900–1930" (Ph.D. diss., University of Illinois at Urbana-Champaign, 1980).

7. Meyer, "British Influences in Psychiatry and Mental Hygiene" (1933), *CP*, 3:401–2.

8. Morton Prince, "Hughlings Jackson on the Connection between the Mind and the Brain," *Brain* 14 (1891): 250–69; Meyer, "British Influences in Psychiatry and Mental Hygiene," 402–4.

9. Grob, *The State and the Mentally Ill*, 65ff.

10. Meyer, "A Review of Recent Problems of Psychiatry" (1904), *CP*, 2:331–85; idem, "A Few Trends in Modern Psychiatry" (1904), *CP*, 2:386–404.

11. Shea, "The Ideology of Mental Health," 83.

12. Sir David K. Henderson, "Introduction," *CP,* 2:xiii. In the same text Henderson also notes that although Meyer did not neglect the role of inheritance, he was "always more strongly attracted to a consideration of habit formation, training, and education than he was to the hereditary or genetic aspects. . . . He wanted something much more elastic than the rigid symptomatology of the Kraepelinian school" (xi).

13. Kurt Danziger, "On the Threshold of the New Psychology: Situating Wundt and James," in *Wundt Studies: A Centennial Collection,* ed. Wolfgang G. Bringmann and Ryan O. Tweney (Toronto: C. J. Hogrefe, 1980), 365.

14. In 1902 Meyer wrote to his wife of his ambition to found "a thoroughly Meyerian psychiatry. . . . Not quite 'German school,' but looking as if it might become something American. In general I am most at home with the psychology of James" (Meyer to Mary Meyer, 8 May 1902, The Adolf Meyer Papers, The Alan Mason Chesney Medical Archives, The Johns Hopkins Medical Institutions). Meyer's esteem for James was reciprocated: "That man has the levelest mind on psychological matters that I know! A splendid character!" James wrote of Meyer after having talked with him at the Worcester conference (James to Clifford Beers, 22 September 1909, The Adolf Meyer Papers). Meyer credited James with helping him grasp the import of Peirce and Dewey's instrumentalism (*CP,* 2:215).

15. Lief, *The Commonsense Psychiatry of Adolf Meyer,* 152.

16. Quoted by Henderson, "Introduction, xii. Cf. Meyer, "An Attempt at Analysis of the Neurotic Constitution" (1903), *CP,* 2:321–30; idem, "The Problems of Mental Reaction Types, Mental Causes and Diseases" (1908), *CP,* 2:591–603.

17. For a discussion of Meyer's representation of human individuality as simultaneously absolutely unique and irreducible and as only definable as a member of a type or class, see Ruth Leys, "Types of One: Adolf Meyer's Life Chart and the Representation of Individuality," *Representations,* forthcoming.

18. Solomon Katzenelbogen, "Dementia Praecox: Formulations by Kraepelin, Bleuler, and Meyer," *Psychiatric Quarterly* 16 (1942): 436–53; Hans Kind, "The Psychogenesis of Schizophrenia: A Review of the Literature," *International Journal of Psychiatry* 3 (1967): 383–97.

19. Meyer's role in the early reception of psychoanalysis in the United States is discussed by John C. Burnham, *Psychoanalysis and American Medicine, 1894–1918: Medicine, Science, and Culture* (New York: International Universities Press, 1967), 157–59; Nathan G. Hale, *Freud and the Americans: The Beginnings of Psychoanalysis in the United States, 1876–1917* (New York: Oxford University Press, 1971), 157–64, 194–200; Ruth Leys, "Meyer's Dealings with Jones: A Chapter in the History of the American Response to Psychoanalysis," *Journal of the History of the Behavioral Sciences* 17 (1981): 445–65; idem, "Meyer, Jung, and the Limits of Association," *Bulletin of the History of Medicine* 59 (1985): 345–60.

20. "The difficulty in understanding Meyer came from a number of sources," one of Meyer's students has sympathetically recalled, "one of which, at least, was his tendency to assume that we had a background and frame of reference comparable to his own. He would often express himself by a series of

oblique references to concepts imbedded not only in psychiatry, but also in psychology, in sociology, in anthropology, in philosophy, in history, and in Greek literature; and then he would pass on to qualifying his core statement with a bewildering series of dependent clauses. Sometimes the dependent clauses came first and he would omit the core statement" (Alexander H. Leighton, "Introduction," *CP,* 4:xiii).

21. Meyer, "Critical Review of the Data and General Methods and Deductions of Modern Neurology" (1898), *CP,* 1:77–148.

22. Louis Hausman, "Introduction," *CP,* 1:xxi–xxii.

23. Meyer, "British Influences in Psychiatry and Mental Hygiene," 400–428. There is also an obvious similarity between Meyer's segmental-suprasegmental concept and Pierre Janet's related theory of the functional, hierarchical organization of the nervous system.

24. Meyer, "The Scientific Study of Behavior and Its Support" (1926), *CP,* 4:132.

25. Leighton, "Introduction," xiv.

26. Meyer, "The Material of Human Nature and Conduct" (1935), *CP,* 3:449.

27. Ibid., 449; idem, "Misconceptions at the Bottom of *Hopelessness of All Psychology*" (1907), *CP,* 2:576.

28. Meyer, "Normal and Abnormal Repression" (1922), *CP,* 4:403.

29. Meyer's therapeutic principles are described by Wendell Muncie, *Psychobiology and Psychiatry: A Textbook of Normal and Abnormal Human Behavior* (St. Louis: C. V. Mosby Co., 1939), pt. 3.

30. It has been estimated that by 1937, approximately 10 percent of all teachers of psychiatry in the United States had been trained at the Phipps Clinic, which remained the center of academic psychiatry in America until World War II. Shea, "The Ideology of Mental Health," 80–82; Frank G. Ebaugh, "Adolf Meyer's Contribution to Psychiatric Education," Supplement to *Bulletin of the Johns Hopkins Hospital* 89 (1951): 71.

31. Grob, *Mental Illness and American Society,* 234–87.

32. Clifford Whittingham Beers, *A Mind That Found Itself* [1908], with a preface by Robert Coles (Pittsburgh: University of Pittsburgh Press, 1981). For accounts of the mental hygiene movement, see Norman Dain, *Clifford E. Beers: Advocate for the Insane* (Pittsburgh: University of Pittsburgh Press, 1980); Grob, *The State and the Mentally Ill,* 144–78; Rothman, *Conscience and Convenience;* Shea, "The Ideology of Mental Health"; Eunice E. Winters, "Adolf Meyer and Clifford Beers, 1907–1910," *Bulletin of the History of Medicine* 43 (1969): 414–43.

33. Leighton, "Introduction," xxii.

34. See especially Klerman, "The Psychobiology of Affective States," 115–31; George Mora, "Adolf Meyer," in *Comprehensive Textbook of Psychiatry,* ed. Alfred M. Freedman, Harold I. Kaplan, and Benjamin J. Sadock, 2 vols. (Baltimore: Williams and Wilkins, 1975), 2:626–32; Barbara Sicherman, "Adolf Meyer (1866–1950): Profile of a Swiss-American Psychiatrist" (Lecture delivered before the Swiss American Historical Society, 2 May 1969).

The Correspondence between Adolf Meyer and E. B. Titchener

Ruth Leys

I insist that Ideas must be razor-sharp. I don't at all mind being wrong, provided only I am clear. To be clearly *wrong is about the biggest service the individual may render to the cause of Thought at large. You insist that Ideas must be flexible, loose-edged, geared with a lot of play in the gearing. You hope, if only you are thus empirically flexible, that somewhere in the loose running of your Ideas you will strike what is right. To be right, even in the midst of muddle, is (I take it) your notion of the biggest service an individual may render to the same cause. If I interpret you aright (and I am always doubtful about that), our aims and ideals will never square.*

E. B. TITCHENER TO ADOLF MEYER, 2 NOVEMBER 1918

The correspondence between Adolf Meyer and Edward Bradford Titchener, leaders of American psychiatry and psychology, respectively, brought together two men who played crucial roles in the emergence of their fields as independent scientific disciplines in the United States. In two compelling sets of letters composed in 1909 and 1918 Meyer and Titchener attempted to define the limits of psychology as a science and to determine its place relative to the other cognitive disciplines of the time. Written during a period of intense debate in the human sciences, the letters provide unique insight not only into the thought of each man but also into the epistemological, methodological, and institutional constraints governing the development of American psychology in the first two decades of this century. They thus have a vital claim on our attention.

The correspondence between Meyer and Titchener testifies to a protracted crisis in the modern history of the human sciences. Experimental psychology, normally associated with the founding of Wilhelm Wundt's laboratory in 1879, had set the stage for the emergence of psychology as an empirical science, but the field still lacked a clear disciplinary identity. Then, in the early years of this century, a number of different systems or approaches—structuralism, functionalism, psychoanalysis, psychobiology, behaviorism, and suggestions stemming from Wilhelm Dilthey and the German hermeneutical tradition—offered competing strategies for obtaining valid or, as Meyer would have said, objective knowledge of human beings and their behavior. The result was a fragmented psychology that lacked consensus as to procedures and institutional structures. Along with others, Meyer and Titchener deplored this state of affairs. In the privacy of their correspondence, the two men attempted to resolve the crisis and to lay down the future foundations of the field.

The immediate stimulus for the correspondence between Meyer and Titchener was Sigmund Freud's visit to Clark University in Worcester, Massachusetts, in early September 1909, a visit that marked a decisive turning point in the reception of psychoanalysis in the United States. Both Meyer and Titchener were in attendance on that historic occasion, and both gave lectures about their respective fields to the assembled audience. What makes their subsequent exchange of letters so interesting is that the two men appeared to represent radically opposed positions—although, as I shall go on to show, there was more agreement than either was able or willing to recognize.

Titchener, an Englishman based at Cornell University who had studied with Wundt, headed what was known as the "structural" school of psychology, an experimental, laboratory psychology emphasizing the analysis of normal, adult mental experience into its supposedly elementary components. In 1909, Titchener was the foremost academic, experimental psychologist in the United States. Meyer, whose arrival in the United States from Switzerland in 1892 has been held to mark the beginning of modern American psychiatry and who, in 1908, had been appointed professor of psychiatry at the Johns Hopkins University in Baltimore, embraced instead the "functional" program of psychology associated with the pragmatism of William James and the Chicago school of functionalism led by John Dewey. Meyer represented a dynamic approach to mind-in-use and to psychology in its application outside the world of the laboratory. Not surprisingly, in his lecture to the Worcester conference, Meyer drew attention to what he perceived as the similarities between his functional conceptions and Freud's psychoanalytic theories.[1]

It was Meyer who, in the aftermath of the meeting, initiated the correspondence with Titchener. Struck by the contrast between the dynamic approach to mental events exemplified by Freud, Carl Jung, and himself on the one hand and Titchener's descriptive methods on the other, but encouraged by his friendly contact with Titchener at the Clark conference, it seemed to Meyer essential that the disparate views aired at Worcester be reconciled if psychology was to legitimate itself as an independent scientific discipline. After a sharp exchange of letters written over a period of six weeks, it became clear—especially to Titchener—that no such reconciliation was possible, and the correspondence was broken off.

At the time of the 1909 exchange, Titchener's influence on American psychology was at its peak. In 1918, in what turned out to be a voluminous exchange, Meyer reopened the correspondence with Titchener in a second attempt to find common ground, only to find that their conflicts were still irreconcilable. By then, the behaviorism of John Broadus Watson had emerged as a new movement in American psychology, and the 1918 correspondence registers behaviorism's challenge to both Meyer's functional psychobiology and Titchener's structuralist school. Meyer and Titchener never overcame their differences, but their attempts to do so greatly illuminate the various assumptions that governed each man's thought. No other documents so clearly epitomize the epistemological and methodological conflicts that shaped American psychology's search for disciplinary identity in the early years of this century.

The correspondence between Meyer and Titchener is difficult to read through. It does not have the world-historical status of the contemporaneous correspondence between Freud and Jung, nor does it have the tragic dimension of the latter as the two men approach their break in 1913 and what is at stake is the very future of psychoanalysis.[2] Yet the exchange between Meyer and Titchener in 1909 and 1918 has a drama of its own. Both participants recognize that the lack of shared norms, assumptions, and procedures jeopardizes the status of psychology as a natural science and that their failure to agree about fundamentals says something potentially ominous about the institutional fate of psychology. The correspondence also has an internal dynamic, as moments of apparently mutual understanding are succeeded by moments of disconcerting disagreement, antagonism, frustration, recrimination—even accusations of deliberate *mis*understanding.

The persistence of both men in the face of radical disagreement suggests the considerable investment each had in the outcome of the debate. Especially in 1909, Meyer is the more patient and good-humored of the two, not only because he has inaugurated the discussion but because he is more committed than Titchener to trying to find common ground. It is an article of faith with Meyer, grounded at once in a personal dislike of conflict and in an understanding of pragmatism, that science is a collaborative enterprise that advances only by virtue of a broad consensus. His scientific and political ideal is one that emphasizes harmony and agreement. Candid and sincere, he dislikes controversy, particularly public controversy, which he regards as inimical to the status of psychology as a science. For this reason he welcomes the opportunity to explore his differences with Titchener in the privacy of a personal exchange.

It is worth pausing for a moment to comment on the function, or rather functions, served by correspondence in the history of early twentieth-century science. By 1900 letters as a mode of scientific communication had begun to be replaced by societies, journals, and even the telephone. Nevertheless, as the extensive correspondence of Freud, Meyer, and Titchener testifies, letters continued to play a multiplicity of roles in the scientific community—as vehicles of exchange, inquiry, persuasion, collegiality, friendship, and self-revelation, among other functions.[3] I suggest that for Meyer in particular, at a moment when public controversy over fundamentals threatened to imperil psychology's successful institutionalization, the correspondence with Titchener served as a supplement to public discussion by providing a privileged domain where the negotiation of interests could take place in safety, away from public scrutiny. "Public discussions are rarely as helpful as personal efforts to clear up points and to reach common ground," he characteristically remarks (28M).[4] It is revealing in this regard that while Meyer's position is carefully argued, the informality of the correspondence medium allows him to state his views with a directness and amplitude that he was never able to achieve in his published work.

Titchener's use of the correspondence is different. A man of the nineteenth century who never learns to drive and who does not like the telephone, letters are his preferred method of communication. Titchener recognizes no significant distinction between the private sphere of the correspondence and the public space of the printed page. His letters are from the first quasi-public documents implicitly intended for a broad scientific audience. Thinking that Meyer might want to publish his first series of letters (13T), Titchener treats the correspondence as an opportunity to state the ideas he is in the process of preparing for publication and to combat those he opposes—especially teleology, which he regards as the greatest enemy of all and which nevertheless in some respects he underestimates. Titchener conceives of the discussion in militaristic and quasi-religious terms.[5] He is engaged in a battle with Meyer for the salvation of psychology and has the zeal of a missionary preaching the truth to the natives. "Psychology has found itself," he asserts, "and knows its business" (2T).

The two men bring different skills to their encounter. In certain obvious respects, Titchener possesses the more forceful intellect and is better equipped than Meyer for the exchange. Known to his colleagues as charming, brilliant, egotistical, and autocratic, he lives for science and demands the same dedication from his students.[6] Precise and dogmatic, he is a gifted and experienced polemicist who likes to debate. Moreover, he has a system to defend, one that is well established and that he has thought through. He is consistent, coherent, and—he prides himself—clear. Clarity for Titchener is the greatest virtue in science: he would rather be clear and wrong, he tells Meyer, than muddled and right, and he thinks Meyer is hopelessly and exasperatingly muddled. Written at speed, sometimes late at night, from the start Titchener's letters are confident, emphatic, and aggressive. Although his tone is more conciliatory in 1918 than in 1909, he remains committed to his own position.

Meyer, by contrast, is unsystematic, rambling, and frequently obscure. He is not as gifted verbally as Titchener, nor does he have Titchener's penchant for debate (moreover English is not Meyer's native language). Yet he should not be underestimated. Intelligent, stubborn, inhibited and prone to indecision, a natural conservative devoted to the Progressive Era's reform goals, oblique and difficult to understand yet capable of pithy remarks—Meyer had the force of personality and leadership skills to impose himself on his colleagues and his era.

Moreover, although both Meyer and Titchener were transplanted Europeans, Meyer was far more at ease than Titchener in his adopted country. By all accounts, Titchener throughout his life remained closely attached to the British and German scientific traditions of his youth: uncomfortable with American practicality and utilitarianism, in a sense he never became part of American psychology.[7] Meyer, on the other hand, felt intellectually at home in the United States. He identified his pluralistic, functional psychiatry with Swiss and American democracy and on this basis contrasted the liberalism of his approach with the dogmatic sectarianism he felt characterized the imperialistic German intellectual tradition—which Titchener represented. (Meyer's evaluation of the virtues of New World democracy was strongly reinforced by the Great War, which provides a tragic setting for the correspondence in 1918 and whose terrible destruction Meyer blames on the cultural and political arrogance of Germany—see 19M and 26M.) Thus if we reread the influential articles Meyer wrote in the late 1890s and early 1900s, we see that from the first he felt comfortable with the broad functionalist trend that was sweeping across America at the turn of the century. He made use of his encounter with the United States to crystallize an approach in psychology that was more in tune with the general current of American thought than was Titchener's structural psychology and that would ultimately exert a more lasting influence.

Finally, if in the correspondence Meyer seems more conciliatory than Titchener, his concessions are more apparent than real, for Meyer is just as tenacious as Titchener, just as convinced that what he stands for is the truth. From Meyer's perspective, what Titchener's system gains in attractiveness by virtue of its logical precision and strict definitions it loses in abstraction and artificiality. In Meyer's view, Titchener's structuralism depends on verbal distinctions rather than empirical observations and accordingly leaves out the kinds of facts Meyer feels must be included if psychology is to be useful and interesting—practical, functional goals that Titchener abhors. Nor are Meyer's arguments methodologically innocent. His idea of common ground presumes a particular conception of science and the psychological enterprise which is precisely one of the issues in dispute between the two men. The dialogue between Meyer and Titchener thus takes place under conceptual auspices that are themselves in question from first to last. Furthermore, the controversy between Meyer and Titchener is part of a wider, ongoing struggle among American psychiatrists and psychologists to achieve professional independence and secure a solid institutional base, and this too may be read in the correspondence. For all the civility of their rhetoric, questions of institutional power are plainly at stake as the two authors seek to determine which of them will define and hence control the field.

Meyer, Titchener, and Positivism

In the decade before the Clark conference, Meyer had participated energetically in numerous scientific societies and organizations, read widely in the psychological and psychiatric literature, and attempted to build bridges to the academic psychologists—including Titchener's group at Cornell. Implicit in all his activities at this time was his conviction that the investigation of the human mind could be made to conform to the norms and methods of the natural sciences. This was to be achieved not by adopting the perspective of the mechanical sciences or an abstract psychology of mental elements, but on the basis of a functional-pragmatic approach that would do justice to the actual, lived experiences of the human subject. "One of the first things that have proved of value in this direction," Meyer wrote in a Jamesian statement in 1908,

> has been the abandonment of fussing over supposed *elements* of psychology and the attempt to explain the chains of events out of such elements. It proved to be much more satisfactory to speak in terms of situation, reaction, and final adjustment. . . . It is better to use the broad concepts of instincts, habits, interests and specific experiences and capacities, than the concepts of structural analysis at the present stage of our biological knowledge.[8]

Meyer was well aware, however, that during the same period Titchener was taking psychology in a very different direction, for by the time of their encounter in 1909 Titchener had emerged as the combative dean of a highly visible (if narrowly entrenched) American school of experimental psychology dedicated to analyzing the structure of the mind into its putative elementary processes by the method of introspection. Now Kurt Danziger and others have demonstrated that in urging the value of his structural approach for the future progress of American psychology, Titchener espoused a distinct conception of the nature and scope of psychology as a natural science. In particular, the confrontation between Meyer and Titchener must be placed in the context of the positivist reorientation of psychology that had occurred in the last decade of the nineteenth century.[9]

Influenced by the German psychologist, Oswald Külpe, and the positivist or empiro-critical philosophy of the physicist Ernst Mach and the philosopher Richard Avenarius, Titchener and his school had reached certain conclusions about the nature of their discipline, and we find those conclusions operating as basic assumptions throughout Titchener's letters to Meyer. The first assumption was that psychology must be defined as a purely natural science. This meant that the distinction, endorsed by Wundt, Dilthey, and the German hermeneutical tradition, between the natural sciences on the one hand and the human or cultural sciences on the other, according to which certain psychological experiences were excluded from an empirical mode of analysis, was emphatically rejected. This, in turn, involved a repudiation of Wundt's distinction between physical causation, which obeyed the laws of mechanics, and mental causation, which was purposive, subjective, and historical in nature. These two types of causation, Wundt believed, meant that psychology as whole could never have the character of a strictly natural science. Denying the existence of mental causation altogether, Titchener followed Külpe in maintaining that the proper domain of psychology was the study of mental events in their dependency on the biological organism, the seat of all physiological processes.

In his correspondence with Meyer, Titchener acknowledges his debt to Mach and Avenarius in the formulation of his research program.[10] What should be emphasized, however, is that in his letters to Titchener, Meyer also appeals to Mach's and Avenarius's definitions of science and psychology to support his psychobiological doctrines. The common debt owed by both Titchener and Meyer to the writings of Mach and Avenarius is sufficiently striking to warrant further comment, especially since the full extent of the influence of Mach and Avenarius on the evolution of functional psychology has not been recognized.

Meyer, like Titchener, was first exposed to the ideas of Mach and Avenarius in the 1890s,[11] but it was not until the early 1900s that Meyer came to appreciate fully the potential significance of those ideas for his own psychiatric work. An important figure in Meyer's intellectual development in this regard, the person on whom more than any other he seems to have relied for his interpretation of the thought of Mach and especially Avenarius, was the Danish philosopher, Harald Höffding (1843–1931).[12] Höffding is today a largely neglected figure in the history of psychology. Yet at the turn of the century he enjoyed a worldwide reputation and saw his works translated into several languages and extensively used as textbooks.[13]

Höffding also had many contacts with American philosophers, including William James, who detected a close similarity between Höffding's views and American pragmatism. These ties are particularly evident in two of Höffding's books, *The Problems of Philosophy* (1903), which James arranged to have translated in 1905, and *Modern Philosophers* (1905), translated in 1915. In his preface to *The Problems of Philosophy,* James summarized what seemed to him the most significant of Höffding's views. Among these was Höffding's "dynamic" notion of truth, his belief that "'knowledge' is a relation of our thinking activities to reality, and that those activities are 'truest' which *work* best—the term 'work' being taken in in the widest possible number of senses. Thought is thus an instrument of adaptation to, and eventually of modification of, its objects. Its duty may, but need not always, be merely to copy the latter." Seen in this light, scientific truths were not simply accurate representations—perfect copies—of an objective reality; instead, they were expressions of specific human interests, or to put this slightly differently, they were *constituted* as truths only within and, in a sense, *by* particular human situations and interpretive contexts. James observed that in adopting such a dynamic theory of truth, Höffding aligned himself not only with the most recent pragmatist literature but also with the "'economical' school of scientific logicians"—the school of Mach and Avenarius.[14] I think it would be truer to say that Höffding at once embraced and modified the positivism of Mach and Avenarius, and I want further to suggest that this aspect of Höffding's thought is of particular importance for understanding Meyer's position vis-à-vis Titchener. The exchange between Meyer and Titchener thus reveals the complex internal differentiations that developed within the human sciences in the United States early this century under the general mantle of positivism.

The Debate between Meyer and Titchener

In the following analysis I mean to facilitate a reading of the correspondence between Meyer and Titchener by isolating several fundamental areas of disagreement all of which reflect their differing interpretations of the work of Mach and Avenarius. The demarcation of these areas of disagreement is, of course, somewhat artificial. As Titchener himself remarks, the assumptions and definitions held by each man so presuppose all the others that serial presentation is bound to be unsatisfactory.

With minor shifts of emphasis, neither man's views changed appreciably over the course of the correspondence. Starting in the early 1900s, Külpe abandoned his earlier commitment to a psychology of sensation and began an experimental study of thinking in functional-teleological terms that challenged the atomistic-sensationalist basis of Titchener's structuralist program. The ensuing controversy over "imageless thought," mentioned in several places in the correspondence (for example, 1M and 2T), helped give rise to behaviorism, but neither the Würzburg-Cornell debate nor behaviorism caused Titchener to alter fundamentally the basic distinctions that governed his approach.[15] Similarly, Meyer's position in 1918 was consistent with the views expressed in his letters of 1909.

What, then, are the issues in dispute between Meyer and Titchener?

The Definition and Subject Matter of Psychology

The first issue in dispute between Meyer and Titchener concerns the definition and proper subject matter of psychology. In his letters to Meyer, Titchener defines psychology as the science of the mind. He explains that the method of psychology is the same as that of all the other sciences, namely observation, which, in the case of psychology, means self-observation or introspection. The primary task of psychology is thus to analyze the mind into its constituent psychic elements by a system of controlled introspection. Of those constituent elements, the most basic is sensation, defined as any sense-process which cannot be further analyzed by introspection. For Titchener, then, a scientific psychology largely reduces itself to the microscopic description of the elementary sensations of the mind; and he justifies his emphasis on the elements of sensation in Machian terms.[16]

Titchener's strictly descriptive approach rigorously excludes as unscientific all functional or purposive considerations from psychology. In highly charged language, he announces his intention of fighting teleology with all the weapons at his disposal:

> The next ten years are going to see a battle between the principles of science, as they were built up by the men of the 19th century, Darwin included,—between them, and the principle of teleology, which has been adopted as a scientific principle primarily by the biologists and secondarily by the biologising psychologists. Evolution, in Darwin's hands, was an anti-teleological instrument. But we are now in one of those waves of popular thought which sweep over countries from time to time . . . and the wave is strongest here in America. The wave, which is the wave of teleological interpretation offering itself as scientific explanation, shows itself in all sorts of

> related movements: in philosophical pragmatism, in the revival of Thomism in the Catholic philosophy, and in your and other men's psycho-biology. . . . That teleology should oust the present principles of science is to me unthinkable. . . . I shall fight you hard, as you invade psychology; I shall use every weapon at my disposal to resist your revolutionary aims; I have not the faintest intention of allowing myself to be killed. (4T)

I have quoted this passage at length because it captures perfectly Titchener's combative tone and the fear of teleology that was, for him, functional psychology's basic defect.[17] Meyer, however, objected to Titchener's psychology on the grounds that by ignoring purposive considerations, it abstracted and isolated the mental elements from the concrete situations or functional settings which constitute them as such. His criticism was not so much that Titchener's analyses were potentially incomplete, although Meyer thought this might be the case. A stronger objection was that by considering the elements of the mind as independent atoms connected together in a purely mechanical fashion, Titchener ignored the fact that the connected whole exercised power over the single elements and hence that the whole and the parts mutually presupposed each other. According to Meyer, the structure of mental experience could not be known independently of the biological setting within which it emerged and out of which it was constituted. Höffding made a similar criticism of psychological atomism[18] and such a situational, holistic account of the nature of the mind was, of course, central to a pragmatist epistemology.

Fortified by both pragmatism and Höffding, in other words, Meyer rejected Titchener's mental elements as so abstract as to be of little interest to most scientists. "The idea of building up living beings out of elements has a ludicrous feature to my mind unless one knows also the compound," he writes (5M). He argues that psychology instead must broaden its approach by analyzing the typical operations of the mind under actual life conditions, that is, in their biological settings and in terms of their functional value. The problem is to discover *how* and *why* mental processes occur and the conditions that call them forth, not to determine supposed irreducible elements of consciousness, and this, in turn, means that it is far better to start from a consideration of the generally observable responses of the organism as a whole to some aspect of its environment than with minute details of a consciousness that can truly be "known" only by its possessor. In short, the individual's overall "adjustive reactions" or instincts must be the unit and prototype of inquiry; Jung's complexes, Meyer notes, are psychodynamic units of this kind (1M, 3M).

All this may be summed up by saying that Meyer and Titchener cannot agree upon the starting point of psychology—on where, practically and conceptually, to *begin*. They are unable to isolate a shared "exemplar," to use Thomas Kuhn's postpositivist term.[19] When Meyer asks, "Why rule out common-sense instead of improving on it?" (5M), he assumes that the experiences of everyday life—appetite (15M) or thumping a chair (19M)—critically analyzed and evaluated, can provide a reliable starting point for psychology. Titchener, however, denies that common sense is a secure guide in science. The everyday situations that form the subject matter of Meyer's psychology are not scientific facts, he objects, but everyday meanings, interpretations, or inferences, which are not open to scientific observation: "[Y]ou don't say how 'activity' can be observed," he complains. "I don't think it can. I think you can observe only facts. And activity is an interpretation of facts" (24T). And on this basis he denies that the mental functions Meyer wishes to study can be the object of scientific inquiry. However, Titchener's disjunction between science and common sense, between observation and interpretation, depends on a positivist opposition between fact and value that Meyer, on pragmatic-functional grounds, is determined to dismantle. "Of course the first question is whether we recognize . . . situations as facts," he retorts. "Somehow some passages of your earlier letters make me still uncertain whether there might be some 'epistemological' flaw in the matter" (31M). Again: "To speak of activities as mere inferences and as post-observational is an inference from your system of definitions" (35M). "Is it possible to follow common sense in its tendency *not* to split fact, value and meaning?" (19M).[20]

Both men realize that their disagreement here is fundamental. The correspondence charts their growing awareness of this fact, as they discover to their growing frustration that they are unable to identify a single concrete, psychological experience or event that can serve as a shared starting point for scientific inquiry. In the ebb and flow of their 1918 correspondence there is a moment when even Titchener himself thinks that this time they may be able to "get over the line" (34T), but that moment disappears as the two men continue to restate their by now familiar antagonisms and differences (see the compelling sequence of letters, starting with Meyer's letter of 2 May 1918 and reaching a climax on 6 June 1918, in which Meyer and Titchener try yet fail to establish a shared standard for discussion).

Characteristically, toward the very end of the correspondence, well after Titchener has given up on it (indicated by a silence on Titchener's part of more than four months after 19 June 1918), Meyer is still trying to find common ground.

The Methods of Psychology

It will be apparent that Meyer's and Titchener's differing definitions of the subject matter of psychology entail very different conceptions of the methods necessary to establish psychology as a natural science. By treating the organism's overall adjustment to the environment as the fundamental unit of inquiry, Meyer sought to broaden the methods of psychology. On the contrary, Titchener restricted the method of psychology exclusively to introspection. He was the leader of the school of "systematic introspection" which flourished in the United States between 1903 and 1913. He rejected the limits previously placed on the use of experimental introspection by Wundt and his school and extended the method to areas such as memory, thinking, and complex feelings that Wundt had explicitly excluded from its legitimate province. As Danziger has observed, Titchener was encouraged in this regard by the phenomenalism of Mach and Avenarius and by their conviction that "science and philosophy must return to their grounding in the analysis of the order of direct experience. Explanatory concepts must not be invented but discovered within the scheme, the regularity, the evidence of experience itself. 'Systematic introspection' was an expression of this outlook within psychology."[21]

According to Titchener, the aim of introspection was to give an analytic description of the "content" of consciousness, that is, of the individual elements of the mind. Introspection reduced complex experience to elements that were held to be identical to the sensory elements of the physical sciences; the only difference was that psychology studied these elements in their dependence on the organism, while physics treated them independently: "I know of no methodological difference between introspection and inspection: they are the same methods applied to what is ultimately the same subject-matter considered from different points of view" (4T). Titchener insisted, however, that the "point of view" of psychology was so different from that of the physical sciences that its method was also entirely different, a point to which I shall return.

By the time Meyer opened the correspondence with Titchener, the latter's exclusive reliance on introspection had begun to be challenged. Many psychologists no longer advocated introspection as the central method of psychology but increasingly supplemented it with the objective observation of others. Thus, James McKeen Cattell, L. L. Judd, E. L. Thorndike, Robert S. Woodworth, and others started to formulate their research problems in terms of the individual's practical performance and the conditions that determined and limited it. The rise of interest in mental testing and the experimental study of mental fatigue further exemplified the same trend.[22]

Meyer's letters reflect this development. "The method of psychology surely is observation," he states. "Primarily it is a matter of introspection. But in as much as we are not inclined to write the psychology of solipsism, we also use the method of inspection, *assisted* by the method of introspection. . . . I should not approach psychology except under its double aspect, that of introspection . . . and that of inspection . . . carried out under the same critical *experimental* conditions demanded in other sciences" (3M). As these remarks suggest, within his functional paradigm Meyer aimed to create methods in psychology that would permit him to apply to the clinical situation the same experimental standards used in the physical sciences. "The fundamental question of science is not the 'what' alone but the 'how'—see Maxwell, if this needs any authoritative proof. . . . The experiment is the unit of scientific experience," Meyer writes (3M), an approach that expands the methods of psychology to include the observation of others: "I truly think it is as much the task of science . . . to create methods of record and analysis of the objective evidence and settings of the mental reactions as it is to introspect their analog in ourselves" (5M).[23]

For Meyer, the specific institutional practice by which the data were to be experimentally observed, and in a sense *produced,* was the psychiatric examination, which, during the years spanned by his correspondence with Titchener, became the cornerstone of his psychiatric teaching.[24] The aim of the examination was to assess not only the patient's physical history but, most important, everything the patient had to say about his or her total life experiences, understood as nearly as possible in the patient's own words—in the "commonsense" language of everyday life. In several important respects, Meyer refined the method of history taking he had inherited from nineteenth-century hospital practice. First, he formalized and standardized the method of examination so that it could be taught in a systematic fashion. He provided students with a basic outline to be followed, specifying the order of procedure, the essential psychobiological data to be ascertained, the various tests to be used to determine the patient's mental and neurological state, and—most important—suggesting the actual questions to be asked the patient, something that had been lacking in previous handbooks of psychiatry. Second, Meyer attempted to free psychiatry from an emphasis on classification, an emphasis he considered premature but which was characteristic of Kraepelinian and other conventional psychiatries. Instead of encouraging students to assign each patient to a specific disease category, Meyer tried to teach them how to generate observations that were independent of and, in effect, prior to questions of nosology. Finally, Meyer taught that the results of the psychiatric examination were to be recorded in a chronological summary of the case in such a way that the factors causing the deviation from "normal" adjustment could be seen to imply a chain of cause and effect that Meyer analogized to the results of a laboratory experiment.[25] As an aid to objectification, Meyer invented the "life chart" as a means of graphically representing each patient's life record. In the section of this essay under the heading "Psychoanalysis, Positivism, and the Self," I shall briefly compare and contrast Meyer's procedures in this regard with those of Freud.

In their dispute over the methods of psychology the future belonged more to Meyer than to Titchener. Titchener's system would fail for a number of reasons. For one thing, he could not argue away the evidence of imageless thought. For another, Titchener's introspective method was based on a traditional equation between the mind and consciousness which the discovery of the unconscious radically called into question. Only by retaining a dogmatic dualism of the mental and physical that consigned all such unconscious mental forces to the physiological level, Meyer argues, is Titchener able to deny the importance of dynamic factors in psychology. "What is the 'functional conception of our mental life'?" Titchener asks. "Where shall I find it? To my thinking, it is organic life that has functions predicable of it, not 'mental life'" (13T). This is a reduction that Meyer cannot accept. "If you wish to limit psychological inquiry to introspection in your own work I am the last man to object," he asserts.

> But if you say that everything outside of that is not psychology, then I must take refuge in psycho-biology as I call it in order to escape your anathema. There I see many fundamental problems of "psychology." What is more confusing, the enumeration of mental elements from the introspectionist's point of view and the overt or

> disguised sensationalism that goes with its aims and interests, or the simple plain and perhaps somewhat slangy descriptions of some of the most vital types of adjustment for a student who goes out into the world with the claim that he had a course in psychology? (3M)

In any case, the general trend in psychology was away from exclusive reliance on introspection. In 1913, that trend reached a climax of sorts in John B. Watson's formulation of the doctrine of behaviorism. By the time Meyer and Titchener had ended their exchange in 1918, even if few psychologists had yet endorsed Watson's radical elimination of all mental experience from psychology, Titchener had nevertheless lost the battle over methodology.

Explanation in Psychology

A third fundamental area of disagreement between Meyer and Titchener concerns the role of explanation in psychology. We have seen that Meyer's functional emphasis on the relational and holistic entailed an emphasis on purposive considerations. Psychology according to this view studied the functional significance of mental experience and therefore did not regard questions of purpose and value as unscientific. In contrast, Titchener's letters to Meyer embody the fundamental positivistic assumption that questions of teleology are extrinsic to a science of psychology. As is well known, Titchener's position on this question, which was shared by many other psychologists, led him to exclude from psychology all questions of meaning and value as unscientific.

Here again both men appeal to the work of Mach and Avenarius to justify their positions, but to very different ends. Titchener's rejection of teleology was based on a positivist conception of causality which held that a complete psychological explanation depended on an account of states of consciousness that portrayed any given state as a continuation or transformation of the states preceding it (following the Machian critique of the concept of cause, Titchener defined causality as involving mere concomitance or covariation). But the phenomena of consciousness appeared to Titchener and his school to be marked by gaps, lacunae, intervals of *un*consciousness: they lacked the temporal continuity that was characteristic of purely material phenomena. Because the principle of continuity was regarded as fundamental to modern science, the demand arose, and we can see this clearly in the writings of Avenarius, to substitute physiological definitions and descriptions (which Titchener, following Avenarius, called the *independent series*) for psychological ones (the *dependent* *series*) wherever possible. More generally, Titchener held that a complete explanation depended on reducing the relation of cause and effect to one of continuity or identity, which, in turn, enabled the establishment of quantitative equations between the phenomena in question.

It followed that psychology could never be a strictly explanatory science like physics, a point on which Titchener agreed with Avenarius. In a passage that makes evident the mechanical-quantitative basis of his conception of causality, Titchener states: "Teleology can't explain any natural phenomenon . . . since the identity in it is an identity of human purpose; whereas in causation the identity is an identity of mechanical energy, cause equals effect energetically" (9T). On these grounds he rejects the notion that mental experience can be the object of causal analysis: "Physics . . . can't deal with mind, since mind is not a form of energy, and can't be included in the machine" (9T). Denying the existence of mental causation altogether, Titchener asserts that only by reference to the nervous system can mental processes be given a causal explanation:

> Psychology is, I hold, strictly a descriptive science. . . . You can get out of it only by mental causation (substantial mind) or by the unconscious [which he regards as a fiction]. But we may make explanations of mental processes by giving their invariable conditions on the side of physics; that indeed is the only explanatory principle possible, so far as I can see. . . . Pure psychology is descriptive, and in the nature of the case must remain so: to get explanation, you must transfer to the other side, to independent experience. . . . So, then, to explain my mental facts I simply wait upon the progress of a causal physiology. (9T)

"In a word," Titchener writes in a passage from his *Textbook of Psychology* to which Meyer will take exception in the correspondence, "reference to the nervous system introduces into psychology just that unity and coherence which a strictly descriptive psychology cannot achieve":

> [T]he explanatory principle for psychology must be looked for beyond, and not within, the world of dependent experience. Physical science, then, explains by assigning a cause; mental science explains by reference to those nervous processes which correspond with the mental processes that are under observation.[26]

Titchener therefore attacks as unscientific Meyer's insistence on the need to study mental events in terms of their functional significance and dismisses Meyer's unit, the "adjustive reaction," on the grounds, first, that it is teleological, and second, that it is borrowed from another science, biology, and is therefore ill suited to serve as the basis for the science of psychology. "'Adjustment' is NOT A SCIENTIFIC TERM at all" he exclaims: "it is a short-hand *biological* expression, used merely for convenience' sake in biology, but not to be used in any other science until analysis there has been fully performed, and indeed to be used EVEN INSIDE BIOLOGY with immense caution" (2T). In sum, he accuses Meyer of giving a merely practical, not a scientific, definition of psychology. "But now the question comes": Titchener remarks,

> Who is to make and to define the pure science? The men who are interested to apply?—That is not the lesson of history. The makers of science have been men to whom the useful was uninteresting. The appliers of science have been the men to whom theory made very scant appeal. You can hardly conceive of a civil engineer propounding a definition of physics, or of a medical practitioner seriously concerning himself to define the limits of physiology. Why then should the psychiatrist offer a novel definition of psychology?

"How, to put it bluntly," Titchener asks, "can the psychiatrist expect that his definition of psychology can be anything more than an amateur's?" (2T).

Not surprisingly, Meyer just as bluntly resists Titchener's efforts to portray him as a scientific incompetent whose practical concern for the care and treatment of patients disqualifies him from defining the field of psychology. Rather, on the basis of his pragmatic-functional views he rejects the dualism of mind and body on which Titchener's dichotomy between physical causality and human purpose is based. Here again, Meyer appeals to the writings of Mach and Avenarius in support of his arguments: "Of course the division of the world into mind and matter is the basis of *your* standpoint. I cannot see that it has any special merit or foundation" (3M). It is precisely the value of Mach and Avenarius, he asserts, to have called into question the radical dualism that characterizes Titchener's views: "You speak of paying regard to Mach and Avenarius. I see scant evidence of that! They are among the very foremost helps in the obliteration of the undesirable split" (5M).

Several articles and reviews, sent to Titchener during the course of their 1918 exchange, helped clarify Meyer's position.[27] He agreed with Titchener that psychology must be defined as a strictly natural science and accordingly concurred with the latter's criticism of Wundt for attempting to exclude certain psychological experiences from the domain of science. Thus Meyer emphatically repudiated the claim, associated with Wundt, Dilthey, Hugo Münsterberg, and others that there are *two* modes of knowledge in the sciences: historical, purposive, or "subjective" understanding on the one hand, and causal, physical, or "objective" knowledge on the other. This approach, by opposing "mind" to "nature," introduced a sharp dichotomy between the human and natural sciences. Rejecting such a view as artificial, as tending either to exclude some aspect of experience from the sphere of psychology or to reduce psychology to physiology, Meyer attempted to unify the human and the natural sciences in a single theoretical framework. His was an experimental or quasi-experimental ideal according to which *all* aspects of experience could be brought into the domain of science and objectively validated.

But the conclusions Meyer drew from his critique of Wundt were not the same as Titchener's. By privileging physics as the only ground of strict causality, Meyer argued, Titchener and others reinstated the artificial distinction between mind and body, which he, Meyer, wished to dispense with once and for all, and in so doing implicitly expressed their solidarity with Wundt. "To some of us it must seem unfortunate," he complained in a review of Münsterberg's *Psychotherapy* to which he alludes in the correspondence (5M),

> to see the . . . over-emphasis of the contrast of "the attitude of appreciation" and "the attitude of physical explanation," the contrast of the subjective and objective, of the purposive and the causal view. . . . We are practically made to believe . . . that translation of the facts into neurological terms furnishes the only real explanatory ground. Is not the role of the psychophysical doctrine chiefly that of eliminating *harmful features* of a dualistic standpoint?[28]

In his letters, Meyer reserves some of his strongest criticisms for Titchener's dualism. Following Mach and Avenarius, Titchener rejected the hypothesis that the mental and physical were two independent metaphysical entities or substances. Instead, Titchener treated mind and matter positivistically as simply two "aspects" of the same world of experience. On this account, experience could be studied from several—or at least two (4T)—aspects or "points of view." Within this framework, Titchener accepted psychophysical parallelism as the doctrine he thought best described the relationship between the mind and body. As simply different aspects of the same experience, mental and physical events did not interact with each other but were parallel phenomena: "The two sets of events, physical and mental, are parallel, but they do not interfere with each other."[29]

But Meyer attacks Titchener's psychophysical parallelism—"that narrow and at best self-evident emphasis of an unessential and scientifically insufficiently founded split of a group of biological events" (3M)—as based on a reinscription of the very dualism of mind and body he intends to dissolve. In opposition to Titchener, he articulates a functional approach to the mind-body problem that treats consciousness not as an independent metaphysical entity to be investigated apart from the body and its setting (James, in his radical empiricism, denies that consciousness exists at all)[30] but as one among many manifestations of organic life:

> The fact is that mental events, the phenomena with which psychology works occur only in sufficiently organized types of living beings. To put the psychological facts on one side and *all* the physical facts on the other expurgates all the life out of psychology. (3M)

> The main purpose of the psychobiological attitude is to eliminate the creation of a phantom called "mind" over and above the biological units which we are and which we look upon as objects of psychology. . . . A common denominator of *function* can be maintained with far less floundering than is the case with the present chasm produced by "parallelism." (5M)

Meyer rejects Titchener's charge that he is universalizing biology and insists rather on the necessity for a broader definition of biology—"call it Huxley's sense of biology" (5M)—to include consideration of mental experience (3M).

Such a broader definition of biology necessarily includes purposive considerations: "In order to give biology a position as common denominator, it will, of course, have to do justice also to the teleological problems" (5M). This was to be achieved by replacing Titchener's mechanical-quantitative definition of causality with a new, energistic conception of both matter and mind that permitted the integration of the physical and the psychical into a single analytic scheme. The "energeticism" of the philosopher-scientist, Wilhelm Ostwald, guided Meyer's observations here. In a book dedicated to Mach, Ostwald attempted an antimaterialist solution to the mind-body problem by treating all qualities of matter and mind as energy, or work. Similarly, Meyer rejected the traditional conception of inert matter that informed Titchener's contrast between the mental and physical in favor of a definition of both mind and matter as combinations of energies, an approach that dissolved the distinction between teleology (mind) and causality (physics) by transforming the received conception of causality into the experimental determination of the functional relations between experiences—both mental and physical—and the conditions that produced them.[31] "To you energy is a physical term. To me it is a fundamental term belonging to all 'natural sciences.' . . . With your parallelistic differentiation according to 'viewpoints,' you naturally create a system of psychological processes devoid of energetic and causal connotation, and that I find the great disadvantage of your formulation" (35M). Physics is not the privileged ground of strict, mechanical causality, as Titchener claims. Rather, all causality is relative and provisional: *experiment,* not mechanics, is the essence of science. For Meyer, this is the true meaning of pragmatism and Mach's work (5M).[32]

On this basis, Meyer refuses to follow Titchener when the latter states that only by reference to the nervous system can mental processes be given a strictly causal explanation. Denying that reference to the nervous system adds in any way to the data of psychology, Meyer in his letters speaks with the authority of the gifted and experienced neurologist he was when he complains about the premature neurologizing to which Titchener's reductionist arguments lend themselves. Quoting Titchener's words back at him, Meyer writes:

> "Reference to the nervous system introduces into psychology just that unity and coherence which a strictly descriptive psychology ogy cannot achieve." That is what I should almost call . . . a bankruptcy of the beautiful structure for which you seem to make such a gallant fight in our correspondence. (5M)

Meyer's position is close to that of Höffding, who observes of Avenarius that in carrying out his physiological reduction, he infers at every stage the constitution of his physiological series from his psychological series, thereby implicitly admitting the existence of a causal relation between psychical states corresponding to the hypothetical physiological states.[33]

Moreover, both Meyer and Höffding argue that there is more continuity in mental experience than is generally recognized. Because Titchener equates the mind with consciousness he is unwilling to explain apparent psychic discontinuities by reference to the unconscious mind. "I do not know what you mean by 'mental activity' and 'dynamic psychology,'" he observes. "You do not define. If by the latter phrase you mean 'a psychology worked out in terms of energy,' or a 'psychology which explains present consciousness by (or from) the purpose or intention of previous consciousness,' then of course I do not accept a dynamic psychology. I cannot find a mental causation, and I cannot accept a teleological principle of explanation" (13T). It is on this basis that Titchener criticizes his contemporary, the psychologist Robert M. Yerkes: "The difference between Yerkes and myself is shown, technically, by his acceptance of mental causality. No system which includes that can be anywhere near mine! . . . He is far nearer to Wundt than he is to me, or than I am to Wundt" (29T). For Meyer, however, the significance of Freud and Jung lies precisely in their demonstration that mental forces just below the threshold of consciousness are at work in the individual where mental gaps appear to exist: "When you come to . . . such a problem as Jung's association-phenomena . . . an essentially introspective psychology must meet the question: *is the degree of consciousness a safe measure for the psychological determination of the stream of thought?*" (3M). Titchener is only able to deny the importance of such dynamic factors in psychology by retaining a rigid dualism of mind and body that reduces such unconscious mental events to physiological processes. Accordingly, Meyer declares that the task of psychology is not to trace psychical phenomena back to their supposed neurological states but to treat psychology as an independent science by studying the functional relations between mental events and determining experimentally the conditions under which they occur. On this basis, he rejects the reductionism implicit in Titchener's position as grounded in an artificial dualism of mind and body that privileges the physical sciences and insists instead on the need to broaden the logic of science to include considerations of teleology or value.

Mach's Principle of Economy and the Hierarchy of Sciences

It will be apparent that Meyer's antireductionism implies an altogether different view from Titchener's of the relation between psychology and the other natural sciences. Once again, the two men use the ideas of Mach and Avenarius to dissimilar ends. Thus both Titchener and Meyer appeal to the empiro-critical principle of the "economy of thought" to justify their respective positions, but the principle means something different in the two cases. According to the principle of economy, the fundamental task of science is observation and description "so as to provide the most economical summary of relationships among experiences."[34] On this account, scientific theories are considered working tools in the service of intellectual economy. Their chief justification is the biological need of the organism to master and control the environment in the most efficient manner possible.

While the principle of economy recognizes that different scientific theories might be necessary at different times and in different situations, in the hands of Mach and Avenarius it leads to a concept of the unity of science based on a hierarchy that makes physics, allegedly the most economical scientific enterprise, the basis for all the others. Following this same reasoning, physiology is regarded as more economical than psychology, which in turn implies the eventual reduction of the latter to the former.

We have seen that Meyer accuses Titchener of such a tendency toward reductionism. Now this is a charge Titchener is at pains to deny. By the terms of his positivist analysis the separate sciences are differentiated from each other, at least initially, not according to their subject matter—as common sense would have it and as Meyer believes—but according to their different aspects or points of view. To use Titchener's formulation in the letters, there is no special class of objects that can be called "psychic" ("*psychisch*"), just as there is none that can be called "physical" ("*physisch*"): experience is simply experience, studied from different points of view (24T). Titchener characterizes the sciences as successive narratives or chapters in the book of nature (4T), narratives which, because they are accounts of the same whole existential universe from different points of view, are coordinate *with* but cannot overlap or be reduced *to* one another. "Wherever one can take a new standpoint over against existence," he writes, "one has a new science; and since the sciences are differentiated by point of view, their renderings of experience must be 'parallel,' in the sense that they lie side by side and cannot meet or fuse" (18T).

In organizing the observed facts of each science into a coherent narrative, the investigator uses the tools of logic in order to work the data up into a communicable system of knowledge in the simplest—the most economical—manner possible. As Titchener will put it in his posthumously published *Prologomena* to his *Systematic Psychology:* "If . . . the business of science is to furnish as simple as possible a description of the existential world, let us add that we mean by 'simplest possible' that which does, in the given circumstances, secure the utmost economy of thought."[35] Yet Titchener explicitly denies that his appeal to the economy of thought implies the actual reduction of psychology to physiology. Mach's economy of thought is a logical, aesthetic, or technological principle, not a scientific one, Titchener asserts to Meyer: it applies to science considered as a *logical* system but not to the *facts* themselves. Implicitly invoking a positivist distinction between observation and logic (interpretation) that pragmatism calls into question, Titchener stipulates:

> The problem of science . . . I take to be description and not understanding. But the system of science, science made available for the generation [sic], holds its facts together by logic. Mach's economy holds, I believe, of this systematic logic. For science it is indifferent whether the description be given in a page of words, or in a single compact mathematical formula; and, as Mach says, the "economical" varies in fact with the public addressed. . . . So the rule that generalised descriptions . . . are to be given in the "simplest possible terms" is a logical ideal, an ideal of the systematic presentation of science—with a touch on it, sometimes, of an aesthetic ideal also,—and with a touch, again if a text-book is in question, of a technological ideal. (27T)[36]

This is the force of Titchener's assertion to Meyer that psychology has only a *logical,* not a *material,* dependence on physiology:

> I don't *explain* or *causally relate* at all, at all! In science all the "explanation" that there is for me is the correlation of a dependent with a (logically prior) independent variable. In psychology the logically prior is biology, in biology the logically prior is physics. . . . So if I "explain" psychology by biology, that means very simply that I take the biological as independent variable in any case where correlation is involved. (32T)

In his *Systematic Psychology,* Titchener defends Avenarius against a similar charge of reductionism.[37] In brief, Titchener conceives of the nervous system as the only possible ground of strict causality in psychology (in the sense of mechanical continuity or covariation defined above) while simultaneously denying that this means any loss of independence for psychology as a science. His position is summed up in the following statement in the letters:

> [T]o explain my mental facts I simply wait upon the progress of a causal physiology. . . . [I]t is, I hope, only a matter of time when physiology will know its nervous system in causal terms. In the meanwhile, my psychology does not fall apart; fact is fact and stays fact . . . and my business primarily and personally is not body but

mind. Physiology can't upset my findings; I am content to go on finding, and to wait the leisure of physiology for their explanation. (9T)

Nevertheless, as Danziger has observed of Titchener's position:

> If psychology was to regard mental data solely in their "dependent" aspect, if mental facts could never explain anything, and if the biological organism provided the only source of explanatory principles for psychology, then it is hardly surprising that psychologists listening to Titchener found themselves wondering why they should bother with mental data at all. Indeed, by dropping them they would do no more than follow the path of progress that Titchener had indicated—psychology would transcend the "natural history" level of mental observation and become a real science.[38]

Just so, in response to the elimination of mental experience implicitly encouraged by Titchener's psychology, Meyer turns Mach's economic principle to other purposes. Rejecting as dualistic and potentially arbitrary Titchener's classification of the sciences as based on different "points of view," Meyer adopts the commonsense approach to experience that Titchener labels "positivist"[39] and assumes as a "given" the existence of various classes of objects or functions (neither purely mental nor purely physical) which it is the task of science to bring under experimental scrutiny. "Here, I really think, is the beginning and end of our differences!" Titchener exclaims. "You—critical common sense, with its various kinds of objects; I—existential experience, with its various aspects" (27T). "It is not exclusively singleness of point of view that is essential," Meyer objects, "and it would be directly wrong to make too much of the 'point of view,' but the postulate of reduction of systematized facts to the standards of critically controlled experimentation or calculation seems to me more fundamental and yet more pragmatically plastic" (17M).

For Meyer—and again, his thought here is close to Höffding's[40]—Mach's principle of economy leads to an emphasis not on the static, timeless character of scientific theories but on their dynamic, time-bound, and symbolic nature. The unity of science is not reductionist in this sense but is based instead on what Meyer calls a principle of "pluralistic consistency," that is, on a commonality of method (the experimental method) between the sciences which complement and, in certain key respects, approach one another but cannot actually be reduced one to the other (which in the last resort means to physics) (5M, 19M, 46M). On this view, physics can be considered the most fundamental science in that it exhibits the workings of the method of science in its purest form; but all the sciences, psychology included, have their own integrity, which is to say their own characteristic subject matter and theoretical-descriptive categories. Thus Meyer treats the mental domain holistically not as a mere summation of component parts but as a new entity or distinct level of psychobiological "integration" whose essence cannot be known but whose conditions of activity as a system of symbolization and meaning can be studied objectively and economically by the psychiatric examination: "[W]ith regard to the adequacy of the various types of description for the various degrees and types of integration, we should simply say that physics and chemistry do not approach the possibility of expressing economically and intelligibly, i.e. scientifically, facts which are simply and specifically expressed in terms of the pertinent level of integration with its special methodological approach" (31M).[41] On the basis of his dynamic interpretation of Mach's principle of the economy of thought, Meyer defends the autonomy of psychology as a science against its threatened absorption into the biological and neurological sciences.

Facts, Values, and Interpretation

It should be clear from the many passages already quoted that Meyer and Titchener appear to adopt fundamentally different conceptions of the nature of a scientific fact. Whereas Meyer's functional approach in psychology posits an intimate connection between fact and value, Titchener's structuralism rests on an epistemology that enforces a radical separation between science and culture. The two men therefore seem to occupy recognizably distinct and opposed positions: for the positivist Titchener, scientific facts are the "pure" data of experience which require no interpretation since they are merely "transcribed" or copied from "the book of nature" by the unbiased observation of the disinterested scientist; for the pragmatist Meyer, scientific facts are always already embedded in an interpretive schema because they are always relative to specific human interests and concerns—they become available, indeed are constituted *as* facts, only within a particular interpretive context or social situation. Yet it is the failure of both Meyer and Titchener to enforce these distinctions that most strikes this reader.

Central both to Titchener's positivism and to the tradition of late-

Victorian scientific naturalism that informed it was the claim that the irreducible elements of the mind constituted the pure data or facts of "existential experience," stripped of all meaning and value. What Titchener meant by "existential experience," Danziger observes, was "what is left of experience when purpose, value, social utility, in short, meaning, have all been removed. According to this metaphysic, there lies beyond the world of ordinary human experience another world of 'sheer existence,' available to us through scientific observation which 'pierces the overlay of interpretation' to reveal the world of 'facts,' 'a world scoured clean of belief and inference and all such evaluative accretion.'"[42] This doctrine was fundamental to Titchener's definition of structuralism from the start and was the basis of his condemnation of functionalism as inevitably construing the material of introspection in terms of meaning and value (20T).

According to Titchener's "context theory of meaning," meaning always involved an act of interpretation supplementary to the observation of the facts themselves:

> I hold that, from the psychological or existential point of view, meaning—so far as it finds representation in consciousness at all—is always context. An idea means another idea, is psychologically the meaning of that other idea, if it is that idea's context. And I understand by context simply the mental process or complex of mental processes which accrues to the original idea through the situation in which the organism finds itself—primitively, the natural situation; later, either the natural or the mental.[43]

To this distinction between fact and interpretation, in which the first term of the opposition is privileged over the second, were related in a systematic fashion all the other dualisms—fact/value, objective/subjective, causal/purposive, science/common sense, theory/practice—to which Titchener appeals in the correspondence.

Armed with these positivist distinctions, Titchener proposed the radical independence of all the sciences, including psychology, from philosophy, history, art, ethics, and religion—in sum, from culture and values. Accordingly, he lumped together all competing psychological systems, including Meyer's psychobiology and Freud's psychoanalysis, as unscientific "value disciplines" or "technologies" because they were concerned with goals, meanings, or values. Titchener claimed that scientific psychology had nothing to contribute to our understanding of social or cultural life: it had no obligation to the social sciences and conducted its work entirely independent of them. It will be recognized that while Titchener repeatedly asserts in his letters that philosophy is irrelevant to scientific psychology (4T, 24T, 32T), his separation of science from philosophy and his denial that he is a positivist are products of that same positivist epistemology. Titchener's system is thus both symptom and reinforcement of the positivist project to demarcate science as a locus of knowledge exempt from all personal, social, and political concerns. As such, his positivism serves as an ideological weapon in the political and institutional struggle to secure structuralism's claim to be the only strictly scientific psychology.

When we turn to Meyer, we are faced with what at first looks like a rigorous antithesis to Titchener's positivist conceptions. In response to Titchener's arguments, Meyer opposes a pragmatic theory of truth which denies the very possibility of isolating scientific knowledge from human experience and the interpretive situations out of which the former emerges and is constituted. For the pragmatist Meyer, scientific truths consist not in conformity or correspondence to an independent reality, as Titchener believes, but are always in the process of formation. To Titchener's essentially specular conception of scientific fact as accurate representation independent of all need or desire (2T, 4T, 13T), Meyer counterpoises an instrumental account of truth as based on specific human interests—interests that are necessarily those of ordinary life and common sense. For Meyer, there can be no difference between scientific truth and what works in practice, a formulation that, by dismantling all the dualisms that structure Titchener's psychology, acknowledges no distinction between science and culture. According to him, pragmatism shows that psychology is not independent of the philosophical, the practical, or the ethical, as Titchener claims, but on the contrary presupposes them. Pragmatism not only validates the scientificity of Meyer's psychobiology but justifies his appropriation of all the "value disciplines," including social psychology and ethics, for science. This appropriation permits him, as it authorizes Dewey and others, to use psychology as an instrument of social reform. When Meyer speaks of his "unblushing assumption that some matters which others look upon sub specie of values are to me plainly objective facts" (26M), he draws attention to one of the most important and obvious differences between Titchener's attempted expulsion of the category of value from psychology and his own pragmatic acceptance of value as inherent in the scientific enterprise.

Here, as elsewhere in the correspondence, Titchener and Meyer mobilize competing interpretations of Mach's writings to support their respective positions. Where Titchener uses Mach to justify the exclusion of value from psychology (24T), Meyer argues that Mach's economic conception of scientific truths as facilitating the individual's adaptation to the environment shows that, according to Mach himself, science is inevitably evaluative in nature (26M). Meyer's position is close to that of Höffding who, in his analysis of the economic theories of Mach and Avenarius, emphasizes the teleological and practical-utilitarian character of scientific laws.[44] And just as Meyer detects an unacknowledged epistemology at work in Titchener's psychology (26M, 28M), so Höffding criticizes as untenable Avenarius's doctrine of pure experience because it denies the historical, situational, and symbolic character of all scientific knowledge and erroneously assumes that we can eventually reach a timeless, objective knowledge free of all auxiliary concepts.[45] In this connection, it is worth noting that although Titchener accuses Meyer of having contempt for the past (24T), Meyer in fact has a far stronger grasp of history than does Titchener for whom the history of science serves the largely ideological function of reassuring himself and others of the progressive and cumulative nature of his enterprise (see Titchener's remarks on the timeless essence of science in 32T).

As a matter of fact, although Titchener strives relentlessly to establish and enforce a distinction between fact and value, the antithesis can readily be deconstructed. Nowhere is this more evident than with respect to Titchener's theory of meaning. Psychologically, Titchener says, meaning is always context, and context is acquired through the "situation" in which the organism finds itself. But the situation, he states, is the "meaningful experience of a conscious present," a definition that, by assuming the existence of another, prior context to determine the meaningfulness of *this* situation, suggests an infinite regress. Put slightly differently, the so-called starting point of his argument is based on presuppositions that render his conclusions circular: what in Titchener's context theory of meaning is stated to be a secondary act of interpretation supplementing an independent process of observation turns out to be primary and constitutive in ways that radically undermine his claim to a discourse of scientificity based on the privileging of factual observation over interpretation.[46] Similarly, Titchener employs an inconsistent metaphorics of reading to describe the relationship between the scientist and nature. In a venerable topos, he figures nature as a book written in a language that he characterizes simultaneously as involving a transparent relation between sign and reality (reality is imaged by representations which, in the first instance, are nature's own and the scientist, with the help of appropriate experimental safeguards, transcribes nature's text in a process that is likened to, though not quite identified with, the almost automatic process of taking dictation) *and* as necessitating a far more complex process of textual decipherment (Titchener's word is "transformation") for which a demanding, esoteric training is required (4T, 24T, 27T, 36T).[47]

In this connection, it is all the more striking that in his letters to Meyer, Titchener figures nature not only as a book to be read but as a mistress to be conquered by stripping her bare of her clothing (27T, 36T). What is interesting about this is less the figure itself, which is hardly original, than the exclusionary social ends it serves to justify: the "production" of woman not as the maker but on the contrary as the object—indeed the very object-*type*—of science. Indeed, from the perspective of postpositivist thought, one might envisage, in place of Titchener's progressivist narrative of the history of science as involving successive acts of taming, stabilizing, and rationalizing (female) nature, an altogether more complex account emphasizing the interaction of different and competing modes of desire, will, and representation.[48]

But analogous contradictions also structure Meyer's account of the relationship between fact and interpretation. On the one hand, Meyer understood himself to be adhering to the pragmatic theory of truth which recognized the situatedness of all knowledge. On the other, Meyer was also convinced that there must be a method capable of eliciting context-free, neutrally describable, in all respects "positive" facts that would not be tied to any particular point of view but would in effect transcend and, in that sense, be prior to, interpretation altogether. The psychiatric examination was developed by Meyer as a technique for eliciting such positive facts, which he accordingly represented as standing above or in implicit precedence to any particular point of view and hence as constituting a body of data on which all scientists must agree. Furthermore, Meyer held that once elicited in this way, the data would not only be prior to interpretation but would themselves provide a sufficient basis for deciding in each particular case which among a variety of alternative interpretations was the appropriate one. On these grounds, he recommended his psychobiological procedures as a solution to the "scandal" of sectarianism that seemed to him to threaten psychiatry's scientific respectability.

But Meyer's project was epistemologically incoherent on two closely related counts. First, as recent writers on the theory of interpretation have emphasized, the realm of facts cannot be imagined to precede interpretation in this way. A thoroughgoing pragmatism might rather have compelled Meyer to realize that the notion of an interpretively neutral method was a chimera and that, inevitably, a particular interpretation inhered in the very procedures he advocated. (This became particularly evident in his attempt to deal with psychoanalysis—a point to which I shall return.) Second, conceding for a moment the possibility of such a method and hence the availability of a set of facts prior to interpretation, Meyer's belief that the mere inspection of those facts would suffice to determine their correct interpretation was also problematic for either the facts in question were imagined as calling for one interpretation rather than another—in which case their neutrality became suspect—or they were genuinely neutral—in which case the choice of one interpretation over another could only be arbitrary.

Similar inconsistencies characterized Meyer's professed pluralism. The pragmatic theory of truth seemed to underwrite Meyer's pluralism and liberalism, for it allowed him to concede that Titchener's interests and concerns might differ from his own. But Meyer's version of the pluralist stance was incoherent in that it posited a condition of openness to all interpretations which could only be that of the preinterpretive moment that the pragmatic theory of truth declared to be an impossibility. Just how ideologically charged Meyer's version of the pragmatic theory of truth turned out to be was expressed in his conviction that the facts with which psychology was concerned must be drawn from the ordinary or common contexts of everyday life. On this basis, he advanced the objection that Titchener's structuralism ignored the ordinary events and situations with which everyone was familiar through personal experience. But this is to say that what was in dispute between Meyer and Titchener were not alternative interpretations of the same facts but rather what, in the first instance, would count as the facts at all. In short, they disagreed about the very subject matter of psychology, or as I put it earlier, about psychology's proper starting point. Meyer's declared epistemological pluralism was thus doomed to come up short for reasons a rigorous pragmatism might have made clear.

Yet we shall hardly be surprised at Meyer's difficulties in this regard if we recognize that the same inconsistency is found in Dewey. In this connection, we may apply to Meyer what Richard Rorty has said of Dewey, that he "was never to escape the notion that what he himself said about experience described what experience itself looked like, whereas what others said of experience was a confusion between the data and the products of their analyses."[49] When Meyer reflected on general epistemological problems, his aim was to resist a positivist epistemology by putting in its place what he understood to be a pragmatist epistemology characterized by relativism, open-mindedness, and tolerance for the opinions of others. But it is also a pragmatist insight that conviction about the truth of one's own beliefs is inescapable—that one cannot stand *outside* one's beliefs, any more than one can stand outside the social and cultural structures and practices in which one is embedded. Accordingly, Meyer's attitude toward his own medical and scientific assertions was not and could not be one of relativism or disinterest. Characteristically, however, Meyer was uncomfortable with this state of affairs. The result was a persistent tendency in his thought to fall back on the notion of a supracontextual framework, a general viewpoint that would have something like the neutral authority traditionally associated with the natural sciences and that would provide a permanent, unbiased matrix for all future investigation. This tendency was powerfully reinforced by the demands of disciplinary professionalization and institutionalization which seemed to make it imperative for Meyer to justify his claim to knowledge by grounding it in sources held to be independent of belief altogether. As a consequence, Meyer's position ended up resembling the perspective of traditional positivist epistemologies (not excluding Titchener's).[50]

The Professionalization of Psychology

As my last remarks suggest, we cannot fully understand the debate between Meyer and Titchener unless we recognize the critical importance of the process of institutionalization and professionalization that occurred not only in psychiatry and psychology but in all the sciences during the period spanned by their correspondence. Between approximately 1880 and 1920 psychiatry shed its former status as a beleaguered speciality isolated from the rest of the medical profession behind the walls of the mental asylum. The rise of medical interest in psychotherapy, the creation of new psychiatric societies and journals, the rapid expansion of a body of "abstract knowledge," the founding of the mental hygiene movement, the integration of psychiatry into the university curriculum—all advances with which Meyer was intimately involved—testify to the increasing professionalization of psychiatry during this period. During the same years psychology underwent a similar evolution, characterized by rapid growth, academic institutionalization, and the establishment of journals and professional associations designed to promote the demarcation and legitimation of the field.[51]

But the growth of professionalism in psychiatry and psychology was neither smooth nor simple. As new disciplines uncertain of their future and jealous of their scientific standing, the process of professionalization was marked by considerable internal friction and dispute. As Titchener and Meyer discuss their respective difficulties in obtaining students and funds it becomes clear that they adhere to divergent models of scientific research and of how the professionalization of psychology is to be achieved. Titchener represents psychology as a strictly academic discipline whose claim to contribute to the advancement of knowledge is based on an explicit disavowal of any vulgar concern for practical results. He grounds his positivist separation between "pure" and "applied" science in radically different goals and attitudes: the aim of science is to explain the riddle of nature; the aim of technology is to solve the practical and material problems of human life. He acknowledges that there is mutual interplay between science and technology but they are "through and through different, and naturally make appeal to different temperaments. The man of science is always in the great minority" (24T); and he characterizes the science-technology relationship in traditional terms by portraying technical innovation as fundamentally dependent on prior advances in "pure" science (2T).

Titchener's description of psychology as an exclusively cognitive discipline divorced from utilitarian considerations and his assertion of an ethics of disinterestedness serve the ideological purpose of appearing to acquit psychology, along with the other basic sciences, of the profit motive. By describing psychology as a scholarly enterprise whose value is independent of market relations, Titchener embraces an aristocratic ideal of science as an impersonal pursuit open only to an elite few. The insistent metaphor of purity that runs through Titchener's letters thus serves the purpose of rendering invisible the economic, political, and social factors that can be shown to have contributed powerfully to psychology's successful institutionalization. At the same time, as a modern professional whose claim to institutional privilege is based on a special competence remote from the practical concerns of the average citizen, Titchener runs the risk of losing the general social support necessary to his enterprise. His complaints to Meyer about the public's indifference to basic science—an indifference he regards as deeply rooted in American culture and as reinforced by the pragmatic movement—register his awareness of that risk (13T, 27T).

In contrast, Meyer adheres to a medical model of scientific research that grounds the legitimation of psychology not only in the production of specialized knowledge but also in the creation of unique client-oriented services of various kinds. Identifying with the democratic, pragmatic trends of American (and Swiss) culture, Meyer seeks to expand the financial and institutional support for psychology beyond the academy to include a middle-class clientele increasingly willing to spend money on all the mental ills the new psychological experts claim the authority to diagnose and cure. Adopting an ideology of social engineering, Meyer justifies the application of psychology to social ends, thereby forging those ties between psychology, industry, and the state that are such a striking feature of psychology's disciplinary identity in the Progressive Era.

The physician-patient relationship provides psychiatry with sources of funds denied Titchener's strictly laboratory psychology. Yet Meyer's more market-oriented conception of psychology faces special problems of professional demarcation, regulation, and control. It is something of a paradox that at the moment psychiatry in America was emancipating itself from the dogma of the organic lesion in favor of a dynamic model, the scientific physician was being encouraged to study almost exclusively the body and its disorders. Owing largely to the success of bacteriology, scientific medicine became oriented to the laboratory and experimental sciences of the German research tradition. The greatly influential Flexner Report of 1910 institutionalized the new paradigm of scientific medicine by calling for a reform of medical education based on the laboratory sciences of chemistry, biology, and physics. Both university and state authorities were anxious to associate themselves with (and benefit from) the Flexner reforms and, partly for that reason, tended to regard skeptically the new methods of hypnosis, psychotherapy, and psychoanalysis which seemed to them to hover precariously between speculation and science.[52] Nowhere was this attitude more evident than at Johns Hopkins, the name of whose most famous medical spokesman, William Welch, was practically synonymous with scientific medicine. One consequence of this was that during his long association with Johns Hopkins, Meyer found himself engaged in a largely unsuccessful struggle to win the confidence of his medical colleagues and to persuade them of the scientific legitimacy of his psychiatric doctrines.

It is therefore not surprising that in his letters Meyer expresses anxiety about the academic respectability and dignity of his field. Burton Bledstein has commented that the "culture of professionalism" has only socially conservative consequences.[53] In Meyer's case, the desire to advance the professional interests of psychiatry and his own natural conservatism were mutually reinforcing. Already before his exchange with Titchener he was disturbed by the developing competition between psychiatrists and psychologists for clients and funds. Concern for professional authority led Meyer in 1909 to oppose lay involvement in the mental hygiene movement and also made him one of the earliest adversaries of lay psychoanalysis.[54] Similarly, from the outset, professional considerations impelled him to demand training in the more established field of neurology as a necessary prerequisite to psychoanalytic practice.[55] More generally, Meyer's desire to safeguard the interests of psychiatry induced him to play a leading role in the creation of monopolistic (or semimonopolistic) devices intended to protect psychiatrists from unwanted competition within the field.

Meyer faced demarcation problems of another, related kind. It has been remarked that the claim to possess exclusive cognitive knowledge is a necessary (though not a sufficient) condition for successful professionalization.[56] In Titchener's case, such a claim was facilitated by the fact that his psychology was couched in an esoteric, theoretical vocabulary that was difficult to routinize without prolonged and specialized training. Meyer's assertion of a distinct, theoretical competence, on the other hand, was compromised by the fact that his dynamic psychiatry was framed in the everyday language of common sense. In a way that was characteristic of American pragmatism, Meyer distrusted as dogmatic and one-sided any theory, such as psychoanalysis, whose specialized terms or exclusive principles seemed to him to ignore the plainly accessible facts or preclude agreement on fundamental issues. In a nonpositivist discourse not fully purged of positivism, he rejected as untrustworthy and potentially dangerous all specialized concepts in favor of the simple words of common usage, words that by virtue of their very ordinariness seemed to him to incarnate reality.[57] "The great myth of a pure Gaze that would be pure Language: a speaking eye," is how Michel Foucault has defined the ideal to which nineteenth-century clinical thought aspired in its effort to construct a natural relation between linguistic sign and symptom.[58] In his writings, Meyer expressed just such a belief in the possibility of erecting a spontaneous relation between word and reality. Self-described as verbally ungifted,[59] he was suspicious, even fearful, of verbal complexity and extolled instead the plain, direct words of common usage. At the same time, there was a tension in his thought between the desire to use words with which everyone was familiar and the demands of professionalism that called for a specialized terminology that could be understood only by the initiate. In this regard also, Meyer was heir to that conflict in the history of clinical thought between simplicity and medical esotericism so brilliantly analyzed by Foucault.[60]

Magali Sarfatti Larson has forcefully reminded us that university training is the most powerful legitimation of any profession's assertion of cognitive superiority[61]—which is why the question of what constitutes appropriate formal training in psychology assumes such importance in the Meyer-Titchener correspondence and why, as educators competing for a limited number of students, the two men touch frequently on their teaching duties and responsibilities (see, for example, 22T, 23M, and 27T). For Meyer in particular, the integration of a common psychology course into the medical curriculum and the requirement of formal medical training in psychiatry are necessary steps in fixing psychiatry's disciplinary boundaries and legitimating its claims to possess a distinct expertise.[62] The two men occupy predictable positions here. Titchener dismisses Meyer's psychobiology course as merely a "psychology for medical students" (24T) and proposes instead that Meyer hire his student, Edwin G. Boring, to carry out psychological research at Meyer's clinic and train the medical students—a proposal that threatens to relegate the psychiatrist to the position of a technocrat capable merely of coordinating the research of others and organizing the practical management of cases (20T). Naturally, Meyer spurns Titchener's suggestion. Emphasizing rather that the relations between "pure" and "applied" science are far more tangled and indeed mutually enabling than Titchener recognizes, Meyer contends that training in clinical methods is essential to mastery in human psychology. In short, Meyer asserts the superior authority of the psychiatrist over all other workers in the psychological sciences by grounding that authority in medical-psychiatric training and by making the psychiatric clinic the institutional center of the field.[63]

The professional conflicts inherent in the two men's positions were exacerbated by the changes in the institutional structure of

American psychiatry and psychology during World War I. The successful mobilization of personnel for the testing of Army recruits and the treatment and rehabilitation of psychiatric casualties brought these fields new prestige. As a consequence, by the war's end there was a growing demand for psychological services of all kinds and a significant improvement in the professional status of both disciplines.[64] The 1918 correspondence between Meyer and Titchener reflects these developments as both men were drawn into the business of providing trained personnel for the war effort. Although in his letters Titchener cites the call for his students as evidence of the success of structuralist psychology (24T), it is rather the case that with the increase of applied psychology during the war years, his system became increasingly isolated from the mainstream of American psychology—a fact of which Meyer is aware when, toward the end of the exchange, he casts doubt on the continued fruitfulness of Titchener's program (46M). However, Meyer also faced problems of professional competition. While he welcomed the growing recognition given to psychiatry and psychology, he was alarmed by the growing competition represented by the success of lay psychologists in the mental hygiene and psychoanalytic movements. In this context, he would do everything possible to maintain the professional superiority of psychiatry by subordinating lay psychology to medical-psychiatric leadership.

Psychoanalysis, Positivism, and the Self

I have reserved until now a consideration of the movement which, in 1909, precipitated the correspondence between Meyer and Titchener and which, from the start, challenged the paradigms of psychological knowledge and representation put forward by both men—I refer, of course, to psychoanalysis. In obvious respects, Titchener's response to Freud's retheorization of the self—conceived not as the autonomous, preexisting consciousness of Cartesian philosophy but as the product of a more or less successful reconciliation between competing, unconscious psychosexual desires—was more straightforward than Meyer's. Late in the 1918 correspondence, we find Titchener defending his structural psychology against Meyer's charge of narrowness and exclusiveness. "So far from feeling that I am hemmed in," he reflects in an autobiographical moment, "I feel on the contrary that the position is immensely fertile." He continues:

> I don't, on the other hand, want to make converts. I think that the great majority of any generation cannot and will not think clearly, and that all one can do is follow out one's light for oneself. To think clearly means years of worrying, and more reading than one likes to look back on. It means therefore a strong animal constitution, and what our enemies call Sitzfleiss [*sic*, Sitzfleisch = perseverance]. Its reward is interior and not external; one keeps in touch with at most a scant half-dozen of likeminded Strebers [= strivers]—and with them one necessarily disagrees on many points!—I have a very great respect accordingly for any man who honestly works, even if he comes out at a wide remove from me.

This passage is immediately followed by the memory of his encounter with Freud at the Worcester conference nine years earlier:

> I had very good talks with Freud, and respect him immensely, though I think his psychology is antediluvian and his constructions largely precarious; but he is a man who has worked and thought and suffered; and I have no stomach for controversy with him,—all the more as the future will finally decide as to what is good and sound in both of us. (34T)

Titchener's unexpectedly conciliatory gesture toward Freud cannot only be attributed to the spirit of greater tolerance that characterized his later years. His remark suggests that powerful processes of identification were at work in his "very good talks" with the "likeminded" leader of psychoanalysis. Yet Titchener is both accuser and defender of Freud: the spell of Freud's "genius" (2T) must be resisted, admiration for the man who (like himself) has suffered for science must not be allowed to interfere with a sober assessment of Freud's work:

> I offered to attempt a translaton out of this psychology of association into modern psychological terms, and Freud laughed at me, and said that if I came to him for half a year I should see that modern psychology needed to be "revolutionised" in his way. Revolutionised, ye gods! That means, set back just about two human generations. And then the man wonders that we do not take his psychologising seriously. Freud is a very great man; but Freud's psychology is a very outworn travesty of psychology. (2T)

Not surprisingly, the terms of Titchener's attempted "translation" of Freud are derived from Mach and Avenarius. Mach rejected the psychological concept of the ego on the positivist grounds that the individual's experience of the self was "not an experience at all but simply a combination of sensations which in themselves are no more mental than they are physical."[65] For Mach, the experience of mental causation and personal agency was an illusion: he dismissed the self as a "metaphysical" construct or auxiliary concept which had no place in a scientific psychology. Avenarius reached the same conclusion by emphasizing the error of "introjection," the tendency to attribute mental experiences to other people when such mental experiences are not given in one's own direct experience. Similarly, Titchener accuses Meyer of the "worst sort of introjectionism" for attributing minds to other people and for claiming that such minds are objectively knowable (24T): according to Titchener, psychology investigates mental experience only in its dependence on the biological organism.

Titchener's rejection of the "psychical individual" had several important consequences. All mental experiences which had previously been attributed to central processes and to an inner self conceived as the source of feeling and action were reinterpreted as the product of peripheral stimulation (see Titchener's reference to his debate with the Würzburg school over this issue in 2T). One major casualty of Titchener's reinterpretation of the self along these lines was the traditional, liberal notion of freedom of the will, a point registered by Meyer: "[Y]our antithesis [between mind and body] looks as if it might in the end deny the freedom altogether" (5M). Nothing was left of the popular idea of individuality except the notion of the self as a temporary and always-changing combination of sensations constructed out of the flux of experience. For Titchener, the tendency to treat oneself and others as permanent personalities had only a social, not a scientific, meaning: "Selfhood thus comes to us from our social experience; the author cannot believe that it would come, save perhaps in exceptional cases, from introspective examination of the background of consciousness."[66] The phenomenon of multiple personality that so captured the imagination of James and others was attributed by Titchener to changing external conditions.

Titchener's response to psychoanalysis, based on these positivist assumptions and beliefs, was simplistic in the extreme. According to Titchener, Freud's psychology of unconscious, symbolic meanings is a logically confused regression to an exploded, unscientific psychology of association (2T, 9T); the "psychodynamic units of events" discovered in Jung's theory of the "complex" are not psychological at all but as yet unanalyzed psychophysical phenomena (2T); lust or sexual desire, for Freud, the fundamental drive in human development, is nothing more than organic sensation (16T); and the dynamic counterplay of motives and the struggle between conflicting tendencies central to Freud's theory of the self is "all popular and interpretive, a matter of 'casuistry' (logical and ethical) in the technical sense of casuistry; worlds away from anything scientific, and patently and obviously teleological and technological!" (34T). In sum, Titchener's introspective psychology remained resistant to Freud's uncommensensical, unpopular conceptions, even as a major wing of American psychology—represented by Meyer—increasingly sought an accommodation with the psychoanalytic movement.

"You said Freud's psychology is that of two generations ago. Is there any possibility of putting its sound nucleus in terms of the psychology of the present generation?" (1M). Meyer's question in his opening letter to Titchener indicates the direction his attempted accommodation with psychoanalysis will take. He acknowledges that psychoanalysis has a "sound nucleus." Yet if what is valuable in psychoanalysis is to be integrated into the legitimate sciences, its findings must—as Titchener says—be reformulated in modern psychological terms in order to meet the same empirical standards that are satisfied in the other natural sciences. Meyer suggests that Jung's work furnishes a natural basis for this operation: Jung's complexes "do indeed offer a very interesting opportunity on which to show how you deal with the dynamic features, and nothing would be more welcome than to have the formulation of that issue from you or one of your men" (12M).

However, Meyer was convinced that any such reformulation would have to remain on functional ground. A psychology of pure introspection which ignored the dynamic factors at work in the mind was, in his view, of little use to psychiatry. Nor, following James, would he abandon the idea of the self.[67] Yet if Meyer was influenced by Freudian theory, he did not identify his views with psychoanalysis. Rather, he attempted to subsume psychoanalysis within what he viewed as his own more objective psychobiological approach—although the process of subsumption was carried out at the expense of modifying Freud's ideas almost beyond recognition.

Take, for example, Meyer's emphasis on the patient's biography. In his letters to Titchener, Meyer argues on functional principles that psychology must start not with the abstract mental elements of Titchener's structural psychology but with the individual's immediate experiences as they are observed by the physician and elicited in conversation with the patient. A narrative component in the form of the patient's biography is therefore an essential ingredient of Meyer's psychobiology: in this regard, his psychology bears a resemblance to Freud's psychoanalysis in which the individual's life story plays a fundamental role. However, Meyer's psychobiological approach made his conception of biography radically different from Freud's. His methodological assumptions, his insistence that facts were not facts unless they were public and shared, naturally tended to valorize the conscious mind, where putative facts were, so to speak, present to both patient and observer, as against the unconscious, whether understood in Freudian terms or simply as a realm of hiddenness and inaccessibility. (Significantly, in 1912 Meyer criticized Freud's concept of the transference in just these terms.[68]) It followed that the narratives Meyer tended to construct differed fundamentally from those of Freud's case histories. Like the psychoanalysts, Meyer was committed to studying the personality in a temporal perspective. But his theoretical and methodological assumptions tended to exclude precisely the concepts of unconscious sexual desire, repressed conflict, and compensatory fantasy that Freud viewed as fundamental and that many psychiatrists through Freud's influence would come to regard as essential to a truly biographical understanding of the human subject. Thus in place of Freud's theory of a crucial discontinuity between a hypothetical "nature" and the "culture" of unconscious sexuality, Meyer substituted a theory of a maturational psychobiological *continuum* leading genetically to a self or ego whose function was efficient adaptation to reality.[69] This functional, adaptive approach was fundamentally alien to Freud's attempt to ascertain the psychological meaning of sexuality for the patient's history as that meaning was revealed in the analytic situation. More generally, Meyer's reformulation of Freud's concept of sexuality as a desexualized "affect" or "go," his depreciation of the unconscious, and his functional emphasis on the patient's current problems rather than on infantile psychosexual conflicts—all anticipated and set the stage for the ego-psychology revisions of the American neo-Freudian Harry Stack Sullivan, and others.[70]

Moreover, whereas in psychoanalysis the subject's identity is established above all at the level of (or in) language, for Meyer the normal function of the individual was guaranteed by the "personality."[71] Meyer did not believe, as Freud emphatically did, that facts have no status as evidence apart from the conceptual, and in an important sense, the linguistic framework that constituted them as such. Nothing could be more emblematic of his distance from psychoanalysis in this regard than his dismissal of language as "the poorest tool we have" for scientific representation (5M) and his recourse instead to various visual devices for recording the patient's biography. The most important of these was the life chart, a device invented by Meyer in order to reduce the "long stories" with which he dealt to a concise, manageable record while creating the same effect of presence and facticity as that established by a photographic image[72] (Figure 2). One might say that whereas Freud turned the visual (the dream) into the verbal, Meyer turned the verbal (the patient's narrative) into the visual. As he made clear in a paper sent to Titchener during their correspondence, Meyer developed the life chart precisely as a solution to the problem of scientific representation posed by Freud's psychoanalytic approach.[73] The overall effect achieved by the chart was of a laconic summary of the "facts" of the case in a graphic representation whose form and temporal characteristics resembled more than anything else the traditional hospital chart. The contrast with Freud could hardly be greater. In particular, everything of interest to Freud, such as the patient's hesitations, unfinished sentences, slips of the tongue, dreams, and phantasies—matters whose significance was only revealed in and through the patient's transferential interaction with the analyst—was omitted by Meyer in the positivist belief that the truth of the patient's biography could be known objectively to both patient and physician by a process of direct observation.[74]

All this may be summed up by saying that Meyer and Freud envisaged fundamentally different kinds of *persons*. Freud's reconceptualization of the self as the site of insistent, psychosexual conflict—a reconceptualization that, as Jacqueline Rose has observed,[75] challenged empiricist accounts of the "real" as involving an unproblematic relation between the internal and external world—made it impossible for those who followed him to equate the self any longer with the notion of the "personality." For Meyer and the American functionalists, however, at the same time as the idea and clinical phenomenon of multiple personality called into question the traditional unity of the self, it also served the conservative purpose of reconfirming the concept of the personality as such. Ian Hacking has recently traced the disappearance of multiple personality—from the start, primarily an American and French phenomenon—to the impact of psychoanalysis.[76] I would suggest rather that the concept of multiple personality did not so much disappear from the American literature—although the more flamboyant cases vanished—as be-

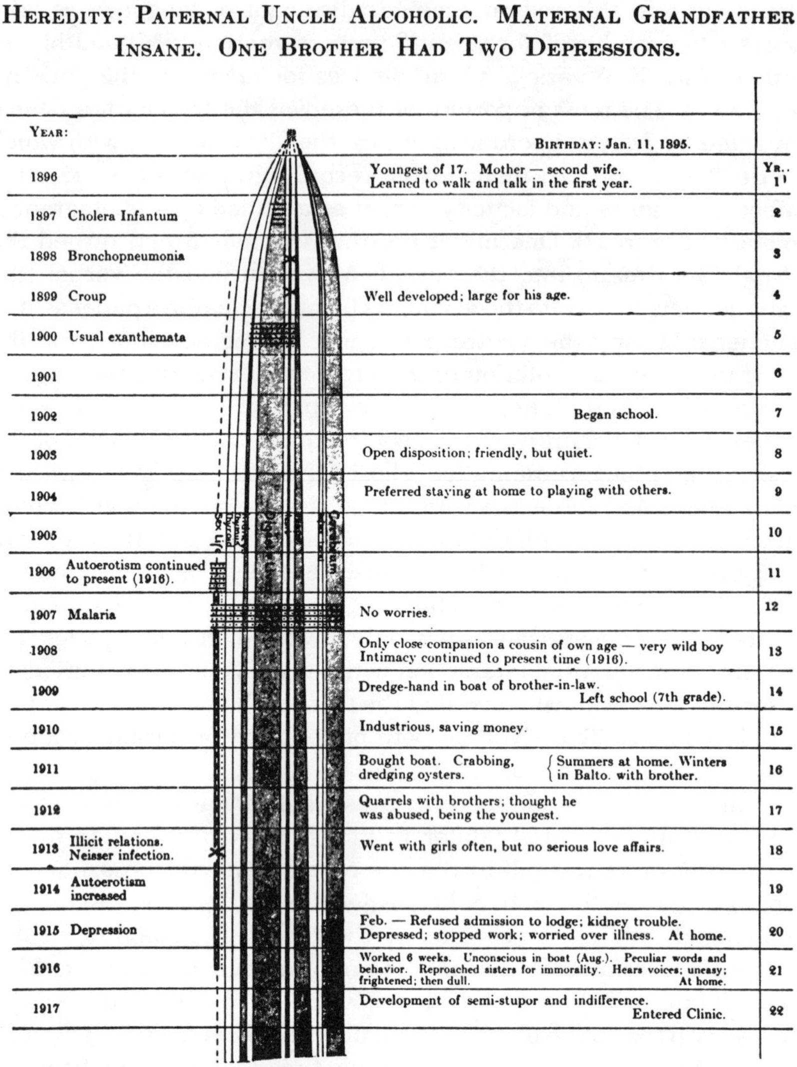

Figure 2. Meyer's Life Chart: Case of Schizophrenia

come domesticated and naturalized in the functionalists' claim that the healthy personality was naturally plural and heterogeneous.[77] In any case, largely through Meyer's influence, the personality construct remained central to American non- and neo-Freudian psychiatry alike.

The Challenge of Behaviorism

Finally, I shall bring my discussion of the Meyer-Titchener correspondence to a close by commenting briefly on the other contemporary movement that challenged both Meyer's psychobiology and Titchener's structuralism: behaviorism. The two sets of correspondence bracket in time a crucial event in twentieth-century American psychology: John B. Watson's launching of behaviorism in 1913. The basic tenets of Watson's foundational paper, "Psychology as the Behaviorist Views It," are well known. Psychology was to abandon as unscientific the study of conscious or internal mental states in order to concentrate exclusively on the objectively observable behavior of organisms. Only in this way would psychology achieve its aim of becoming an experimental science and fulfill its theoretical goal of the prediction and control of behavior. Recognizing no distinction between human beings and lower animals, Watson included higher mental processes in the repertory of behavior by treating thought itself as subvocal speech and so reducing it to sequences of motor actions. In this way, he sought to describe all normal and abnormal reactions objectively by viewing them as a system of habitual responses to the environment.[78]

In attempting to account for the emergence of behaviorism in 1913, commentators have recently emphasized the debt Watson's behaviorist project owed to the positivist movement in American academic psychology. Thus Danziger has persuasively argued that Titchener's positivism led almost inescapably to behaviorism. Basing himself on the ideas of Mach and Avenarius, Titchener denied the explanatory status of mental events and treated meaning and value as merely auxiliary to the data of existential experience. As a result, Titchener encouraged psychologists to cease bothering about mental data altogether and made virtually inescapable Watson's turn to behaviorism in 1913. Danziger writes:

> Such matters as meaning and purpose clearly do not belong to [Titchener's] psychology of consciousness, and therefore they are relegated to the area of behavioral response. Titchener had legis-

> lated sensation to be devoid of meaning; meaning appeared by the addition of a "context." But that addition, as Boring quite correctly concludes, is simply the response of the organism to the original sensation. Because the addition of "context" is itself frequently not a conscious act, "the test of such a meaning can only be behavioural." Meaning is a matter of discriminatory response, and Titchener's context theory of meaning finally fathers behaviorism.[79]

From the start, Meyer recognized the intellectual lineage between Titchener's structuralism and Watson's behaviorism. Thus in an important exchange of letters with Watson in 1916, Meyer reproached the behaviorist for directly encouraging Titchener and his school:

> Titchener could not find a greater support theoretically than by your formulations. He will at once say: Do as you please; but you do not touch "*my* problems." And I am afraid many will feel with him; whereas with my point of view, I feel that I can rise above Titchener's viewpoint and taken in all that is substantial in his and yours.[80]

As a matter of fact, Titchener's reaction to Watson's behaviorism was just as Meyer feared in terms of reinforcing Titchener's dualism and leaving his structuralist research problems untouched. Treating Watson's behaviorist project as a contribution to the research program of Mach and Avenarius in psychology—that is, as a contribution to understanding experience considered as dependent on the central nervous system—Titchener assimilated Watson's behaviorism to the same positivist project that informed his structuralist enterprise. I believe this helps explain the leniency of his overall appraisal of Watson's proposals as not only technological but, more fundamentally, biological in nature and therefore as supporting Titchener's structuralist program: "[I]t is . . . clear that behaviorism and psychology are . . . correlative; and that . . . it is impossible to have a science of behaviorism independent of all psychology. It is equally impossible . . . to have an independent science of psychology; the two halves are essential to the single whole."[81] In the correspondence, Titchener shows the same indulgence toward Watson: "In my critique of Watson I . . . showed that what he had so far said was both inadequate and incoherent. I don't think that the b-ists are at all bothered about fundamentals. I think they like to do a certain sort of work (which is perfectly good work of its kind) and they like to damn what they think is psychology; and I heartily doubt if they have thought their own position through" (29T).

Meyer's response to behaviorism was different. Like Titchener, Meyer was on friendly terms with Watson, whom he met at Hopkins in 1908 soon after Watson had arrived at the university to take up a position as professor of psychology, and with whom he believed at first that he shared the same scientific and professional interests. However, after 1913, even as he continued to support Watson by inviting the behaviorist to move his psychology laboratory to the Phipps Clinic, it became increasingly obvious to Meyer that their differing theoretical viewpoints could not be reconciled. This was especially apparent when Watson assimilated Meyer's concept of "twisted habits" to the "conditioned reflex" concept in order to explain mental disease in strictly behavioral terms.[82] Indignantly repudiating Watson's effort to appropriate his teachings to the behaviorist cause, Meyer complained: "Behaviorism physiologizes the data of experience, while some of us consider it wise to speak in our first preliminary surveys of common experience, actuated by the sense of economy concerning the advisability of translation of the immediate data into a special jargon. Psychobiology sees no harm in using the data as they present themselves, and the usual terminology."[83] "I might be called a behaviorist who does not damn psychology" Meyer claims in a letter to Titchener (31M) thereby—like Dewey, Edwin B. Holt, and others—defining behavior along functional-purposive lines to include the role of mental experience and the human personality.

Moreover, as we have seen, Meyer's functional psychology recognized no distinction between science and ethics, whereas Watson's behaviorism, like Titchener's structuralism and on the grounds of the same positivist epistemology, assumed a complete separation between fact and value. According to Watson, it was not the province of psychology to set moral standards. Rather, psychology's aim was to provide the techniques for social control by which whatever standards society desired could be achieved. In effect, Watson was a moral relativist who displaced ethical questions into the social and political realm on the grounds that they were irrelevant to the development of a technology of behavior control which alone was the legitimate concern of a scientific psychology. In words which—apart from their behaviorist application—could have been written by Titchener himself, Watson would write: "I have no sympathy with those psychologists and philosophers who try to introduce a concept of 'meaning' ('values' is another sacred word) into behavior. . . . The question of meaning is an abstraction, a rationalisation and a speculation serving no useful scientific purpose."[84]

The disparity between the approaches of Meyer and Watson in this regard was particularly evident with regard to sexual conduct and morality. Watson agreed with Freud that the sexual drive or instinct was of fundamental importance in the life of the individual. True to his behaviorist principles, however, he did not interpret sexuality psychically but treated it, rather as Titchener did, as an organic response of the body—a response that according to Watson was, in principle, open not only to objective observation but to outright manipulation as well.[85] For Meyer, on the contrary, human sexual behavior could never be merely a matter of the reflex response of the sexual organs, as Watson claimed, because sexual reactions always took place in a social situation and always involved social values. Thus, Meyer rejected Watson's account of sexual behavior as mechanistic and fatalistic, an account that he suspected of leading all too easily to the notion of human sexual desires as demanding satisfaction and hence of justifying sexual behavior at odds with conventional wisdom. What was needed, he argued in response to changing American attitudes toward sexual morality, was a new consensus or code of conduct that would achieve a balance between individual freedom and social responsibility.[86]

In this context, it is ironic that two years after the close of their correspondence Titchener should have held Meyer in some sense responsible for the sexual scandal that in 1920 ruined Watson's academic career. In August of that year, Meyer was informed by the psychologist G. Stanley Hall that Watson was conducting an extramarital affair with his research assistant, Rosalie Rayner, daughter of a prominent Baltimorean, and that an ugly scandal was brewing. Stung by Watson's apparent disregard for the reputation of the Phipps Clinic, Meyer immediately asked Watson for an explanation. Meyer knew that Watson's conduct was not likely to be tolerated by a university administration highly sensitive to public opinion and in the weeks that followed attempted to persuade Watson to rectify the situation. When it became apparent that Watson had no intention of giving Rayner up and that a public scandal could not be averted, Meyer placed statements Watson had sent to him about his private life into the hands of the university administration with the result that Watson was asked to resign his position.[87]

When Titchener heard of these events, he blamed Meyer for the fiasco. In a letter to Yerkes that is indicative of the strength of his final assessment of Meyer's intellectual capacities, he wrote:

> I am terribly sorry for the Watson children, just as I am sorry for W. himself; he will have to disappear for 5 or 10 years, I am afraid, if he ever wants indeed to return to psychology. . . . But what makes me indignant, is that A. Meyer and the Clinic in general couldn't have used their arts to keep W. straight. They are so blamed keen on theory—in which they are after all only logical infants—that they forget that the business of the psychiatrist is to prevent and cure. A little decent advice (for W. is intrinsically a very decent and eminently likeable person) would have prevented the family tragedy. And it is the children who suffer most.[88]

In actuality, when confronted with the crisis caused by Watson's adultery, Meyer attempted to remedy the situation by pointing to what he viewed as exactly the "logical" connection between Watson's positivist beliefs and his willingness to flout his marriage vows. "I cannot help seeing in the whole matter a practical illustration of the lack of responsibility to have a definite philosophy, the implications of not recognizing meanings, the emphasis on the emancipation of science from ethics etc.," he reproached Watson:

> It may not affect your psychology, or rather you may consider it necessary to keep your psychology free from contamination in order to focus its methods. Unfortunately it blinds you to matters which after all are vital and which in this case threaten the very existence of your psychological research.[89]

In short, Meyer's response to the crisis caused by Watson's sexual conduct was consistent with his pragmatic refusal to separate facts from values—one of the key issues at stake between himself and Titchener.

After a final restatement of their respective credos, Meyer and Titchener broke off their correspondence in December 1918. Although they occasionally corresponded in later years, so far as I know they did not meet again. Neither man was subsequently able to produce the book on which he was working at the time of the exchange and which each had intended as a summary of his life's work. The incompleteness of the correspondence thus anticipates the inability of either man to produce the comprehensive statement that each aspired to make. Just so, their failure to reach agreement mirrors the factionalism and sectarianism that have continued to mark psychology's disciplinary history throughout this century.

Notes

1. Adolf Meyer, "The Dynamic Interpretation of Dementia Praecox" (1909), in *The Collected Papers of Adolf Meyer,* ed. Eunice E. Winters, 4 vols. (Baltimore: Johns Hopkins Press, 1950–52), 2:443–58 (hereafter cited as *CP*).

2. *The Freud/Jung Letters: The Correspondence between Sigmund Freud and C. G. Jung,* ed. William McGuire, trans. Ralph Mannheim and R. F. C. Hull (Princeton: Princeton University Press, 1974).

3. Krzysztof Pomian, "De la lettre au periodique: La circulation des informations dans les milieux des historiens au XVIIe siècle," *Organon* 10 (1974): 25–43. Cf. F. L. Holmes, "The Fine Structure of Creativity," *History of Science* 19 (1981): 60–70.

4. "I am very anxious to get common ground with psychologists," Meyer would later write to Titchener's student, Edwin G. Boring, "since the continual division into camps hurts the recognition of psychology as a natural science tremendously" (Meyer to Edwin G. Boring, 24 May 1920, The Adolf Meyer Papers, The Alan Mason Chesney Medical Archives, The Johns Hopkins Medical Institutions).

5. Cf. Rand B. Evans, "E. B. Titchener and His Lost System," *Journal of the History of the Behavioral Sciences* 2 (1972): 168.

6. Edwin G. Boring, "Edward Bradford Titchener: 1867–1927," in *Psychologist at Large: An Autobiography and Selected Essays* (New York: Basic Books, 1961), 246–65; idem, "The Society of Experimental Psychologists: 1904–1938," *American Journal of Psychology* 51 (1938): 410–23; idem, "Titchener's Experimentalists," *Journal of the History of the Behavioral Sciences* 3 (1967): 315–25.

7. Edwin G. Boring, *A History of Experimental Psychology,* 2d ed. (New York: Appleton-Century-Crofts, 1950), 410–20; idem, *Psychologist at Large,* 246ff.

8. Meyer, "The Problems of Mental Reaction Types, Mental Causes, and Diseases" (1908), *CP,* 2:598.

9. Kurt Danziger, "The Positivist Repudiation of Wundt," *Journal of the History of the Behavioral Sciences* 15 (1979): 205–30; E. B. Titchener, *A Textbook of Psychology* (1910), with an introduction by Rand B. Evans (Delmar, N.Y.: Scholars' Facsimiles and Reprints, 1980), v–xiii; David F. Lindenfeld, *The Transformation of Positivism. Alexius Meinong and European Thought, 1880–1920* (Berkeley and Los Angeles: University of California Press, 1980).

10. Although Titchener's debt to Mach and Avenarius was known to his contemporaries, he reserved his most explicit discussion of their views for his posthumously published (and unfinished) *Systematic Psychology: Prolegomena* (1929; reprint, with a foreword by Rand B. Evans and Robert B. McLeod, Ithaca: Cornell University Press, 1972). The Meyer-Titchener correspondence is therefore especially valuable for documenting this aspect of Titchener's thought.

11. Meyer, "British Influences in Psychiatry and Mental Hygiene" (1933), *CP,* 3:403. Meyer credited Avenarius with anticipating pluralism, "at any rate not a dualism of . . . materialism v. idealism" (Post-Retirement Notes and Conversations with Eunice Winters and Anna Mae Bowers, VI/8/35, The Adolf Meyer Papers). Although Avenarius was at the University of Zurich when Meyer

was a student, Meyer first read him soon after his arrival in the United States, encouraged by his friend Joseph Kodis, whose wife had been a pupil of Avenarius. Through his friendship with the monist Paul Carus, Meyer also read Mach at this time.

12. "Of . . . philosophical works I have probably been most grateful to Höffding's writings, some of which I think are available in English, especially his *History of Modern Philosophy* and *Problems of Philosophy*" (Meyer to R. H. Harper, 13 September 1915, The Adolf Meyer Papers). See also Meyer to Arthur O. Lovejoy, 15 January 1916, The Adolf Meyer Papers; Meyer, "British Influences in Psychiatry and Mental Hygiene," 403. Meyer later recalled that "Avenarius [was] a very interesting philosopher . . . best interpreted in Harald Höffding's *Moderne Philosophen*. . . . Höffding was not only an eye-opener but I had the feeling 'that is it'" (Post-Retirement Notes and Conversations with Eunice Winters and Anna Mae Bowers, VI/8/180, The Adolf Meyer Papers).

It must be emphasized that in using Höffding's interpretation of Mach and Avenarius for his own pragmatic purposes, Meyer ignored the neo-Kantian framework of Höffding's presentation. My thanks to Gary Hatfield for helpful discussions of Höffding's work.

13. Frithiof Brandt, "Harald Höffding," *The Encyclopedia of Philosophy* (New York: Macmillan Publishing Company, 1976), 4:48–49; Kalle Sandelin, *Harald Höffding in Memoriam* (Copenhagen: Gyldendal, 1932).

14. Harald Höffding, *The Problems of Philosophy,* trans. Galen M. Fisher with a preface by William James (New York: Macmillan, 1906), ix–x.

15. For the debate over imageless thought, see George Humphrey, *Thinking: An Introduction to Its Experimental Psychology* (London: Methuen and Company, 1951); Lindenfeld, *The Transformation of Positivism,* 225ff.

16. Danziger, "The Positivist Repudiation of Wundt," 218–20.

17. Titchener interprets Darwin's evolutionary theory positivistically as fundamentally hostile to the principle of teleology, whereas for functionalists such as Meyer the signal importance of the Darwinian revolution was its teleological emphasis on adaptation as a principle of biological analysis. Cf. Robert Richards, *Darwin and the Emergence of Evolutionary Theories of Mind and Behavior* (Chicago: University of Chicago Press, 1987).

18. Höffding, *The Problems of Philosophy,* 15–18.

19. Thomas Kuhn, "Postscript" to *The Structure of Scientific Revolutions,* 2d ed. (Chicago: University of Chicago Press, 1970), 174–210. Pickering explains that "For Kuhn, an exemplar is a shared example, upon which scientists base their work at the research front. He emphasized that such a shared example involves the concrete demonstration in some practical situation of the utility of a cultural product—a new experimental technique, a new theoretical model, or whatever—and that it is precisely through such demonstrations, through *practice* involving exemplars, that new concepts are related to the natural world and acquire their meanings" (Andrew Pickering, "Interests and Analogies," in *Science in Context: Readings in the Sociology of Science,* ed. Barry Barnes and David Edge [Cambridge: MIT Press, 1982], 125).

20. In this context, it is not surprising that Meyer would later express sympathy for the Gestalt school of psychology.

21. Danziger, "The History of Introspection Reconsidered," *Journal of the*

History of the Behavioral Sciences 16 (1980): 254.

22. Ibid., 257. See also Michael M. Sokal, ed., *An Education in Science: James McKeen Cattell's Journal and Letters from Germany and England* (Cambridge: MIT Press, 1980).

23. Meyer describes his experimental approach to psychiatry in "Principles in Grouping Facts in Psychiatry" (1905), *CP,* 2:138.

24. Meyer's extension and adaptation of the medical examination for psychiatric evaluation may be viewed as a contribution to the modern production of the "individual" as described by Michel Foucault, *Discipline and Punish: The Birth of the Prison,* trans. Alan Sheridan (New York: Pantheon Books, 1977), 184–94.

25. See especially, Meyer, "Outlines of Examinations" (1918), *CP,* 3:224–58; idem, "Outline of First Year Course" (1938), *CP,* 3:259–70.

26. Titchener, *A Textbook of Psychology,* 39–41. In a letter to the psychologist Robert M. Yerkes, Titchener makes the same criticism of Meyer's functionalism (Titchener to Robert M. Yerkes, 16 November 1909, The Robert M. Yerkes Papers, Yale University Library).

27. In chronological order, they were: Meyer, "Misconceptions at the Bottom of *Hopelessness of All Psychology*" (1907), *CP,* 2:573–80; idem, "Pathopsychology and Psychopathology" (1912), *CP,* 2:640–53; idem, "Objective Psychology or Psychobiology with Subordination of the Medically Useless Contrast of Mental and Physical" (1915), *CP,* 3:38–43. Titchener comments at length on this last paper in 24T.

28. Meyer, review of Münsterberg's *Psychotherapy* (1909), *CP,* 2:637. Höffding makes a similar criticism of Münsterberg's antithesis between science and values in *The Problems of Philosophy,* 23–24. Münsterberg's debt in this regard to Dilthey and the German hermeneutical tradition is discussed by Matthew Hale, Jr., *Human Science and the Social Order: Hugo Münsterberg and the Origins of Applied Psychology* (Philadelphia: Temple University Press, 1980), chap. 6.

Recent criticisms of attempts to distinguish the human sciences from the natural sciences on the grounds of method include Mary Hesse, *Revolutions and Reconstructions in the Philosophy of Science* (Bloomington: Indiana University Press, 1980); Richard Rorty, *Philosophy and the Mirror of Nature* (Princeton: Princeton University Press, 1979), chap. 5; idem, "Method, Social Science, and Social Hope," in *Consequences of Pragmatism: Essays 1972–1980* (Minneapolis: University of Minnesota Press, 1982), 191–210. Meyer would have been in substantial agreement with Rorty's antifoundationalist, pragmatist position but for his (Meyer's) residual positivism which, characteristically, ends up dominating his enterprise. On this point see under "Facts, Values, and Interpretation" in this essay.

29. Titchener, *A Textbook of Psychology,* 14.

30. William James, *Essays in Radical Empiricism* (Cambridge: Harvard University Press, 1976).

31. For Meyer's debt to Ostwald, see "The Philosophy of Occupation Therapy" (1922), *CP,* 4:88. Cf. Meyer's remark: "More and more we realize that what figures to our mind as *matter* is much better expressed in terms of combinations of electrons, if not simply of energies, which throw off many of the forbid-

ding and restricting features of those masses which form the starting point of our concept of inert matter" ("The Role of the Mental Factors in Psychiatry" [1908], *CP,* 2:584). Höffding gives a brief evaluation of Ostwald's theory of energetics in *Modern Philosophers,* 125–29. Cf. Erwin Hiebert, "Wilhelm Friedrich Ostwald," *Dictionary of Scientific Biography* (New York: Charles Scribner's Sons, 1978), 25: suppl. 1, 455–67.

32. In notes written immediately after the termination of his 1909 correspondence with Titchener, Meyer rejects the definition of science as mechanical. The "discovery of facts, and of new ways of handling things and the spirit of experimentation with limited hypotheses rather than the assumption of a universal principle [of mechanism] accounts for the progress," he observes. This conception, Meyer adds, is the one of common sense and also of "most religions, of the voluntaristic philosophies, and the raison d'être of James's tychism" (Scientific Notes and Records, XI/1/2, The Adolf Meyer Papers).

33. Höffding, *The Problems of Philosophy,* 38–39.

34. Danziger, "The Positivist Repudiation of Wundt," 212. Cf. John T. Blackmore, *Ernst Mach: His Work, Life, and Influence* (Berkeley and Los Angeles: University of California Press, 1972), chap. 12; Lindenfeld, *The Transformation of Positivism,* 81ff.

35. Titchener, *Systematic Psychology,* 64.

36. Cf. Mary Henle, "E. B. Titchener and the Case of the Missing Element," in *1879 and All That. Essays in the Theory and History of Psychology* (New York: Columbia University Press, 1986), 147.

37. Titchener, *Systematic Psychology,* 134–35.

38. Danziger, "The Positivist Repudiation of Wundt, 216.

39. Titchener denies that he adopts any philosophy, positivist or otherwise, and instead accuses Meyer of "positivism" (24T, 27T), by which he means Meyer's willingness to abide by common sense and hence to dissolve the distinction, so central to Titchener, between science and interpretation or values. Meyer accepts the label of "critical common-sense" (26M) or "neo-positivism" (31M).

40. Höffding, *The Problems of Philosophy,* 84; idem, *Modern Philosophers,* 13–40.

41. "I used integration when Sherrington used it for the nervous system," Meyer recalled. "I thought, as long as it was accepted by neurologists, it was a good term, and I demanded it also for the psychological integration" (Post-Retirement Notes and Conversations with Eunice Winters and Anna Mae Bowers, 31 July 1942, The Adolf Meyer Papers).

42. Danziger, "The Positivist Repudiation of Wundt," 223. Cf. Rand B. Evans, "The Origins of Titchener's Doctrine of Meaning," *Journal of the History of the Behavioral Sciences* 11 (1975): 334–41.

43. Titchener, *Lectures on the Elementary Psychology of the Thought Processes* (New York: Macmillan, 1909), 175.

44. Höffding, *The Problems of Philosophy,* 75ff.

45. Ibid., 98–103. Danziger observes that in introducing his concept of existential experience Titchener makes one of his rare points of disagreement with Avenarius, who takes phenomenal experience as his starting point and accordingly includes the experience of value in psychology (Danziger, "The

Positivist Repudiation of Wundt," n. 77). The disagreement is noted by Titchener when he comments to Meyer: "You seem . . . to use 'observe' . . . as more or less = vorfinden. You then 'find' all sort of things about you, much in the sense of Avenarius' positivism. (He, it is true did not find values, but he found valuations)" (24T). Cf. Höffding, *Modern Philosophers,* 138–39.

46. Cf. Mary Henle, "Did Titchener Commit the Stimulus Error? The Problem of Meaning in Structural Psychology," *Journal of the History of the Behavioral Sciences* 5 (1969): 279–82.

47. For the topos of the book of nature, see Ernst Robert Curtius, *European Literature and the Latin Middle Ages,* trans. Willard R. Trask (Princeton: Princeton University Press, 1953), 319–26. The model that ultimately informs Titchener's secularized conception of reading nature is divine revelation, as his passing reference to God as the author of Nature in 34T suggests.

48. For the figure of nature as a woman, see Carolyn Merchant, *The Death of Nature. Women, Ecology, and the Scientific Revolution* (San Francisco: Harper and Row, 1980). I will only add in connection with the tangled question of Titchener's attitude toward the struggle of women to enter science at this time that he created the "Experimentalists," an informal, influential society of experimental psychologists from which women were excluded, precisely in order to protect a "pure" psychology of introspection from the inroads being made within the American Psychological Association by an (increasingly feminized) applied psychology. As a consequence, he helped ensure that women's experience in science was one of containment and segregation rather than expansion. Titchener appears to have dissociated his liberal views on race from his attitude toward women—not an unusual phenomenon. See Edward H. Beardsley, "The American Scientist as Social Activist: Franz Boas, Burt G. Wilder, and the Cause of Racial Justice, 1900–1915," *Isis* 64 (1973): 50–66.

Although Meyer's functional approach at first appears more receptive to the presence of women in psychology, he was no less sensitive than Titchener to the demands of professionalization and no less inclined to subject women to an interpretive process that worked in the direction of their professional containment and control. On the one hand, Meyer's residual but in the end fundamental positivism helped defeminize psychology. Specifically, Meyer's insistence on the necessity of medical training served to justify the subordination of the lay psychologist to the hospital-trained physician—a policy that in combination with the barriers to the advancement of women and minority groups being erected at the turn of the century by the Flexner reforms had the effect of tending to segregate women in the less prestigious fields of clinical and applied psychology. On the other hand, eschewing the fact-value distinction that helped disguise the social interests informing Titchener's representations of women, Meyer on pragmatic grounds developed a prescriptive account of female identity as reproductive and maternal in essence that repeated and reinforced traditional medical-scientific justifications for limiting the role of women in science.

For the history of women's struggle to enter psychology in this period, see Margaret Rossiter, *Women Scientists in America: Struggles and Strategies to 1940* (Baltimore: Johns Hopkins University Press, 1982); Elizabeth Scarborough and Laurel Furumoto, *Untold Lives: The First Generation of American Women Psychologists* (New York: Columbia University Press, 1987).

49. Richard Rorty, "Dewey's Metaphysics," in *Consequences of Pragmatism,* 79–80.

50. My analysis of the tensions and contradictions in Meyer's pluralism is indebted to helpful discussions with Stanley Fish, Michael Fried, and Walter Benn Michaels. In this connection, see especially Stanley Fish, *Is There a Text in This Class? The Authority of Interpretive Communities* (Cambridge: Harvard University Press, 1980); idem, "Interpretation and the Pluralist Vision," *Texas Law Review* 60 (1982): 495–505; Michael Fried, "How Modernism Works: A Response to T. J. Clark," *Critical Inquiry* 9 (Autumn 1982): 217–34; Steven Knapp and Walter Benn Michaels, "Against Theory," ibid. 8 (Summer 1982): 732–42; idem, "A Reply to Our Critics," ibid. 9 (June 1983): 790–800; idem, "A Reply to Richard Rorty: What is Pragmatism?" ibid. 11 (March 1985): 466–73; idem, "Against Theory 2: Hermeneutics and Deconstruction," ibid. 14 (Autumn 1987): 49–68.

51. In a large literature, see especially Joseph Ben-David and Randall Collins, "Social Factors in the Origins of a New Science: The Case of Psychology," *American Sociological Review* 31 (1966): 451–65; E. Richard Brown, *Rockefeller Medicine Men: Medicine and Capitalism in America* (Berkeley and Los Angeles: University of California Press, 1979); Thomas M. Camfield, "The Professionalization of American Psychology," *Journal of the History of the Behavioral Sciences* 9 (1973): 66–75; Magali Sarfatti Larson, *The Rise of Professionalism: A Sociological Analysis* (Berkeley and Los Angeles: University of California Press, 1977); Dorothy Ross, *G. Stanley Hall: The Psychologist as Prophet* (Chicago: University of Chicago Press, 1972); Paul Starr, *The Social Transformation of American Medicine* (New York: Basic Books, 1982). My discussion of Meyer's and Titchener's definitions of professionalism is especially indebted to Larson's impressive analysis.

52. C. P. Oberndorf, *A History of Psychoanalysis in America* (New York: Grune and Stratton, 1953), 114.

53. Burton Bledstein, *The Culture of Professionalism: The Middle Class and the Development of Higher Education in America* (New York: Norton, 1976), 92.

54. Norman Dain, *Clifford W. Beers: Advocate for the Insane* (Pittsburgh: University of Pittsburgh Press, 1980), 143.

55. Ernest Jones to Meyer, 30 November 1910, The Adolf Meyer Papers.

56. Larson, *The Rise of Professionalism,* 31ff.

57. Meyer, "Preparation for Psychiatry" (1933), *CP,* 3:79–80; idem, "A Discussion of Some Fundamental Issues in Freud's Psychoanalysis" (1909–10), *CP,* 2:604–17; idem, "Constructive Formulation of Schizophrenia" (1921–22), *CP,* 476.

58. Michel Foucault, *The Birth of the Clinic: An Archeology of Medical Perception,* trans. A. M. Sheridan Smith (New York: Vintage, 1975), 114.

59. Meyer, "British Influences in Psychiatry and Mental Hygiene," 404.

60. Significantly, Meyer—who started his career by condemning all existing systems of classification—ended it by proposing a psychiatric nosology of his own, one so terminologically barbarous that it never caught on. Meyer, "Leading Concepts of Psychobiology (Ergasiology) and of Psychiatry (Ergasiatry)" (1938), *CP,* 3:285–314.

61. Larson, *The Rise of Professionalism,* 50–51.

62. In 1914 Meyer, John Broadus Watson, and Knight Dunlap jointly inaugurated a psychology course for students at the Phipps Clinic, but their differing theoretical viewpoints could not be reconciled and Meyer abandoned the attempt after one year. From then on he taught the course alone and attached great importance to the task.

63. Meyer, "Conditions for a Home of Psychology in the Medical Curriculum" (1912), *CP,* 3:35–36.

64. Daniel J. Kevles, "Testing the Army's Intelligence: Psychologists and the Military in World War I," *Journal of American History* 55 (1968): 565–81; Franz Samelson, "World War I Intelligence Testing and the Development of Psychology," *Journal of the History of the Behavioral Sciences* 13 (1977): 274–82; Michael M. Sokal, "The Origins of the Psychological Corporation," ibid., 17 (1981): 54–67. For a general review of the role of testing in American psychology, see Michael M. Sokal, ed., *Psychological Testing and American Society, 1890–1930* (New Brunswick, N.J.: Rutgers University Press, 1987).

65. Danziger, "The Positivist Repudiation of Wundt," 210.

66. Titchener, *A Textbook of Psychology,* 17, 546–47.

67. In his famous meditation on the philosophical problem of personal identity, James, in his *Principles of Psychology,* argued that a rigorous introspection revealed no such thing as a metaphysical or transcendental "soul"; but he did not follow Titchener in rejecting the concept of the self. Rather, he treated the self as neither completely identical with the body nor as utterly independent of it but as a "logical postulate" inseparable from certain movements of the body and which, in a surprising metaphor, he figured as involving the notion of an inherited title that never lapsed: our sense of personal identity, James suggested, was achieved by a process analogous to an orderly, unbroken chain of legal inheritance. As Michaels has shown, such an analogy naturalized and made crucial to the concept of the self a certain idea of property: the mind was owned, James argued, albeit by a self whose precarious unity was easily fragmented into various component parts by acts of dispossession or alien appropriation. The radical alterations of the self that occurred in hypnotism and cases of "multiple personality" were interpreted by James as involving violations of property rights. See Walter Benn Michaels, *The Gold Standard and the Logic of Naturalism. American Literature at the Turn of the Century* (Berkeley and Los Angeles: University of California Press, 1987), 7–9.

68. Meyer, "Conditions for a Home of Psychology in the Medical Curriculum," 36.

69. I have adapted and applied to Meyer Jeffrey Mehlman's description of the tension between the two conceptual schemes that inform Freud's enterprise on the one hand and American ego psychology on the other—a tension (roughly, between an abiological theory of the unconscious and biologism) that Jean Laplanche has brilliantly demonstrated also functions systematically within the general economy of Freud's own thought. Jean Laplanche, *Life and Death in Psychoanalysis,* trans. and intro. Jeffrey Mehlman (Baltimore: Johns Hopkins University Press, 1976), ix–x.

70. Helen Swick Perry, *Psychiatrist of America. The Life of Harry Stack Sullivan* (Cambridge: Harvard University Press, 1982), 232–41. For the revisionist return to a psychology of common sense among the neo- and post-Freudians,

see Russell Jacoby, *Social Amnesia: A Critique of Contemporary Psychology From Adler to Jung* (Boston: Beacon Press, 1975).

71. For a similar description of Janet, see John Forrester, *Language and the Origins of Psychoanalysis* (New York: Columbia University Press, 1980), 18.

72. Meyer, "The Life Chart and the Obligation of Specifying Positive Data in Psychopathological Diagnosis" (1919), *CP*, 3:53–56.

73. Meyer, "Objective Psychology or Psychobiology," 39–40.

74. For an analysis of Meyer's life chart, see Ruth Leys, "Types of One: Adolf Meyer's Life Chart and the Representation of Individuality," *Representations*, forthcoming.

75. Jacqueline Rose, *Sexuality in the Field of Vision* (London: Verso, 1986), 100.

76. Ian Hacking, "The Invention of Split Personalities (An illustration of Michel Foucault's Doctrine of the Constitution of the Human Subject)," in Alan Donagan, Anthony N. Perovich, Jr., and Michael V. Wedin, eds., *Human Nature and Natural Knowledge* (Dordrecht, Holland: D. Reidel, 1986), 79. For the invention of new kinds of persons at the turn of the century, see also idem, "Making Up People," in *Reconstructing Individualism: Autonomy, Individuality, and the Self in Western Thought*, ed. Thomas C. Heller, Morton Sosna, and David E. Wellberry (Stanford: Stanford University Press, 1986), 222–36; Arnold I. Davidson, "Sex and the Emergence of Sexuality," *Critical Inquiry* 14 (Autumn 1987): 46–48.

77. "A multiple personality is in a sense normal," asserts the sociologist George Herbert Mead (*Mind, Self, and Society from the Standpoint of a Social Behaviorist*, ed. and intro. Charles W. Morris [Chicago: The University of Chicago Press, 1934], 142).

78. John B. Watson, "Psychology as the Behaviorist Views It," *Psychological Review* 20 (1913): 158–77.

79. Danziger, "The Positivist Repudiation of Wundt," 223–24. Cf. Brian Mackenzie, *Behaviorism and the Limits of Scientific Method* (London: Routledge and Kegan Paul, 1977).

80. Meyer to Watson, 2 June 1916, The Adolf Meyer Papers.

81. Titchener, "On 'Psychology as the Behaviorist Views It,'" *Proceedings of the American Philosophical Society* 53 (1914): 6.

82. John B. Watson, "Behavior and the Concept of Mental Disease," *Journal of Philosophy, Psychology, and Scientific Methods* 13 (1916): 589–95.

83. Meyer to Watson, 29 May 1916, The Adolf Meyer Papers.

84. John B. Watson, "Is Thinking Merely the Action of Language Mechanisms?" *British Journal of Psychology* 11 (1920): 103. For a brief statement of Watson's views on ethics, see his "An Attempted Formulation of the Scope of Behavior Psychology," *Psychological Review* 24 (1917): 329–30.

85. For Watson's views on human sexuality, see his "Image and Affection in Behavior," *Journal of Philosophy, Psychology, and Scientific Method* 10 (1913): 421–28; idem, "Emotional Reactions and Psychological Experimentation," *Journal of Psychology* 28 (1917): 163–74; idem, "A Schematic Outline of the Emotions," ibid. 26 (1919): 165–96; John Watson and Rosalie Rayner, "Controlled Emotional Reactions," *Journal of Experimental Psychology* 2 (1920): 1–14; John Watson and Karl S. Lashley, "A Consensus of Medical Opinion upon

Questions Relating to Sex Education and Venereal Disease Campaigns," *Mental Hygiene* 4 (1920): 769–847.

86. These themes are discussed in Adolf Meyer, "Normal and Abnormal Repression" (1922), *CP,* 4:401–6; idem, "Freedom and Discipline" (1928), *CP,* 4:411–17; idem, "The Meaning of Maturity" (1932) *CP,* 4:425–34; idem, "Spontaneity" (1933), *CP,* 4:460–83. It should be added by way of clarification that in his writings Watson was no more able than Titchener to segregate "facts" from "values": his books and articles embody the social and political values typical of his class and time, including rather conventional sexual attitudes. However, Watson's assumption that behavior as a whole was fully determined—that it necessarily changed with changing stimulus situations—implicitly threatened the stability of traditional sexual arrangements. As a matter of fact, there are passages in Watson's later writings than can be seen as justifying in retrospect his own sexual conduct in behaviorist terms.

87. These events are analyzed in detail in Ruth Leys, "Meyer, Watson, and the Dangers of Behaviorism," *Journal of the History of the Behavioral Sciences* 20 (1984): 18–49.

88. Titchener to Robert M. Yerkes, 25 November 1920, The Robert M. Yerkes Papers, Yale University Library. Titchener's sympathy for Watson's plight contrasts with Meyer's more critical reaction: "Frankly—I have little patience with either Thomas [the sociologist, W. I. Thomas, who in 1919 was forced to resign from the University of Chicago for sexual improprieties] or Watson. Neither in their life nor in their philosophy have I seen a constructive effort. I do not think their instincts led to anything but a mess. What on earth *did* they attain?" Meyer to Ethel Dummer, 9 November 1920, The Adolf Meyer Papers.

89. Meyer to Watson, 17 August 1920, The Adolf Meyer Papers.

The Meyer-Titchener Letters, 1909 and 1918

The Correspondence of 1909

1 M

September 18, 1909

Dear Professor Titchener:—

I am so determined not to let the strong impressions of the Worcester meeting[1] pass into the field of repressed complexes that I venture to ask you whether you would be willing to give me a few hints as to how to find the working hypothesis which would avoid unnecessary conflicts. Your excellent reviews of certain phases of psychology[2] make me realize the difference between our standpoints, but also the necessity that those who wish to teach should understand each other and not leave to the student the task of adjustment. I should formulate such an effort as follows:

There are evidently a number of standpoints which are entitled to the term psychology. If I understand it correctly your standpoint is that of seriously analyzing the nature and conditions of what is accessible to introspection and presents itself as mental function under the conditions of well controlled experiments. This form of psychology would to my mind correspond to the minute histological studies and certainly has a very important place, although it necessarily is of interest chiefly to a relatively small group of investigators,—whereas the rest will profit from certain results and correct their illusions without necessarily being able to participate in the work.[3] As I see it you are concerned with such questions as whether or not there are imageless /thought/ processes etc.,[4] very much as we histologists try to determine whether there is nerve activity without neurofibrils and the like. At the same time there are innumerable and important problems in neurology which do not depend on such detail and which form legitimate topics of enquiry. In psychology there are similar problems of a most sweeping character and I might even say of fundamentally much greater importance to the average student. Psychology, as I see it, is the study of all those reactions which the neurologist can only describe by metaphor and which for convenience sake I call the reactions of the individual as a whole in contrast to reactions of individual organs. Genetically we would feel inclined to look for adjustive instincts as the fundamental elements which have become differentiated into actions and reactions of various degrees of specialization, as I tried to sketch the matter in the Psychological Bulletin, June 1907/ p. 179/.[5] Out of the wealth of differentiated reactions we physicians would pick out those which are most subject to fluctuation under more or less definite conditions. So far only extraneous conditions have received much attention— the poisons, fatigue, etc. But there are other influencing factors, and among these I should like to be set right concerning Jung's complex-theory.[6] You said Freud's psychology is that of two generations ago. Is there any possibility of putting its sound nucleus in terms of the psychology of the present generation? The best place to attempt this would be in Jung's complex-theory. Now, of course, one might turn down the problem with the remark that psychology is not far enough advanced or not concerned with these matters at the present time, and that the problem is not mature; but that would remind me of kindred claims of those who would make the science of neurology dependent on sufficient knowledge of neurofibrils and other detail structures. To this we might reply that the work of neuro-physiology has moved along excellently with mere working hypotheses in the field of histology and maximum utilization of the functional phenomena. The whole problem of Jung's work is comparable with any problem of neurophysiology, and all we want is to see it carried out with conscientious methods and in terms which should not be misleading. The best help in an effort to strike a common ground would, therefore, be a statement from you as to how you think the problems of Freud and Jung would have to be formulated in order to receive a card of admission to the domains of legitimate enquiry into those reactions which we cannot understand under any other heading but as psycho-biology.[7]

I am afraid that I am asking altogether too much, but I assure you that I shall be grateful for whatever you will be willing to formulate. This is not a matter for publication; even a hasty dictation of the main points would be sure to have a great value for me. Whether I can repay you for your trouble in any way is uncertain; I may have to charge it up to the account of indebtedness which has accumulated in the past. If I can turn the amount into a capital of working material from which students may derive some benefit and which might keep me from creating confusion, you would possibly have to be content with the results.

I have another letter from Mrs. D.[8]; she is very, very eager to see her son in a paying position; she cannot understand why there should be any doubt about his qualifications. If you see any chance for getting him employment anywhere it would be a God-send in this rather tragical situation.

I ought not to mix my own appeal for help in psychological problems with this sad reminder, as I do hope that you won't consider both situations equally hopeless. It may be that you can make matters easy for you by merely pointing to some literature which you would consider essential for me to digest before bothering you personally.

The week in Worcester was really delightful and extremely stimulating; I only wish these occasions would come oftener.

With my best regards to you and to Mrs. Titchener, I remain,

Very sincerely yours,
Adolf Meyer

1. The meeting to which Meyer referred was the celebrated Clark University Conference on Psychology and Pedagogy held at Worcester, Massachusetts during the second week of September, 1909. It was at the Clark conference that Titchener and Meyer met Sigmund Freud, Carl Jung, and several other European scholars. Titchener, Meyer, Freud, and Jung were among those receiving honorary degrees. See Rand Evans and William A. Koelsch, "Psychoanalysis Arrives in America: The Psychology Conference at Clark University," *American Psychologist* 40 (1985): 942–48.

2. Titchener delivered two papers at the Clark Conference: "The Past Decade in Experimental Psychology," subsequently published in the *American Journal of Psychology* 21 (1910): 404–21; and "The Experimental Psychology of the Thought Processes," which was not published but was based on lectures published in a book of the same title, *Lectures on the Experimental Psychology of the Thought-Processes* (New York: Macmillan, 1909).

3. Titchener had distinguished between structural and functional psychology by analogy to the difference between anatomy and physiology in his "Structural and Functional Psychology," *Philosophical Review* 8 (1899): 290–99.

4. In 1909, Titchener was just beginning to get deeply involved in the imageless thought controversy which centered on the question of whether thought was reducible to the sensations or images of orthodox psychology. The controversy, in which Titchener opposed his old Leipzig friend Oswald Külpe

(1862–1915), would damage the faith of many psychologists in the reliability and generalizability of introspection. For details of the controversy see George Humphrey, *Thinking: An Introduction to Its Experimental Psychology* (London: Methuen and Co., 1951). Two of Titchener's relevant articles are: "Description vs. Statement of Meaning," *American Journal of Psychology* 23 (1912): 165–82, and "The Method of Examination," ibid. 24 (1913): 429–40.

5. "Misconceptions at the Bottom of *Hopelessness of All Psychology*" (a review of *Die Hoffnungslosigkeit aller Psychologie,* by J. Möbius), *Psychological Bulletin* 4 (1907): 170–79. Reprinted in *The Collected Papers of Adolf Meyer*, ed., Eunice E. Winters, 4 vols. (Baltimore: Johns Hopkins Press, 1950–52), 2: 573–80 (hereafter cited as *CP*).

6. Carl Gustav Jung (1875–1961), in 1909 Freud's chief disciple in Europe, gave three lectures at the Clark conference under the general title "The Association Method." The series was translated by A. A. Brill and published in the *American Journal of Psychology* 21 (1910): 219–69. Meyer had begun a correspondence with Jung in 1907 and had met him for the first time in Zürich in the summer of 1908. For an account of their relationship, see Ruth Leys, "Meyer, Jung, and the Limits of Association," *Bulletin of the History of Medicine* 59 (1985): 345–60.

7. "Psychobiology" was the term Meyer introduced around 1908 to characterize his functional approach in psychiatry.

8. This name has been abbreviated in the interest of the patient's confidentiality.

2 T

September 19, 1909

My dear Meyer,

I heartily appreciate the spirit of your letter; and though your questions are not easy to answer, and the answer would vary somewhat — especially in degree of assurance — if given by different psychologists, I will try to answer them in a general way.

Psychology is the science of mind, neither more nor less; and mind is a species of the genus experience, and a species which can be (and has been) adequately differentiated from other species of experience. Psychology may, therefore, be narrow and useless; but, as a science, it has a definite field, and to extend or change the name or the field is simply to invite confusion.

The method of psychology is observation, precisely as the method of science at large is observation. In the case of the natural sciences we speak of observation in general, or more specifically of inspection; in psychology, for historical reasons, we call our method introspection. But there is absolutely no difference between inspection and introspection as methods. The difference lies only in the nature of the subject-matter, i.e. in the species of experience, to which the method of observation is applied.

These two points are sufficiently worked out in the introductory sections of my Text-book of Psychology.[1]

Psychology, as thus defined, is the counterpart, in the classification of the sciences, of all the "natural" sciences. It is, that is to say, a very wide term, covering what will presently be, I suppose, a number of separate and coordinate sciences. Since, however, the mind appears only in connection with the living body, the animate world, psychology is especially and more narrowly the counterpart of the sciences of the living body, anatomy, physiology, histology, &c.

Whether we can draw an analogy here, and say that there is an anatomy of mind, a physiology of mind, an histology of mind, &c., is a question that must be decided simply by appeal to the facts. And since the facts are not yet adequate to its answer, psychologists are divided. Just as physiology proper (apart from the philosophy of life) is divided into mechanistic and vitalistic camps, so are psychologists divided into energistic and non-energistic &c. camps. But it is always to be remembered that these divisions are inside divisions, and that they are based upon secondary issues. As you do much the same sort of work in the physiological laboratory, whether you are mechanist or vitalist, only that your wishes and expectations are different, so in psychology you do much the same sort of experimental work whatever your view of mind, although you will theorise the results in different ways.

However, it is very natural to confuse this secondary set of questions (about there being counterparts in psychology of gross anatomy, physiology, histology, &c.) with a much more fundamental matter. The primary problem of all science is Analysis. Whatever you are doing, whatever you are working on, whatever view you hold within psychology, you have first of all to analyse the experience before you. Precisely as you have to analyse Matter or Body, so have you to analyse Mind, if you are to possess a science at all.

And analysis is at first a descriptive analysis. It may be disputed whether science ever gets beyond description; whether the distinction of description and explanation is not a difference of degree or extent rather than of kind. But whatever opinion one may hold on that point, the first analysis made is of the descriptive kind. So it follows that the great task before a scientific psychology, at its beginning, is a descriptive analysis of mind. This is what you regard as parallel with "minute histological studies" and consider to be "of interest chiefly to a relatively small group of investigators." I believe that you take this view because you have confused the secondary questions, of division of labour within psychology, referred to above, with this ultimate question of the primary problem of psychology as science.

There is, in any case, a great difference between histology and /even/ the minutest psychological analysis. For histology works on the dead tissue, while psychology refers always to the living mind; and histology is a static science, ignoring time, while psychological analysis regards duration, the temporal attribute, as one of its keenest instruments of dissection.

But we may leave these differences aside, and say, if we like, that no analogy is perfect. There then still remains the fundamental confusion, I believe: you do not realise that whatever science does, it begins by analysing, and that if psychology is to be a science, it can do nothing else. The more minutely it can analyse, of course, the better; for the more microscopic the vision, the greater the factual knowledge. What has not the microscope done for physiology! The whole of modern preventive medicine, one might almost say, depends upon the microscope. And so, if one were to press what I do not think is a true analogy at all in this connection, — but if we were to press your analogy, we might argue to the same end with regard to preventive psychological medicine. I do not wish to do that; but I wish to insist as strongly as I can that psychology has the right and the duty to analyse mind as well as she possibly can.

Sept. 20.

All this is prefatory: and I hope that in general it is clear. Now I come to the questions that centre about your proposed definition of psychology.

We must all admit that practice and theory interlock and help each other. There were bridges built before there was a mathematical physics. But bridge-building helped towards pure physics; and very certainly mathematical physics has helped the bridge-builder. There were cures made and operations performed before there was a science of physiology; but certainly pure physiology has been of aid to medicine. Demons were exorcised, and David played the harp before Saul, when there was no science of psychology. But by all analogy the working-out of a science of psychology should advance psychiatry. It seems indeed, if we look at the history of science, as if there were no great advance possible in the applied field until some group of men had devoted themselves to pure science, to the apparently useless and remote, to interests that lie as far as can be from application. When pure science has been studied, then — even, so to say, against the will of the men who have given themselves to it — we invariably find a great progress in application.

But now the question comes: Who is to make and to define the pure science? The men who are interested to apply? — That is not the lesson of history. The makers of science have been men to whom the useful was uninteresting. The appliers of science have been the men to whom theory made very scant appeal. You can hardly conceive of a civil engineer propounding a definition of physics, or of a medical practitioner seriously concerning himself to define the limits of physiology. Why then should the psychiatrist offer a novel definition of psychology? What claim has he, that should empower him to do this? How can he expect to do it adequately, when psychology has its own technique, attitude, procedure, — things that must be gained by special study extending over many years? How, to put it bluntly, can the psychiatrist expect that his definition of psychology can be anything more than an amateur's?

You write as follows. "Psychology is the study of all those reactions which the neurologist can only describe by metaphor and which . . . I call the reactions of the individual as a whole in contrast to reactions of individual organs. Genetically we would feel inclined to look for adjustive instincts as the fundamental elements which have become differentiated into actions and reactions of various degrees of specialisation."

Now it is clear at once that this is a practical and not a scientific definition: that is shown by the fact that your next following sentence speaks of what "we physicians would pick out." The scientific man, the theorist, does not pick out; he takes what is there. — But it is clear also that the definition, like all practical definitions, is proximate and secondary only, not a technical definition at all. Look at your terms: reaction, individual, organ, adjustive, instinct, element, differentiation, action, specialisation. What in the world do all these things mean? What is the universe of discourse within which they are relevant? Every single one of them demands its own definition.

So far as I can see, if I come to the definition with goodwill and not too much scientific temper, the definition which you offer is a logical construction from biology. On both counts it is bad. First, as a logical formulation: because a definition should be induced from the facts and not be based upon inference. Secondly as a logical construction from biology: because in accepting biology as your standard science, and translating out of biology into psychology, you have universalised biology. You make the same mistake that a philosopher makes when he theorises the whole universe of experience in terms of a single science; the same mistake that the evolutionary enthusiasts made when they tried, at first, to carry Darwinism straight over into ethics.[2] No single science can be adequate, either to experience as a whole, or to a coordinate science. Hence biology, however far it go, can never be legislative for psychology. That is my general objection to your definition.

But further. Every science comes to use proximate terms, short-hand expressions, which everybody within the science is supposed to understand and to be able to derive, but which on that very account cannot possibly be used as terms of general scientific application. Biology uses in this way terms like adjustment, reaction, differentation. All these terms are simply short-hand expressions for long and complicated causal nexuses: and to pass as general scientific currency, they must of course be fully explicated into causal terms. "Adjustment" is NOT A SCIENTIFIC TERM at all: it is a short-hand biological expression, used merely for convenience' sake in biology, but not to be used in any other science until analysis there has been fully performed, and indeed to be used EVEN INSIDE BIOLOGY with immense caution. "Instinct" is a popular term, taken over from the faculty psychology of the 18. century, which has as yet a very dubious standing even as as short-cut term in modern psychology, to say nothing of modern biology: we are trying to let it lie in suspense for a while, and in the meantime we prefer to talk of "nervous settings," "nervous Einstellungen," "nervous tendencies" — colourless terms which are used by biologists and physiologists /alike/, and carry no /hypothesis/ so far upon them. — And so with your other terms.

I say, then, first, that your definition is faulty because it is a logical construction, and does not represent the Inbegriff[3] of psychological experience; secondly, that it is bad because it describes psychology in terms taken from the coordinate science of biology; and thirdly that it is bad because the biological terms which it employs are not terms of general scientific currency, but are the short-hand or slang of biology, and themselves within biology need constant retranslation into causal sentences. You forget, as the practical man always does forget, that the science which you are defining has a long history, and has achieved its present status with immense pains. You seek to plunge us back into the obscurities and confusions of fact, and the reliance upon logic and reflective thought, which it has taken us centuries to transcend. Can you wonder that we shrug our shoulders, and pass by on the other side?— that we go our own way serenely in the laboratory, and show no particular interest in your theoretical discussions?[4]

Now I digress a moment to my discussion of the thought- element. That seems to you to be hair-splitting and irrelevant to life. Well, — but you want to know, I suppose, whether mind is furnished solely from the periphery or partly from the centre? If thought is all ultimately the product of peripheral stimulation, you wish to know that: if the cortex itself originates a wholly new form of mental experience, you surely want to be assured of that? So far from the discussion being up in the clouds, it seems to me (from the outside) that the value of a settlement of the thought-controversy would to you, as psychiatrist, be rather large. Yet it is only by the minutest of histological enquiries, carried out by the most refined of techniques, that we can hope to resolve this controversy.

Then as to Freud. His psychology is, basally, the psychology of associationism. The fundamental fallacy of that psychology is that it looks upon "ideas" not psychologically, as very fluid existences, but logically, as hard static meanings. The idea of the associationists is always a meaning, a symbol, even when it is not termed by them a "symbolic" idea. The result of this confusion is manifold. First, we have the absurdities of cortical localisation: an "idea" is "deposited" in a single "psychical cell." So neurology is held back by a false psychology. Secondly we have the absurdities of the "laws of association" within psychology itself: static meanings are hooked together by "relations" of sorts; the game is played with all logical precision, but is therefore a logical and not a psychological game. We have slowly and painfully worked our way out of this logical construction, and have sought to analyse both the idea and the connection of ideas as these things occur in experience existentially. We have thus freed the physiologists from all sorts of mythology, although very few of them (Kries is one)[5] have the eyes to see this fact; and we have given mind itself a new lay-out, a new patterning and progress, which ought to open the eyes of the psychiatrist. But Freud, with all his genius, theorises his facts by association. His second main point of doctrine is that of the Affektbetrag.[6] "Feeling" is a quantitative something, that may attach to an idea, and thence be transferred bodily to other ideas. Now the question of Gefühlsuebertragung[7] is a very difficult question, but it is a question which we have attacked; something is known of it; whereas Freud's Affektbetrag is really only another meaning, another symbol, mechanically transferred from idea-symbol to idea-symbol. — I offered to attempt a translation out of this psychology of association into modern psychological terms, and Freud laughed at me, and said that if I came to him for half a year I should see that modern psychology needed to be "revolutionised" in his way. Revolutionised, ye gods! That means, set back just about two human generations. And then the man wonders that we do not take his psychologising seriously. Freud is a very great man; but Freud's psychology is a very outworn travesty of psychology.

By these digressions I have tried to reach the question: What do you want with a psychology anyway, a theoretical psychology? You are primarily biologists, all of you; you deal with the whole man, the psychophysical organism; you deal neither with mind (psychology) nor with body (physiology). No doubt, you will be all the better for knowing psychology and physiology; but what you are actually doing is to apply psychophysics or (if you like) biology. And since, in psychophysics, body is prior to mind, and not contrariwise (as we have learned from Fechner long ago),[8] it is naturally and properly the body that you deal with first — first in logic, I mean; mental symptoms are for you only symptoms, on the same level for curative purposes with contractures or tics. What you are doing is applied biology; and it is thus natural, again, though it is by no means proper, that when you theorise psychology you do so from the biological point of view. But why try to theorise psychology? It is man, if anything, that you should theorise, not mind. I see no harm in your looking on Man as differentiated out of fundamental elements which are adjustive instincts: you are then, in biology, using biological slang, and biology is responsible to science for what use you make of such terms. I may very gravely doubt, as a theoretical psychologist, whether this use of slang will carry you very far: but if you find that it does not carry you as far as the present generation can see, then I find no harm in your attitude to it and use of it.

You will reply that this gives up the whole thing: you asked for a bridge between psychology and psychiatry, and I tell you to stay behind with the biologists! Not quite. I said that the more psychology you know the better it will be for you; I illustrated this by reference to the thought-controversy; and I tried to show how associationism might lead you astray, both in physiology and in psychology. You will read the mental symptoms better, even in your biological universe, if you read them as the psychologist would. All the same, I must say that I regard this as a counsel of perfection. That is to say, psychiatry, as a practical matter, will have its own technicalities and rules of thumb, and these will always suffice for the rank and file: just as is the case with the civil engineer and the general practitioner. Only a few of the most active minds will concern themselves, or need to concern themselves, with current neurology or current psychology. In the meanwhile, what is now scientific psychology will slowly filter down and oust the older psychology, and so the psychiatrist will presently find his notions of mind insensibly changing. What psychology herself will have done is another and a very interesting question. But from all appearances the advance in pure science is henceforth, since the advent of the critical method, to be quantitative rather than qualitative. I mean that science will increase in range, but is hardly likely to shift its standpoint.

You ask definitely about Jung's complex-theory. That is not a psychological theory at all. It is a psychophysical theory; or rather it is a psychophysical short-hand for a group of not yet analysed phenomena. The word "complex" is happily chosen, since it carries no hypothesis; and indeed Jung has oftentimes shown the effects of his psychological training, and has instinctively avoided his master's dogmatic fallacies. What we shall find psychologically in the "complex" I don't know, because I haven't tried, and so far as I know nobody has yet tried. And I am, as you see, inclined to agree with you that, from your point of view, it doesn't very much matter. As I said in the last paragraph, the psychologising of such matters is only for the élite in psychiatry. As you say, "the work of neuro-physiology has moved along excellently with mere working hypotheses." Things work in practice astonishingly well that in theory — that is, in scientific fact — are astonishingly wrong or imperfect. Trouble comes only when this working is made the excuse for a re-theorising (as in Freud's case, and in your own so far as you hold to your definition of "psychology") which ignores the actual status and advance of theory at the time. Adopt any working hypothesis you like, and we shall not quarrel with you. But if you leave your work, and come up into the theoretical attic, you must expect criticism of the theoretical sort unless you show knowledge and just estimation of what science has so far done. Jung's "complex" strikes me as a very happy introduction of an important discovery; it is definite enough to work with, and modest and non-committal enough to leave room for psychological analysis.

As I said, I very heartily appreciate the spirit of your letter, and I have let myself run on and out in reply. What I do not at all accept is your initial statement that "there are evidently a number of standpoints which are entitled to the term psychology." Psychology has found itself, and knows its business; you simply run against fact if you try to change the scientific constitution of our knowledge of human experience. Your question is: How far must I know, take account of, be trained in psychology, in order to be an efficient psychiatrist? You can help us tremendously if you share our outlook, and we can help you; but you can't reconstruct psychology, as science; what appears to you to be ahead of the age looks to us either out of date or logically confused.

Write again on anything that isn't clear!

Yours,
E. B. Titchener

1. E. B. Titchener, *A Textbook of Psychology*, Parts 1 and 2 (New York: Macmillan, 1910). The textbook mentioned in the 1909 correspondence is Part 1, published in June 1909. It contained chapters on methodology and elementary processes such as sensation and feeling. Titchener was eager to replace his outdated *Outline of Psychology*, originally published by Macmillan in 1896, and had the first half of the book published early. Part 2 contained sections on perception, association, memory and imagination, action, emotion, and thought.

2. Titchener is referring to the school of Herbert Spencer (1820–1903) of which he had been a disciple while he was a student at Oxford.

3. Inbegriff = content, essence.

4. Titchener's reference is to the parable of the good Samaritan.

5. Johannes von Kries (1853–1928), German physiologist, was closely allied to the new experimental psychology. He was associated with Hermann Helmholtz in Berlin (1876) and with Karl Ludwig in Leipzig (1877–80); he spent the rest of his career at Freiburg. He is best known for his duplicity theory of vision in which he correctly attributed low illumination vision to retinal rods and daylight vision to retinal cones.

6. Affektbetrag = quota of affect. According to Freud's economic hypothesis, the "quota of affect" is the element that remains invariable despite the various modifications the "affect" undergoes in displacement and qualitative transformations.

7. Gefühlsuebertragung = emotional transference.

8. G. T. Fechner (1801–87), founder of psychophysics. His *Elemente der Psychophysik* (1860) was a founding text in experimental psychology. Volume 1 is available in English translation as *Elements of Psychophysics*, trans. Helmut E. Adler (New York: Holt, Rinehart and Winston, 1966).

3 M

September 23, 1909

My dear Professor Titchener:—

I am very grateful to you for your letter of Sept. 19, 09. I only hope my reply will not tire your patience.

Your definition of psychology, of course, stands on a very old and correspondingly firm basis. I should, however, have to say: Psychology is the science of that species of experience or happenings which can be adequately differentiated from other species of experience or happenings by its having the characteristics of consciousness of varying degrees. This empirical characterization would naturally have to yield to other definitions taken from the functional sphere = states and reactions working with a principle new in nature's evolution, possible from a certain stage of organization, consisting in reactions capable of association of a kind to be defined, or of adjustments if that term can in some way be made respectable. I must say, however, that it seems to me absurd to try and make an absolute definition of a science. Let it show what it does. To say that psychology is the science of mind, is not especially illuminative if you do not give the definition of mind, and I should prefer not to ask for that, but rather for the facts to be dealt with and the way it is done.

The method of psychology surely is observation. Primarily it is a matter of introspection. But in as much as we are not inclined to write the psychology of solipsism, we also use the method of inspection, assisted by the method of introspection of states of the same or of analogous character. Psychology, (neither in its narrower sense nor in the broader one) is not the counterpart of all the natural sciences. It is a part thereof, and a specially limited part, as I said, is that of self-inspection. What you split off as "mind" would at best be the subjective "counterpart" of a certain realm of biological states and functions which in experience are not found without, and cannot be thought of except as involving with necessity the characteristic mental states and reactions as obtained by introspection. In my scheme these states and functions stand in contrast to the non-mental biological functions: digestion, respiration, elimination, circulation, etc., i.e. all those functions which are possible without the participation of states and functions which with necessity imply the mental characteristic, apart from the general biological characteristic of growth, structural organization, and metabolism. The latter in turn must adhere to every psychological function: i.e. every psychological function has also certain physical aspects. The spirit with flesh and bone makes the "mental" reaction and its organ. Science does well to treat them as a unit.

Here, of course, is, after all, a rather fundamental difference. I should not approach psychology except under its double aspect, that of introspection (of what one is and has and does), and that of inspection (what others are and do) carried out under the same critical experimental conditions demanded in other sciences. I surrender the quest for the final "essence" or "what" and realize that science deals especially with the question of pushing the "how" to the limits of its power, leaving the "what" to the demand for differentiations; and I am naturally bent on the analysis of what is "essential" in the line of what yields to the question "how."

In this respect, I have no interest in the questions of an analysis which divides mind and body as real contrasts.

In all this, science is either description and statement of problems or of parts which lend themselves to explanation or reconstruction or demonstration of the principle of reconstruction. Honesty and wisdom alike force us to start from our experience as we have it at our best. There clings to us a certain individualism and we must realize that we are bound to be biased either by nominalistic and logical tendencies or by our seeing things from the "working" point of view, the one as abstract thinker, the other as bent on concrete things. As soon as you emphasize the time feature, you let up on the nominalistic and logical side and join those of us who have a functional bias; but you arbitrarily do not go further. There is, of course, no histology about this, but a description of detail with the time-aspect made obligatory, but I felt and feel now (from your last paragraph of page 2) that you insist that the method of analysis must necessarily enter into the minutiae, as histology does. Histology is a part of the general study of organization. You might say no! It is part of anatomy! The form of "analysis by cutting up"! But what is analysis without control by synthesis? And does not the scientific work set in in its most active phase where the synthesis is attempted and achieved? Anatomy is not a fundamental science; nor is histology by itself. The microscope has not done such marvelous feats through analysis of the tissues, but through extending the analysis of certain conditions under which the tissues work, especially the condition of symbiosis with microorganisms. We can safely say that microscopy has done most for physiology through its keeping it from mechanistic self-satisfaction. The same service might be accepted by psychology from those who want to include the objective valuation of the processes, i.e. more than the mere time element, viz. also the other conditions under which the events take place. But why not make sure of some broad psychological waves before turning on the microscope?

The main point of contention would probably be: Is it right to class the objects of psychology as "events" and "their conditions"? Let us argue then as to the importance for preventive medicine if we will; it is certainly a fact that the heuristic results in psychopathology are most abundant in the direction of knowing about conditions of happenings, and not only that of discrimination of detail features. All I claim is that psychology is concerned with the determination and analysis of conditions as well as of details of structure. The two do well to maintain a certain balance. The vital — and by that I do not mean necessarily the practical — advances in every science occurred in fields in which this balance of analysis and experimental synthesis was strikingly even.

Pure science — who shall say what is pure? And what is useful? I should simply say: To the one are given the instincts of analysis, discrimination and description and if he is true to the facts and presents the results in a form which can be grasped and used with other instincts in the lead, we give him all the glory of pure science. Others are equally disinterested workers in pure science with a preeminently synthetic mind and a keen sense for the study of conditions of synthesis. They are usually the lucky discoverers and those who also discover the gems of simple observation and discrimination. They are nearer the practical life, the former nearer the contemplative life. They are where things happen; should that disqualify them for the ranks of pure science?

It is clear to me, that I would be an amateur whenever I should try to make final definitions of psychology, but perhaps one who feels under compulsion to be an amateur about the tentative lay-out, because he finds no such help (except perhaps in Dr. Sanford's sketch)[1] in the psychologist's camp as would make it unnecessary to be a filibuster. But I also consider myself an "amateur" with neurology and within everything I do — I cannot see a difference: an honest investigator of facts for the truth's sake; an investigator of experience with a keen conscience about the necessity of letting everything pass through the trial of critical test and repetition; anxious to find generalizations which cover the facts and allow of combinations with other generalizations and other fields of trial and test. I do pick out as every scientist does. No scientist can take up everything. The one has this problem or craving and the other an other; and yet he takes the facts he finds, and I try to make sure that what I take, is there. I distinguish between workable and remote problems, and do not dictate to others. The first and fundamental condition is, of course, a familiarity with the fundamental issues and methods of the domain, and the ability to think and work in terms acceptable and controllable and standards of accuracy and reliability. And that is what I am trying to attain, but with a sense of economy: simple methods for simple things, and more detail when we need it.

A science should not expect to have an a priori definition. Definitions are especially dangerous when built on assumptions based largely on logical tradition. If I cannot accept the contrast of body and mind as a scientifically essential one, could we get a definition in which that bone of contention would be left out?

I did not, in my first letter, attempt a definition of psychology, but a characterization of the situation in which those things are and happen which are likely to come under the heading of any psychology however defined. The detail or the definition as such would then be an issue of methods to be applied. The setting is, of course, that of biology with me, and with you? I am not universalizing biology. But I frankly admit that biology is a special department of science generally, worth keeping apart from the departments of physics and chemistry and its go-betweens, because it is limited to organisms of a definable constitution, definite conditions of origin and probable span of life and possibilities of function and development, and as far as I can see the psychology which the physician and the scientist study is concerned with phenomena and experiences limited to this part of our environment or of the world. If I were to identify mind and soul and all the derivatives and connections of the soul, I should be guilty of the mistake you ascribe to me, paragraph 1, page 4. I am not universalizing biology. But I limit myself to biology in order to keep out the spooks and the logical products of mental functions which as such are not psychological — such as this letter, your library, the phonograph-record, the kymograph tracings— products, only psychological by relation. I see no sciences as self-contained spheres; but sciences are groups of methods applied to groups of facts — groups worth making. To carry Darwinism straight into ethics is quite a different thing. I limit psychology to biology and consider biology the more embracing unit, because individual and social biology is the field which covers my operations. Within this field physics and chemistry have their application and fundamental value too. But psychology refers to functions (and sufficient organization for such functions) with which as a rule we can leave physics and chemistry to take care of themselves unless we need their terms and methods and facts for the determination of the events and facts under study in psychological happenings and possibilities. But that does not mean that we ignore the physical aspect.

"Adjustment is no scientific term." May be. It states a biological problem, ever at hand, a setting, as worthy as any setting borrowed from physics. It is really a broader term than any other we might borrow from physics alone. It is more universal in a universe with time and space and not merely with noumena.

Psychology has not a long history as a science, and I am afraid it still has its shell on its back in many of its manifestations. We do not want to go back to obscurities. You are right that mine are largely theoretical discussions, but in a struggle for a different base of work for myself and others. The standpoint of tradition is not final. There are more standpoints than one concerning the ultimate splitting up of the domain of experience into sciences. As I said I am not a pan-biologist, nor a pan-psychologist but a student of what I find and where I find it. Of course the division of the world into mind and matter is the basis of your standpoint. I cannot see that it has any special merit or foundation in fact except its venerable chronicity, or to put it more modestly, it is a question which has bewildered so many people that there is something radically wrong with it and really a question which we do not have to settle for everybody and finally. The fact is that mental events, the phenomena with which psychology works occur only in sufficiently organized types of living beings. To put the psychological facts on one side and all the physical facts on the other expurgates all the life out of psychology which is not returned by the meagre time and supplement, and it makes a hopeless mess also in that physical field which we call biology. It creates affiliations between psychology and metaphysical traditions which cannot be a topic of scientific decision as yet; and where it is most needed it leaves confusion as the attitude of physicians shows every day.

Dr. Gay[2] who now works on serum-pathology with Dr. Southard,[3] told me once he would not have anything to do with psychopathology if it were merely materialism. I feel that I do not care to have anything to do with psychology, if it must preordain the solution of the question whether the contrast of physical and mental is not after all more logical than valuable in science, and if it claims that mental functions are not physical as well as mental. Take Woodbridge's attitude.[4] He states the views better than I, and might certainly seem to share my view that another stand point in psychology is possible if not mandatory. Bakewell[5] in the discussion called him down for his rank materialism. What a poverty of conception of modern developments! Can we seriously maintain the contrast "idealism" and "materialism" when we view modern science? Or do I step on the ground of confusion here?

As scientists we must quit starting from a priori divisions.

If you wish to limit psychological inquiry to introspection in your own work I am the last man to object. But if you say that everything outside of that is not psychology, then I must take refuge in psychobiology as I call it in order to escape your anathema. There I see many fundamental problems of "psychology." What is more confusing, the enumeration of mental elements from the introspectionist's point of view and the overt or disguised sensationalism that goes with its aims and interests, or the simple plain and perhaps somewhat slangy descriptions of some of the most vital types of adjustment for a student who goes out into the world with the claim that he had a course in psychology? I must say that in reading your books, I am charmed with the simplicity of some of them, but also overawed by the struggle over abstruse and remote problems in some other chapters, and when I return to the psychology I work with and try to use your schemes, I am thrown on my own resources most of the time, in quite a different way from what is the case when I consult chemistry and physics. Chemistry is the same in the most scientific part of chemical work and in the work of chemical analysis which presents itself to us. And I repeat that the difference is not that of "application." If psychology would frankly embrace the domain of study of conduct and behavior and its detailed workings, it would be a different matter. Instead of that, it prefers to roost in an eagle's nest. Why not come down to life? Would the psychologist's psychophysics do any better? Not that I can see. The issue of the thought-element certainly has a decided interest for me, but as I said not more so than the question whether neurofibrils are essential for the nerve-functions which we study en bloc with full scientific pride. My question would probably be formulated differently. Even in sensations the "mind" is I suppose, not finished [*sic,* furnished] solely from the periphery; the question is mainly one of the share, and the bulk of the problem is that of the conditions under which thoughts occur and play their part in attitudes and reactions. Without more knowledge of the new lay-out than I may have acquired quite innocently, I have long fought the mythology part in my conceptions of aphasia and the like. But the symbol concept to which you object, I have used, but not only for "ideas" but for all mental activity. I have indeed identified as mental activities those in which "symbols" or symbol-like actions — of the mental type — are inserted — another heresy which ferments in me and may yet yield something. I wish I had your attempt at translation of the Freud views into modern psychological terms. I don't believe I would merely turn it down; and I would not want my psychology to be an outworn travesty of psychology if I could help it.

Mental symptoms are not as you say merely "symptoms" to me. They are activities and attitudes, and in turn means and conditions for the whole chain of events. As to calling what I work on "man" and not "mind,"— "mind" has no meaning to me beside that of certain attitudes and functions and functional possibilities, i.e. organization of man, and I should especially distrust any parts which have not a dynamic or determining value in definite experimental developments.

When you come to the psychological presentation of such a problem as Jung's association-phenomena, you may find a very interesting domain in which an essentially introspective psychology must meet the question: is the degree of consciousness a safe measure for the psychological determination of the stream of thought? Where is the psychologist's problem in this field? I take the complex-process as a condition of mental constellation in which certain avenues of reaction remain freer than others and the obstruction must be expressed in terms of (1) a (psychological?) constellation of the past, and (2) the effect which remained from it in the balancing mechanisms which have to meet new adjustments. The safest description is that of the conditions of the original reaction, its foundation and its actual nature and the final adjustment as shown in the readiness for new reactions, and the behavior in the same. With these records I shall be able to get guides and standards for the estimate of similar events. This I would consider one of the types of psychological problems the student must learn to master and we must learn to get accurate methods for; methods good enough, but not cumbersome.

I am so conscious of the rambling character of these notes jotted down on re-reading your letter, that I hesitate to send them. I would sum up my reply this way:

(1) I cannot believe that the contrast of mental and physical has scientific value.

(2) All psychological facts (reactions and attitudes) should be viewed by introspection and by inspection. Psychology is the domain

thus covered, not merely the introspective side of the problem.

(3) That which we meet as mental reactions and attitudes are always phenomena in living beings of sufficient organization; their study is therefore best considered as part of biology — the conditions and kinds of reactions which include as an essential feature subjective phenomena of consciousness.

(4) Instead of merely concerning ourselves with the time- feature of these reactions and the possibilities of extreme differentiation (into sensations, thoughts, etc.) I should also take other objective conditions and features into consideration and take as the most general unit of reaction that which I call an adjustment. I do this for reasons which I had wanted to discuss in my Worcester paper,[6] but which involved certain issues of logic of science which would have taken much more time than I could have asked for. The main contentions are these: The fundamental question of science is not the "what" alone but the "how" — see Maxwell,[7] if this needs any authoritative proof from one not an amateur. The experiment is the unit of scientific experience. In it we can specify parts if they are again defined by other accepted experimental equations. We may suppress these other parts of the full experiment, the constellation and result, and merely pick out the single fact, the "what," but it always has its value only because we accept the "panning out" in the experiments implied (duration, velocity, direction, impetus and what not). Where the definition of the "what" becomes difficult to bring to an ordinary denominator, where we deal with reactions and events of a biological and especially of a psychological character, we do best to give always the initial constellation, the reaction and the readjustment or result. It is also better to work with elementary gesammtreactionen,[8] rather than with minute details to start with. The unit and prototype is the adjustive reaction. No psychological fact can be sized up sufficiently well for psychopathology to make superfluous the effort to reach this ideal standard.

(5) The unit of psycho-dynamic events is therefore not to be compared with the unit of associationism. In this you do Freud injustice and also in the incrimination concerning the brain-mythology. The unit is an experience (to be stated in terms of an equation of actual events unless psychology devises simpler schemes) inevitably conceived as psycho-physical if you wish to raise that self-evident issue. How much introspection will do in the sizing up of things is to be seen. So far we prefer to trust the appearance of the same or kindred factors in other experiences (or adjustments) as shown, for

instance, in the association experiment and "psychoanalysis" by memories which come up and their reaction, and we are directly forced to mistrust introspection as an adequate guide or measure, owing to the peculiar lack of parallelism of psycho-dynamic force and consciousness.

(6) Psychopathology needs definite dynamic units in the life of the patients determining the developments. These must be psychobiological. Let us begin with habit conflicts and their influence on the stream of events. Let us take up the effects of events of the Jung-complex type where they occur as long as we cannot always make them to order for the laboratory. Let us look for a formulation of some psychological problems which figure in life—not as applied psychology but as psychology of nature's simplest and yet most vital experiments. Let us study especially the effects of "experiences" on further developments. It may be that some of them may yield more striking results than the ordinary laboratory experiments, just as Jung's work totally eclipsed Stern's.[9] Stern certainly sketched a wide range of possibilities and problems; Jung brought somewhat for an accounting for the observations, something touching the dynamic needs.

I realize that I throw a veritable medley on your desk. I am very sorry that I have not been more concise, but fear that if I tried to rewrite this I would have to put it off too long. I know you will be nachsichtig.[10]

Is there any hope of a connecting link? Where is psychopathology to land if the physician and the psychologist disown it on account of psycho-physical parallelism, that narrow and at best self-evident emphasis of an unessential and scientifically insufficiently founded split of a group of biological events? I do not want to reconstruct psychology. But I should like psychology to consider some legitimate issues and fundamental needs.

Faithfully yours,
Adolf Meyer

1. Edmund Clark Sanford (1859–1924), experimental psychologist and college president, taught for many years at Clark University. Meyer was probably referring to Sanford's *A Course in Experimental Psychology*, 2 vols. (1894–98), a laboratory manual dealing with sensation which was widely used in academic circles prior to the appearance of Titchener's *Experimental Psychology*, 4 vols. (New York: Macmillan, 1901–5).

2. Frederick Parker Gay (1874–1939), physician, made numerous contributions to the emerging fields of bacteriology and immunology. Between 1906 and 1907 he was on the bacteriological staff of Danvers (Massachusetts) State Hospi-

tal for the Insane. Subsequently, Gay was on the pathology faculty of Harvard Medical School and the University of California at Berkeley.

3. Elmer Ernest Southard (1876–1920), neuropathologist and neuropsychiatrist, in 1909 was on the staff of the Danvers State Hospital for the Insane at the same time as Frederick Parker Gay, before becoming director of the Boston Psychopathic Hospital in 1912. Author of over two hundred publications, including *Neurosyphilis* (1917), with H. C. Solomon, and *Shell-Shock and Other Neuropsychiatric Problems* (1919), Southard was well known to his contemporaries for his belief in the somatic origin of mental disease.

4. Frederick James Eugene Woodbridge (1867–1940) was professor of philosophy at Columbia University from 1902 and the university's dean of the faculty of political science, philosophy, and pure science, 1912–29. Editor of the *Journal of Philosophy, Psychology, and Scientific Methods*, Woodbridge held a philosophical position close to that of Meyer.

5. Charles Montague Bakewell (1867–1957), idealist, in 1909 was Sheldon Clark professor of philosophy at Yale University, a position he held until his death. The discussion to which Meyer refers took place at the annual meeting of the American Philosophical Association held at Johns Hopkins University from December 29–31, 1908. At that meeting, which was held jointly with the American Psychological Association, the Southern Society for Philosophy and Psychology, and the American Association for the Advancement of Science, Woodbridge gave a paper, "Consciousness, The Sense Organs, and the Nervous System" which was criticized in the discussion period by Bakewell. Woodbridge's paper, which cited Meyer's article "Misconceptions at the Bottom of *Hopelessness of All Psychology*" (1907), was published in the *Journal of Philosophy, Psychology, and Scientific Methods* 6 (1909): 449–55.

6. Meyer, "The Dynamic Interpretation of Dementia Praecox," *American Journal of Psychology* 21 (1910): 385–403 (*CP*, 2: 443–58).

7. James Clerk Maxwell (1831–79), physicist, made revolutionary investigations in electromagnetics and the kinetic theory of gases. Both Meyer and Titchener, although on different grounds, were indebted to Maxwell's empirocritical views concerning the nature of science.

8. Gesammtreactionen = reactions of the whole.

9. William Stern (1871–1938) in 1909 was professor of applied psychology at Breslau, later at Hamburg and at Duke University, Durham, N.C. A pioneer of applied psychology, in 1903 he established a periodical *Beiträge zur Psychologie der Aussage* (*Contributions to the Psychology of Testimony*) for studies in legal psychology. At the Clark conference, Stern summarized his work on testimony in his lecture "Abstracts of Lectures on the Psychology of Testimony and on the Study of Individuality," *American Journal of Psychology* 21 (1910): 270–82.

10. Nachsichtig = lenient.

4 T

September 25, 1909

My dear Meyer,

I don't know which strikes me the more forcibly about your letter: the utter candour and sincerity with which you write, or the hopelessness of argument without any common standing-ground. Be sure, at any rate, that I appreciate the former. As to the latter, — it is nonsense to try to meet you point by point: that would take books. I must pick out a few general impressions, and seek to remove some of the needlessest misunderstandings. I wish that one could present half-a-dozen considerations together: serial presentation is unsatisfactory, since one's views naturally hang together and imply one another. However, here goes.

First, there are two things in your letter that irritate me; & I get them off my mind at once.

(1) You recur perpetually to philosophy. If you had spent five solid years in philosophy, as I did,[1] and if you had fought your way out of philosophy into science, you would know science (as distinct from philosophy) when you saw it. Philosophy is quite irrelevant to our present discussion[2]: there was no word of it in my letter: it can come in now only as a diversion, out of idle intellectual curiosity, or out of intellectual cowardice: and from both of these vices we are, I hope, both of us free. Yet you rake in solipsism and materialism and idealism, as if you know what those terms meant, and as if I should unerringly take your and their meaning. And you refer me to Bakewell and Woodbridge on a psychological matter, and you talk of the essence and the ultimate what and all sorts of things! — No, if you want to talk philosophy, we must change the venue and change our technique. I am talking science.

Your man who is afraid of materialism (Lord knows what he means by it!— there are plenty of sorts) is simply an intellectual coward: he ought to be willing to accept a personal devil if that is where the truth[3] leads him. As to Bakewell and Woodbridge, they are amiable and talented persons; but they have small tincture of science; and they are, even in philosophy, not yet international authorities. In any case, let us be clear in what universe of discourse we are; as I said, I am talking science.

(2) The second thing is the undercurrent of feeling your letter shows that psychology has a quarrel or an issue with your work as work. It has not. And I am not unjust to Freud as man or to Freud's work. All these things concern me but little. I can wish you both

godspeed in your attempt to better the lot of humanity.[4]

The issue is raised by you and Freud yourselves, when you seek to invent a theoretical psychology. When you do that, I have the right and the duty to scrutinise your proposals, and to criticise them in the light of my knowledge and experience. Freud says outright that he will revolutionise (umstülpen) modern psychology; and he does, in fact, offer a technical psychology: you are unfair to him, if you have failed to see that. It happens that this new and revolutionary psychology is, in essentials, an old friend of ours; and we know how to handle it, and what to expect of it. But all this does not the least affect Freud's work or his "psycho-dynamic unit of events," — because his work and that unit are not psychological. (Not in our sense psychological: I come back to the question of definition presently.) You are more radical than Freud, because you wage war on psychology as such, — apparently because it cannot do what we never intended it to do; you want to substitute what you call a psycho-biology (and the "psycho" is, on your own showing, altogether redundant) for modern psychology. Are we to sit still and let you kill us?

Now I leave emotion and come to the factual discussion. (3) We might let you kill us, if we were moribund anyhow. But just because we are theorists we have an historical perspective. And this is the great big salient thing about our whole controversy.

The next ten years are going to see a battle between the principles of science, as they were built up by the men of the 19th century, Darwin included, — between them, and the principle of teleology, which has been adopted as a scientific principle primarily by the biologists and secondarily by the biologising psychologists. Evolution, in Darwin's hands, was an anti-teleological instrument. But we are now in one of those waves of popular thought which sweep over countries from time to time, and the conditions of which can hardly be traced till later; and the wave is strongest here in America. The wave, which is the wave of teleological interpretation offering itself as scientific explanation, shows itself in all sorts of related movements: in philosophical pragmatism, in the revival of Thomism in the Catholic philosophy, and in your and other men's psycho-biology. In essentials, it is a reversion to Aristotelianism, nothing more nor less. The main difference is that the concept of substance has been largely eliminated from it: matter has become energy, mind has become the sum-total of mental processes, disease has become the sum-total of symptoms. Aside from that, the history of science is repeating itself in a very pretty way, and in a very usual way. I am not sure that I cannot see, dimly, the conditions of all this movement as a reflex of European thought; but I am not yet sure enough of my historical ground to venture anything very definite on that score.

To me, this is all amazingly interesting. I cannot take sides as whole-heartedly as men like Poulten and Bateson,[5] because I know something of the history of science, and of human thought in the large; and I know that these movements, although they spend themselves and pass, always modify that which is left. So I am open-hearted to them, and want to know — more especially — how I myself shall be modified by them. That teleology should oust the present principles of science is to me unthinkable; yet I am sure that in some way the teleological movement will affect those principles. That is my personal interest in this correspondence. I shall fight you hard, as you invade psychology; I shall use every weapon at my disposal to resist your revolutionary aims; I have not the faintest intention of allowing myself to be killed. But I am already looking ahead to our reorganisation after the fight.

— Let me add two footnotes. (a) To talk in this way about philosophy, as an objective psychological datum, is not, of course, to talk philosophy itself. What I objected to, in your letter, was the talking of philosophy as if one's philosophical creed or belief had anything to say in a scientific discussion.[6] (b) To my mind the setting of things, in this way, in their perspective, is as much of a "discovery" as the doing of any act can be. The man who knows is as likely to discover as the man who does! Whether his discoveries are as "valuable" depends partly on what you mean by valuable and partly on the adoption of "value" as a scientific criterion — one of the very things in dispute.

Now I pick up some minor points of misunderstanding.[7] (4) You apparently think that the definition of a science delimits the field of that science. That is, you seem to think of sciences as made, by definition, compartments of a limited space, compartments made mutually to exclude one another, so that the area of science is a priori restricted and its expansion forbidden by definition. But I think that every science seeks to read the whole world, the whole universe of human experience, from a special point of view: that and that only. Hence I regard the sciences rather as successive chapters of the book of experience, each chapter covering the same ground (or as much of it as it can) from its own standpoint.[8] The definition of /a/ science is thus simply the chapter heading. The chapter itself may be long or short; may be corrected, added to, in every new edition of the book. A new heading simply means the writing of a new chapter. There is no overlapping, no mutual exclusion or restriction of any sort. Only, the one thing needful in writing this book is to know your chapter heading, to write relevantly, not to muddle up the contents of different chapters, narratives written from different points of view.[9] The chapters group themselves into Parts, and the grouping shifts from one generation to another. An original single chapter often splits up into several, as knowledge grows. But every chapter deals, from one point of view, with the whole of experience, and the cardinal sin of the scientific writer is muddle. Hence I think that a definition, in this sense of a chapter heading, is indispensable. I have never meant anything else by a definition, and I have put this idea of it clearly in my Text-book.[10]

(5) You are not familiar, I think, with my definition of introspection. I define introspection, as psychological method, as consisting of "attention and record" (Text-book, 20): clear experience and permanent account of it. You leave out the second half of the method, and so can twist it into solipsism. My "record" covers your inspection-element in introspection, factually, and covers it, I believe, more truthfully.[11]

(6) Of course every individual man of science selects, because he is selectively built. I have worked this out fully in my doctrine of attention.[12] But science is not selective, because if the world of experience is a cosmos, every fact in it is indispensable to every other fact; there are no gradations of value. One of the most marked features of the history of science is the tremendous systematic importance won by facts which, at the time of their discovery, seemed insignificant. This is not surprising, but inevitable, on scientific principles. We must, then, distinguish sharply between the man of science as individual human being and the science which that man of science represents. The man of science is selective against his principles, because he cannot help himself. The man of action is selective of set voluntary purpose, because he wants to get out of experience what is useful to his present need. If the man of science lets himself go, follows his bent to the utmost, it is only from a conviction that by using his individual powers to their limit he can best advance, in the long run, the non-selective course of science. But this conviction is something very different indeed from any inherent selectivity in science.

(7) I said nothing in my last letter about psychophysical parallelism. Everything that I there said was entirely compatible with any alternative working hypothesis — for instance, with an extreme mental energism. You have not only read p.p.[13] into me, but you have

done much worse, — you have philosophised p.p. itself. However, that I have already commented on.

At the end of your letter you call p.p. various names. Well, but what do you gain by underestimating your opponent? P.p. appealed to men like Goethe and Fechner. It was originated by one of the most creative minds we have ever had, — Spinoza. It was adopted by Wundt from Fechner, although Wundt would gladly have bettered Fechner; it was adopted by Ebbinghaus[14] from Wundt, although Ebbinghaus would still more gladly have bettered Wundt. All the recent work in the Zeitschrift f. Psych. has made in its favour, oftentimes very clearly in spite of the authors' will and desire. It has resisted the most ingenious and the most brutal attacks. Yet you call it "that narrow and at best self-evident emphasis of an unessential and scientifically insufficiently founded split of a group of biological events." Ye gods! I gave it a whole year of my spare time, some years ago, and was doubtful even then whether I had earned the right to an independent judgment.[15]

I think that these are the most salient points: if I have missed anything, it is not by intention. Now I take up your conclusions.

(1) I do not make physical and psychical "contrasts." But I think that the terms characterise the two main Parts of the whole book of experience, as scientifically written, and I think that any muddlement of the two standpoints is death to scientific clarity.[16]

(2) I believe that introspection, as attention and record, is adequate to the whole of psychology. I know of no methodical difference between introspection and inspection[17]: they are the same methods applied to what is ultimately the same subject-matter considered from different points of view. These points of view, however, are the remotest possible within the range of science.

(3) I have no objection to a science of the organism, i.e. to a psychophysics or biology. Only, to be science, it must be causal and not simply teleological.[18] And, just because it is psychophysics or biology, it is different from either physiology or psychology, and occupies a separate chapter in the Book. It belongs, however, to the same group of chapters.[19]

(4) I have no quarrel either with Maxwell, though the terms "what" and "how" and "why," being extremely abstract terms, need a definition at the outset. It would be necessary to say, e.g., whether the "what" is qualitative only, or quantitative as well. It would be also necessary to say whether quantity, if admitted, was understood as magnitude merely or as divisible magnitude; and so on. Avoidance of

these understandings at the beginning means muddle later. But in general the problem of science, as I give it in my Text-book, is Maxwell's, and indeed that of numberless others, although the terms of it are cut a little differently — especially in order to pay regard to the Mach-Avenarius discussions which postdate Maxwell.[20]

I have no objection to psychopathology's working with the unit of the adjustive reaction. Not the least. Only the term adjustive reaction is (1) teleological, and so to my mind less than scientific[21]; it must, to be science, lead beyond itself to causal statement; and (2) the term is borrowed from a definite science, from biology, and therefore cannot pass muster as the "unit" and "prototype" for work in a separate science,[22] written from another point of view, namely, psychology. Biology cannot legislate to psychology, any more than it can legislate to physics or ethics. But within biology the biologist can do as he pleases; and if psychopathology finds biology's proximate terms useful, so much the better for psychopathology. I have no quarrel.[23]

(5) I have not compared this unit with the unit of associationism; that would be a very thick-headed thing to do. I compared the unit of Freud's overtly expounded psychology with the unit of associationist psychology. Here I am right.

Neither have I ever supposed or suggested that introspection could be adequate in the field of adjustive-reaction units. Introspection is valid only in psychology. It is neither a biological nor a physiological method, under the definition of it as given in (2) above.

A satisfactory definition of psychology, i.e. a chapter heading indicating its point of view, is quite possible without reference to consciousness, and has been given by me without such reference more than once.[24]

(6) Psychopathology, again, has every right to use its habit-conflicts. This quite apart from any question of whether Stern is bested by Jung or Jung by Stern: that is irrelevant.[25] But before habit-conflicts are accepted in psychology, we want to know what they mean. If they are biological events, they belong to the chapter written from the standpoint of biology; and must appear in psychology, if at all, as seen from a different angle and so modified and transformed.

(7) All "issues" are "legitimate" in psychology which arise from its chapter heading.[26] The law of the conservation of energy is not a psychological issue; neither is the adjustive reaction of biology. Both may come into contact with psychology, in the particular case; neither could be derived from psychology.

There are no "fundamental needs" in any science, because science as science is in search of facts.[27] "Need" is a practical, not a scientific concept. I may personally need something for my purposes; but then I need as individual, not as incorporation of science.[28]

No, I cannot help you further towards a connecting link. You are working out an applied biology. In so far as you thus deal both with mind and with body, you will be the better applier if you know psychology and know physiology. But you cannot make direct use of either of these sciences, because your unit is the proximate total biological unit of the adjustive reaction. Perhaps at best psychology and physiology will save you from error in working with your unit. They will prevent your reading into that unit mental or physical factors that are not there. They may save you from logical constructions that do not accord with the facts. Possibly they may go further, and positively suggest to you the make-up of your unit; but after all you are little interested in the make-up, since you accept it as given.[29]

You will doubtless set problems to psychological analysis, as Jung has already done. Whether psychology hurries to solve them will depend on circumstances; what we have in hand to do, and how nearly the problems accord with our current work. We shall solve them ultimately.[30] But on our own behalf, not on yours.

I don't seem able to get nearer; and perhaps it is something to have realised clearly what the other standpoint is, and how it differs from one's own. After all, a rapprochement would be absurd if it were intrinsically unscientific.[31]

Yours,
E. B. Titchener

1. Titchener started out as a student of philosophy at Brasenose College, Oxford University. Late in his Oxford career, his interests gravitated toward biology (with John Scott Burdon-Sanderson), animal intelligence (with George John Romanes), and human psychology.

2. Meyer's marginal note, "Why?"

3. Meyer's marginal note, "!"

4. Meyer's marginal note, "!"

5. Edward Bagnall Poulten (1856–1943), English zoologist, Hope professor of zoology at Oxford University, 1893–1933; William Bateson (1861–1926), English biologist, professor of biology, Cambridge University, 1908–9.

6. Meyer's marginal note, "!"

7. Meyer's marginal note, "Titchener's!"

8. Meyer's marginal note, "*book*! What did I say p. 4?"

9. Meyer's marginal note, "And the contents?"

10. Titchener, *Textbook*, pp. 1–6.

11. Meyer's marginal note, "No!"
12. E. B. Titchener, *Lectures on the Elementary Psychology of Feeling and Attention* (New York: Macmillan, 1908).
13. p.p. = psychophysical parallelism.
14. Hermann Ebbinghaus (1850–1909), experimental psychologist known best for his work on memory. He was also editor of the *Zeitschrift für Psychologie*.
15. Meyer's marginal note, "And I?"
16. Meyer's marginal note, "?"
17. Meyer's marginal note, "except limitation."
18. Meyer's marginal note, "of course!"
19. Meyer's marginal note, "Where is the chapter?"
20. Meyer's marginal note, "Successfully?"
21. Meyer's marginal note, "?"
22. Meyer's marginal note, "circle".
23. Meyer's marginal note, "and who correlates?"
24. Meyer's marginal notes, "Where in such a way as to make consciousness necessary by implication?"
25. Meyer's marginal note, "I would only speak of giving most satisfaction!"
26. Meyer's marginal note, "deus ex machina."
27. Meyer's marginal note, "?"
28. Meyer's marginal note, "!"
29. Meyer's marginal note, "!?!"
30. Meyer's marginal note, "Please do not bother!"
31. Meyer's marginal note, "!"

5 M

September 28, 1909

My dear Professor Titchener:—

First some notes I wrote before receiving your letter:

I have just started to read your new textbook. It /prompts/ me /to/ formulate my attitude. Much of what I said in my scrappy letter of to-day must look as if it went far from the target.[1] I think I can give some points a better show.

1: Psychology must be observing, not only self-observing. Our psychology therefore works with necessity through personal experience and its biological manifestations and observations of others with the same manifestations; and since we have only psychological terms for those events in others, we cannot refuse taking the manifestations as part of our psychological problem.

/We may say:/

2: Among biological functions there are some for which we have none but psychological terms. We study them introspectively and in their manifestations in others and for the conditions and dynamic value they possess in the course of existence and function of ourselves and the other observed persons. These functions are a subject of psychobiology and not merely of non-mental biology because they necessarily imply the conscious process or aspect obtained in introspection and manifested in various ways of symbolization. Introspection or, where that is not available, utilization of sufficiently safe symbols and manifestations and the study of the conditions and effects in chains of events of experimental definition and purity of varying degree constitutes the problem and aim of psychology in partly intro- and partly in-spection.

3: Introspection does not furnish safe measures without very special helps in certain domains of psychology. It is, therefore, only a part method /the results/ to be supplied by chains or groups of introspections if you please, or determination of chains of reaction which /would be/ unequivocal. I refer to the /study of the/ repressed factors in many mental conflicts and disorders. Hence the emphasis may fall on the non-introspective aspects or at least on chains of introspective reports.[2] [Short cuts nevertheless do belong to psychobiology and can only be taken in as such, and not easily in terms of non-mental biology. On the other hand the possibility of introspection is so limited that a "kinematogram" of the introspective material is not possible, and the description is bound to be somewhat arbitrary.]

4: The ideal is a maximum efficiency in the differential estimation of the events, not /necessarily/ photographic accuracy of really subordinate incidentals. It is as much the task of psychology to teach economy of its processes as it is to teach accuracy generally.[3]

5: For the objectivation of psychology we use expressions which must be taken from a development of biology and not merely from neurology. Neurologizing transcriptions may be colorless, but they are also too indirect. But for this end we have to broaden the logic of science so that its expressions can do justice to the type of events at hand. For this it must get rid of the phobia of teleological conceptions, or rather learn to formulate them so that they need not give reason for phobias. I believe this is possible, if we learn to use the type of equivalent of mathematical formulas which are adaptable to biology. Mechanics gets along with very simple forms of mathematics. Biology reckons with necessity with formulas of the type of "functions." To devise the plan and standardize the methods is one of the tasks of the logic of psychology.

6: The main purpose of the psychobiological attitude is to eliminate the creation of a phantom called "mind" over and above the biological units which we are and which we look upon as objects of psychology. Most minds can only think in terms of causal chains. A common denominator of function can be maintained with far less floundering than is the case with the present chasm produced by "parallelism." What physicist would tolerate such a split in his field! Why should any scientist subordinate his logic to a traditional overrating of a feature of a set of facts, simply because the function under study happens to be the one through which psychology itself becomes possible!

7: As to the question of the utter hopelessness and uselessness of an effort of getting the facts in line for a presentation of psychology which would take this position and yet would avoid retrogression and confusion, I am not quite hopeless yet. What is psychology in your or any psychology, will remain psychology and will find its place if a qualified man takes it up. The broader field, what is not given by your exclusively introspectional psychology may have to be rendered in modest attempts, and I believe by no means necessarily in opposition or in disharmony. I admit that I attempt my share with fear and trembling, but also with times of enthusiasm and satisfaction.

8: My whole plan turns against scientific dogmatism. What is good /also/ in common-sense is the best part of science and if there is much need of correcting common-sense there is also plenty of opportunity to improve the scientific attitude. There is no reason why the best types of each should be in conflict with each other. My melioristic temperament demands greater modesty on the part of science. The idea of building up living beings out of elements has a ludicrous feature to my mind unless one knows also the compound, and it seems at least wise to describe both sides as well as we can so that we keep our knowledge as balanced and as true to our broader experience as possible (in the same way as the chemist describes the behavior of the compound and not only the composition).

Now one question in which I know you can give me a most valuable advice. Which is the best of the empirical psychologies of the 18th century or the best modern presentation of the whole group?

Further, which is the best attempt since then of giving an empirical (and possibly biologically useful) description of mental functions apart from James?[4] An analogon of Bain,[5] but less diffuse and with some actual knowledge of more modern demands of concrete observation?

Since /scribbling/ the above I have read your letter and the pertinent discussions of your Text-book.[6]

I am really under very great obligations for your reply to my letter. I am glad that I wrote perfectly frankly but am sorry that you came to the conclusion of hopelessness of argument and absence of any common standing ground. Personally I am not of the give-up kind and I gladly acknowledge that your statements are in many ways helpful to me as they show me clearly what I am confronted with, and also that there is some common ground in view, even in your statements.

Both in your letter and in your book you are by no means as clear as you think with regard to the meaning of position and conditions of accuracy of what you call record, and especially the extent to which you accept record material as pertaining to psychology when it has to be expressed in terms non-psychological; that is a vital issue especially in animal psychology and in our work, but I feel it has been altogether too narrowly taken, too little defined by psychology as a "science" as you want to limit it. You limit psychology to introspection and refer inspection to physics. I think what you gain in "clearness of thought" there you gain at the expense of confusion in fields which cannot afford it. You find yourself forced to "attribute" minds to other human beings, you say the psychologist is "justified in believing that other men have minds" etc.; you feel like making its range coextensive with that of animal life. You accept animal, society and madman (what a term!). You accept gestures as well as words and then call the repetition "introspection." And finally you refuse it the value of scientific observation. With what justification? Are words any better? I truly think it is as much the task of science — call it psychophysics if you like — to create methods of record and analysis of the objective evidence and settings of the mental reactions as it is to introspect their analog in ourselves. There, then, comes the light: in your new "chapter" of psychophysics or biology! Who is going to shape them, going to write the chapter headings? Or where would you direct me for them?

With regard to the sense in which I speak of adjustive reaction you do me hopeless injustice when you say "that after all you are little interested in the make-up of the unit since you accept it as given." That was one of the main points which I discussed in my notes for an alternative lecture at Clark. I almost believe that statement makes us quits concerning any slips in our mutual sizing up. If we had to stop there we should have to work in serene indifference. I had of course no idea of prescribing to the psychologists as researchers the task of tackling the psychological analysis of the problems that Jung and others have on hand. But I had thought that possibly the psychologist as a teacher might feel some interest in showing students how to size up these problems: in the first place what he calls them when he meets them, that is, whether they are problems of biology; second, how we can do justice to them without conflict with the tenets of standard "sciences." That, of course, "may take books to explain" but I believe it is also feasible to give a sketch of the perspectives. And in this respect, I believe it is the task of a teacher to show the student the relationship of the facts in one's science to those of another science or how the same facts appear to the different sciences. If the teacher cannot do that, the student will always be in a mess. I believe with Sanford that the "physician's attitude" is not a bad one to cultivate first.[7] But of course you seem to be interested only in the science not in the sphere which the science should comprehend and conquer! I do not quarrel with you on what you wish to call psychology and how you wish to limit it. But I claim that in common parlance there is a whole domain of events (incorrectly?) called psychology which nobody else dares handle; let us call it psychophysics or biology with some qualification such as psychobiology, because the biologist has been made to believe that anything which has any contact with psychology must be avoided — see Uexküll,[8] and in turn Jennings,[9] who would no doubt side with me. This branch of biology has to cover those actions and reactions which involve with necessity that which by introspection or analogy we accept as psychological event. You are probably narrow if you deny biology the character of science when it dares include these events. But that is a matter of definition of science. If you want historical perspective, call it Huxley's sense of biology.[10] As far as I can see we psychopathologists stand at a juncture in many ways similar to that at which the physiological chemists stood. The main trouble is that we have even more complex units to ascertain and to analyze than they had and still have. And the greatest difficulty of it all is the diversity of methods of the sciences that should furnish us the safest methods and setting, and that unwillingness of yours to come to any terms. If there were a common denominator, such as biology seems to furnish, many stumbling blocks would seem to vanish. You yourself admit that the range of psychology is even narrower than that of biology. What is in the way to joining biology? Evidently the overawing contrast of the subjective and objective character of two methods, raised to such dignity as to give the right of way to the theories which thrive /when given/ the right to split what can be split that way, viz. the manifestations in the animal kingdom. And that you call the double aspect of the whole world! You say yourself, p. 15,[11] that mankind has assumed two substances, matter and mind, and that the hypothesis of these stable substances must be surrendered. But you will not surrender the excessive respect for the double-aspect theory of the world[12] which to my mind is but a subordinate consequence of our biological organization, the way our "mind" works.

In order to give biology a position as common denominator, it will, of course, have to do justice also to the teleological problems. That question I had had in mind for Worcester, but for obvious reasons I refrained from an attempt which may well be made in a circle of friends or a close circle of critics, but not where larger responsibilities might be affected. I do not consider it hopeless nor is it necessary to stop with Aristotle or Thomism or with Driesch.[13]

You speak of paying regard to Mach and Avenarius. I see scant evidence of that! They are among the very foremost helps in the obliteration of the undesirable split. (You use them only in the rather confusing §§ 1 and 2. I should like to see their effect on readers who are not /somewhat/ familiar with what you are driving at and who can make the necessary corrections in the shifting between subjective and objective experience (p. 11, line 24) and supply the "principles" you merely allude to in p. 4, l. 12 from their experience.) Is it not well to teach the student to handle the facts (which they meet and are asked to use even by you) and to learn to see their relations? Who is to do that?

Here then, most certainly, we would need the "chapter" on psychophysics or biology or as I say psychobiology, to contrast it with the rest of biology, the non-mental regulations. You offer it. Where are its headings?

In the question of parallelism I may or may not have the right of an independent judgment. I see the havoc it plays, the indifference it breeds towards the most important issues of clearness, merely to satisfy clearness in an esoteric circle. It is an issue of metaphysics, but a very serious one. If we can eliminate it, the better for science. I have a right to ask: Can you join me in an effort to reach a definition or stand-point of psychology which would be on neutral ground and which would subordinate all contrasts which could possibly be spared?

You say you do not mention p.p. But your whole scheme of limiting psychology to introspection could not exist without the overemphasis of p.p. The question might certainly be asked: is there enough objective distinction to the psychological functions to make them worth studying objectively in others, not merely in terms of physiology but also [in] terms of psychology? Why rule out common-sense instead of improving on it? I should assent to calling the hybrid biology instead of psychobiology, although with the latter term I only meant that "part of biology which deals with reactions including psychological reactions" in the narrow sense in which you use the word. The result need not be "death to scientific clarity." The difference of the subjective and objective points of view can readily be submerged and to my mind had best be submerged just as I should welcome the submerging of the contrasts of teleological and causal point of view and several other contrasts criticised in my review of Münsterberg in Science.[14] In your note to (3) of my conclusions you certainly join me on common ground, viz. where you see a place for "psychophysics or biology" and for "special chapters different from either physiology or psychology." "It belongs, however, to the same group of chapters." To know this group of chapters of "psychophysics" would bring a very direct answer to most of my questions.

I am very anxious to get at all the definitions of psychology which do not involve "consciousness." We might perhaps in that way find common definitions for those biological reactions which would be legitimate topics of psychobiology.

I should now like to take up certain points in your Text-book.

You say on p. VII "if psychology is to be taken seriously, its problems must now-a-days be treated in some detail," and I should add, in an intelligible setting. Your "setting" is given in pp. 1–41, and I must confess that at least three headings have confirmed my first impression that it is not the kind of setting I should allow my students to maintain. They should at least know the relation to a functional setting, if they did not accept it.

In the first place your definition of a science. You define primers of science; the same issue of chapters and chapter-headings. But let that pass! You next attach it to some man and special lines of inquiry. That would be all right; but then comes the addendum which is positively misleading and not true. You say "throughout the whole of experience," instead of "wherever it applies." "The science of mechanics begins when men begin to interpret the universe in mechanical terms, when the world at large is looked upon as a vast machine, working precisely as a tool of an engine works." My common-sense revolts against such a construction, and I look for a wish fathering this claim. You need this attitude towards the whole world for your dogmatic and arbitrary division of psychology and physics. Mach has a much saner view of the origin of mechanics and of any science. There is a process of specialization; a class of workers' forms; schools or methods of instruction; principles to be communicated, comprehensive, compact, consistent and facile conceptions of facts; economy of communication and of apprehension; new questions, new answers, etc. The material in which this organization takes place is experience. There is multiplicity but no "chaos" except to the confused human being; every human being has a nucleus of orderly experience and expands from it along lines of opportunities of application and of imagination. But science is usually economical of the latter unless special hopes or tendencies get the better of experience in the narrower sense. Mythology animated the world, but it did not seriously lead science to look upon "the world at large" as mind. Without parallelistic bias you would not universalize the "points of view."

I can see clearly the spirit of your attitude. But can you tell where it is worked out to its logical consequences so as to /warrant our using its formulation/ as an introductory setting for students? I prefer to put the question in this manner, rather than try to criticise it further in detail and in its broader bearings. Mach and Avenarius, and a number of others have used similar avenues; but I have not seen it used for the same purpose and ends at which you arrive with it. To say the least this attempt is not easily assimilated because it is arbitrary in spots and not clear enough and not true enough to the actual demands of orderly analysis. Your division of experience into dependent and independent will be carried by but few readers, especially because, in addition, you shift the sense of "experience" (as in p. 12, l. 24). Instead of insisting on science being some man's consistent adherence to a definite point of view — which fits your relation to your psychology— I would rather call science organized and critical experience free of one-man power or aspirations thereto.

Instead of saying: "experience is relative; to reduce the relativity, certain rules must be observed. Common-sense has adjusted itself to this requirement, but it behooves us in science to do better and to be even more accurate" etc.— you say that the two forms of experience are different. You prefer an "absolute" point of view[15] (just as the theologian and philosopher bows to his kinds of absolute). Scientific experience (within psychology as well as within "physical sciences") is the systematic arrangement of those data of experience which have the criterion of being generally acceptable to individuals under the best conditions of experience, stripped of the variables for the sake of economy and clearness of thought, and stripped especially of the numerous accompaniments experienced in their connection by persons at different times or by different persons. You charge me with biologizing the universe. You mechanize, opticize and psychologize it with your principle of point of view. The main claims to attention in your split of the data of experience into mental and physical is the extremeness of these two possible points of view, and the "independence" and "dependence"; first you say they have the same sort of material or subject-matter (p. 6, line 10) and p. 8–27 it becomes the same stuff, the same material, without any reminder that physics covers the whole range of "matter," and psychology the experience (as function of sufficiently organized biological units) in a limited sphere.[16]

Experience taken objectively is one type of reaction of things to other things, and if /studied as it appears in psychological action/, limited to a type of reaction which you yourself say occurs only in animals. The functional experience offers two possibilities of approach: the reaction by introspection and that of inspection of one's self or others; moreover, we can study the products of mental activity (books, records of mentation), for their relational and other features and values; but these problems are kept out of functional [sic, structural?] psychology.

Your whole problem of the attitude in science could be much better illustrated by a comparison of Goethe's Farbenlehre[17] and general attitude, and that of "science." It is admirably presented in Chamberlain's Kant[18] — a bright literary product, worthy of some leisure hours.

What you /next/ call common-sense is a very conventional creation to suit your own purposes. My common-sense is probably somewhat different from yours; and it would be much better to teach students to size up their own personal common-sense, not merely in the sense of tradition, but of /personal or individual/ "Mutterwitz"[19] and to show how it is to be transformed to reach the attitude and standard of science.

When on p. 10, l. 13, you say "so far there is a general agreement," I call that a presumption which is bound to revenge itself. The agreement is a question of tradition and also dependent on the individual. Common-sense is more or less uncritical or critical individual "experience"; but it is not hopeless; it is subject to training. That is the main thing the student should go to college for.

Your argument puts the student on a path which may be stimulating, but is not helping him as much as it should. Your common-sense deals with too many questions which I am pretty sure my wife (without psychological or philosophical training) would never ask; and you mix matters hopelessly as when you refer to Fig. I[20] and mingle the spatial character of the object and product of "mental experience" with what is implied by the statement that "mind is not spatial." That mind is free to act as it pleases is quite obviously too naive even for your pupils to think and your antithesis looks as if it might in the end deny the freedom altogether. The influence between body and mind is given over to the "nobody knows," while it certainly is possible to restate the question to any reasonable mind to a fair degree of satisfaction. The contrast of p.p. and interaction does not become clear and certainly does not relieve the difficulty, that there might be an obliteration of the parallelism and therefore no interaction in the old sense, but interaction of different sets of biological functions is not even mentioned. The problem can be solved easily enough to the satisfaction of clearer thought and so as to make the feeling of puzzle unnecessary. Your "exhaustive account" on p. 14, l. 1–5, creates more "poor common-sense" than clearness when held together with the mental event. This is not parallelism but may very easily be crossing without intersection and without any hope of a formula of stating the relation. Parallelism, I admit, is compatible with doing some kind of justice to all the observed facts; we never come into contradiction of facts merely on account of the parallelism. But see the results. You say you avoid perplexing questions!

The questions you raise on p. 14 of your introduction as avoided by parallelism are an /interesting collection/. I mean "Where does the body and the mind begin?" and the rest of the questions. You say it is a hard matter to answer them. Is it as hard as the many fool-problems parallelism has driven some neurologists into? and many real ones? such as: What does the parallelism consist in? What is parallel? Who deals with the parallel part on the "physical" side? To whom does the psychologist throw that job? Can we have any decent psychology without considering the laws of make-up and function of that parallel part of the organism? To my mind it would be a very desirable thing to teach the student to ask his questions properly; to tell him that instead of asking where does the body end and the mind begin (a question I regret I have never heard) he might possibly wonder which objective reactions can be safely called as having something to do with that "parallel-arrangement" and which not; or "do the senses belong to the mind or to body" is a poor question unless you say what you mean by sense —etc. etc. That the lawn-sprinkler simile is rather blunt you will admit.[21] Sorrow and fear are reactions which you can describe biologically, or introspectively+objectively; if you do not go out of your way, the practical diction is perfectly true, and not only by accommodation.

In your first letter you say psychological analysis regards duration, the temporal attribute, as one of its keenest instruments of dissection (a statement which I should like to see in your "introduction"). Does it not also need other data from the camp of the "objective world" to define the conditions under which the events take place? Do you not presuppose other domains of biology on every turn of the road, and also physics and chemistry? In our interests as psychopathologists the conditions of the flow and contents of events are partly designated with psychological terms, partly with biological ones or in case of intoxications in our naivety in chemical terms.

Your definition and use of "consciousness" is another point which must confuse the student unnecessarily. In the first rejected meaning it is of course better abandoned and replaced by "awareness." /The/ sense /you accept/ is arbitrary and objectionable. To speak of the direct object of psychological study as "always a consciousness" seems to me hazy and avoidable, because consciousness is really used in quite a different sense by those who have a definite reason to use it, viz. we physicians, who cannot get along without the term. Münsterberg mixes the senses very badly and made me specially conscious of the difficulty about this expression.

{S} 8 is most vital. Here you emphasize the record. You praise the poorest tool we have, viz. language, and accept it, apparently only when it is used for recording of introspection, not also as a record of the event itself (in "loud thinking"). Similarly you accept verbal descriptions of gesture. Would not the kinematograph combined with phonograph make a better record? and one leading over to a valuable record of the event as it takes place apart from attempts at introspection? and would not that very quickly suggest the real relation of things? I mean the need of some knowledge of how to record and interpret the objective evidence of the happening which you also introspect? You accept the utterances and behavior of the "inmates of hospitals" and systematic tests. You make the reader think that there too only the introspective part of the "record" of mental activity is looked for. This specification of introspection in the whole realm of psychology, from the obliteration of solipsism (in the sense of limitation of psychology to introspection) to the extension of the analogy of other persons' reactions to the animal and "madman," appears to me unfortunate. The language and gesture and the nature of the activity and behavior are direct objective data which I want recorded, and which I test or supplement by additional "introspection," but after all with introspection in the usual sense /i.e./ chiefly as a supplement and not as the essential basis of the record.

I am tempted to stop at your samples of introspective psychopathology, where you speak of paranoia on p. 30, when you say the self-importance is "merely," etc. Some knowledge of paranoia would make me hesitate; and the backwardness of the sample (cp.[*sic*,cf.] p. 39) is not the fault of the opportunities for study offered by us.

The reasoning on p. 36–41 affects me strangely. The first task for the psychologist would to my mind be not the analysis into the simplest components, but the identification of the object of analysis and the ways of determination of the identity or homology in successive experiments. The next /step/ is not necessarily analysis into irreducible partitions but the behavior of the event under varied conditions; in this analysis and synthesis in your sense are but one side of the problem. And then you might get some replies to the "why" in a less bewildering manner than that sketched from p. 39 on. I don't mean to say that it is bewildering to me; it is only a surprise that the burden should all be thrown on the nervous system before the poor student. "Reference to the nervous system introduces into psychology just that unity and coherence which a strictly descriptive psychology cannot achieve." That is what I should /almost/ call /something like a/ bankruptcy of the beautiful structure for which you seem to make such a gallant fight in our correspondence. Reference to the body does not add to the data of psychology; but if furnishes an (or the ?) explanatory principle. Perhaps "mental science explains mental processes by reference to those nervous processes under observation." This part of the job interests me because it throws a light on the consistency of your other definitions of the task of psychology. Or does psychology really have to shirk "explanation" at least as a rule? I might ask you what kind of neurology you actually /and preferably/ use to hold your psychology together? I feel at home in neurology and know that from a certain point on I have to use functional neurobiological if not directly "psychological" terms, in which I do not mention much of the nervous system, and where I need my critical teleology. Perhaps you could show me how you /practically/ attend to this feature in your actual science of psychology and it might be that different standards in the carrying out of that task might account for some of our differences.

You say: a rapprochement would be absurd if it were unscientific. Surely. Therefore let us understand on ground of science: How had we best attend to the explanatory member of the psychological trinity? and how can we formulate the "chapter" on psychophysics in terms of a sufficient biology?

Here are my questions and difficulties on more concrete ground than I had expected to write. Do pardon the very hasty and lamentably blunt way. I know we must limit ourselves to mere sketchy statements. But I truly believe, I have come to some points worth formulating and if you feel like jotting down some hints and helps, and a few points as to the literature on the underscored issues, I should feel we had done better than tried to "kill each other." We would have worked together. And for that and the stimulus you have my gratitude.

Very sincerely yours,
Adolf Meyer

1. Although Meyer dates this letter September 28, 1909, he appears to have begun it on September 23, 1909, the same day as 3M, before he received Titchener's letter of September 25, 1909 (4T).

2. The text from this point to the end of the paragraph was struck out in the carbon of Meyer's letter. The original is not extant.

3. Meyer refers here to Ernst Mach's principle of the economy of thought according to which the fundamental task of science was observation and description "so as to provide the most economical summary of relationships among experiences" (Kurt Danziger, "The Positivist Repudiation of Wundt," *Journal of the History of the Behavioral Sciences* 15 [1979]: 212). On this account, scientific theories did not copy or mirror reality but were considered working tools in the service of intellectual economy; their chief justification was the biological need of the organism to master and control the environment in the most efficient or economical manner possible.

4. William James (1842–1910), leading American psychologist and philosopher, was author of the influential *Principles of Psychology* (1890) in which he insisted that psychology had the status of a special science and in which he elaborated a functional approach to the study of mental states. Titchener defined his structural approach in psychology in opposition to James's functional views, whereas it was Meyer's ambition to build an American psychiatry on the basis of James's functional principles. At the time of their correspondence in 1909, both Titchener and Meyer were personally acquainted with James.

5. Alexander Bain (1818–1903), Scottish psychologist, logician, and writer on education, was author of the widely read *The Senses and the Intellect* (1868),

The Emotions and the Will (1880), and other works. An early advocate of the application of physiology to the elucidation of mental states, Bain expounded the association psychology of Mill and his contemporaries.

6. Meyer refers to Titchener's letter of September 25, 1909 (4T) which arrived subsequently to the beginning of this letter.

7. We have been unable to identify this reference. Possibly, Meyer refers to a remark made by Sanford at the Worcester Conference.

8. Baron Jakob Johann von Uexküll (1864–1944), German biologist and comparative psychologist, supported the views of the German-American zoologist and physiologist Jacques Loeb (1859–1924), who led the mechanist movement in comparative psychology. In 1899, von Uexküll with T. Beer and A. Bethe published a joint paper in which they proposed discarding all psychological terms in the explanation of the behavior of lower animals and substituting objective terms instead.

9. Herbert Spencer Jennings (1868–1947), experimental biologist and professor of experimental zoology at Johns Hopkins University. An opponent of mechanists such as Jacques Loeb and vitalists such as Hans Driesch, Jennings in his classic *Behavior of the Lower Organisms* (1906) insisted on the contribution of inner experience, including sensation, emotion, and thought, in the determination of human conduct, and provided a functional or holistic account of behavior.

10. Thomas Henry Huxley's (1830–1897) definition of science as organized common sense played a decisive role on the development of Meyer's psychiatry of common sense. See especially in this connection Meyer's paper "British Influences in Psychiatry and Mental Hygiene" (1933), *CP*, 3:400–428.

11. Meyer's page, paragraph, and line references here and at other places in the 1909 correspondence are to Titchener, *A Textbook of Psychology*, Part 1, the pagination of which is the same as in the first edition of the completed *Textbook*, published in 1910.

12. Meyer refers to Titchener's criticism of metaphysical dualism associated with the work of Ernst Mach and Richard Avenarius.

13. Hans Adolf Eduard Driesch (1867–1941), German biologist and philosopher, was a major figure in the rise of experimental embryology at the turn of the century. An advocate of vitalism, Driesch attributed embryological development to an agent outside the machine (for which he borrowed Aristotle's word "entelechy"). Driesch was invited to deliver the Gifford lectures in natural theology at the University of Aberdeen in 1907 and 1908. The lectures were published as *Science and Philosophy of the Organism* (1908).

14. Hugo Münsterberg (1863–1916), a student of Wundt and successor to William James as director of the psychological laboratory at Harvard University. His work on industrial efficiency, the psychology of testimony, psychotherapy, vocational training, education, and film earned him the title of "founder" of applied psychology in the United States. Meyer's reference is to his 1909 review of Münsterberg's book *Psychotherapy*, reprinted in *CP*, 2:635–40.

15. The text from this point to the end of the sentence was struck out in the carbon of Meyer's letter.

16. Following Avenarius, Titchener held to a conception of causality that led him to substitute physiological definitions and descriptions (which Avenarius

called the independent series) for psychological definitions and descriptions (which Avenarius called the dependent series) wherever possible, a position that Meyer rejected as a threat to the autonomy of psychology as a science.

17. Johann Wolfgang von Goethe (1749–1832) published his *Farbenlehre* (translated as *Theory of Colors*) in 1810.

18. The reference is probably to Houston Stewart Chamberlain's *Immanuel Kant, die Personlichkeit als Einfahring in das Werk* (c. 1905).

19. Mutterwitz = common sense.

20. The figure is the Müller-Lyer illusion, similar in principle to that reproduced in Figure 1, p. 20.

21. Opposing the commonsense view that we cry because we are sorry or run because we are frightened, Titchener wrote in his *Textbook*: "To suppose that the sorrow and the fear are literally the cause of tears and bodily movements would be on a par with supposing that the idea of watering the lawn can, literally and directly, turn the tap and set the sprinkler in motion" (p. 15).

6 T

October 1, 1909

My dear Meyer,

Life has her ironies! I have just been offered a glorious research position, with an adequate salary.[1] I cannot accept it, but must fritter away another year of my life, because our Trustees think it so vastly important that I should "fulfill my obligations" to the Cornell undergraduate, and instill into him just those doctrines which you find so heartily narrow and confused! I am inclined at the moment to wish that I were still narrower and still more confused, so that my services might the more readily be dispensed with.

The book I shall not attempt to defend; its many defects do not touch the question of the merits of the position. On the position itself I shall hope to write to you later, though I shall for some while be overwhelmed with routine work and lecturing.

Yours,
E. B. Titchener

1. Titchener was offered the headship of the Department of Psychology at Clark University by G. Stanley Hall on September 21, 1909. Titchener stipulated the terms—$4,000 per year and $400 per year for an assistant. Hall made the offer to take effect at Titchener's convenience "after Christmas." According to Hall "no professor here has ever been paid a higher salary than this." (G. Stanley Hall to E. B. Titchener, 21 September 1909, The E. B. Titchener Papers, Cornell University Archives.) Cornell retaliated by offering Titchener an equivalent position, which he accepted—the first research professorship in the university's history.

7 M

October 4, 1909

My dear Professor Titchener:—

This offer to you and our correspondence should not be called "life's ironies." It seems to me that both have their justification and most certainly the fact that you should get an absolutely /free/ research position. That part is sure to come and I never should worry for those who would have the good sense to create it. And as to the doctrines— I wish there were no adjectives. Those miserable things are difficult to control and their relativity makes it possible that the one uses them very lightly and the one who is affected sees rather more in them. The "narrow" I might still allow to stand without much reserve. I truly believe that the history of science shows us that any conception which tends to eliminate the causal point of view and to insist too much on the analytical descriptive issues may do for the individual but is not the best for teaching in its broader and more effective sense; and as to the word "confused," that I would take with a grain of salt in a very relative sense. It may be that because I have to apply it very often to my own attempts at reaching clearness that I have used the word rather too freely.

I know the great demands on your time and only feel sorry that the beginning of the term overtook us. I am to some extent in the same predicament but I am still "going" under the impetus as far as time permits, and I hope that neither you nor I will have to regret the time spent on a clearing of the situation.

When I shall get further with my attempts you will no doubt have a rich critical harvest /or rather a rich chance for criticism/ if you care to go over the attempts, and that is just what I am looking for most of all, namely, the working together of those who with or against their will have to direct the mental attitude of students beside living their life as investigators.

Please accept my heartiest congratulations and my wishes that the University's demands may not interfere with an ultimate response to a call in another direction.

Very sincerely yours,
Adolf Meyer

8 M

October 13, 1909

My dear Professor Titchener:—

Pardon me for troubling you on one of the questions that I raised in my last letter, to which I should very much appreciate an answer. Before I enter more definitely on the recasting of my lectures I should like to form a more definite idea of the empirical psychology at its best, and I would like to know which is the best example of the conceptions of the 18th Century and those of the present day? Another question would be whether any one from your stand-point has given a thorough review of Judd's psychology,[1] and if so where it is to be found?

Believe me,

Very sincerely yours,
Adolf Meyer

1. Charles Hubbard Judd (1873–1946), educational psychologist, student and translator of Wundt, in 1907 became director of the Yale Psychological Laboratory, and in 1909 professor of education at the University of Chicago. Meyer's reference is to Judd's *Psychology, General Introduction* (1907), in which Judd developed a functional account of mental life.

9 T

October 17, 1909

My dear Meyer,

I have three letters to thank you for, — and I should have written earlier had I not been overwhelmed with departmental duties. I cannot give very much time to an answer, even now, but I will do my best.[1]

(1) As to your question about the 18th cent. and its modern presentation.

There is , of course, no history of psychology yet written. There could hardly be, since the meaning of the term "psychology," as a specific thing, dates only from the middle of the 19th century. There are the German works of Dessoir[2] (on modern German psychology) and of Sommer[3] (psychology and aesthetics), both written in competition for a Berlin prize. There is the often-quoted article on Associationism in the Britannica.[4] There is the book on Kant's psychology by your namesake.[5] There are historical summaries in Wundt's big work,[6] and there are references in Baldwin's Dictionary.[7] Historical articles appear from time to time in the technical journals. I may at the moment miss something; but I can think of nothing more. If you want to know the 18th cent., you have to read it. There are dissertations on special things, like Braunschweiger's on attention.[8] — You see, nobody was competent to write this sort of history before the men of the present generation, men of your own and Münsterberg's and Külpe's[9] and my own age: competent, I say, to write this sort of history, a history of psychology proper; and we have all been too busy with the spreading of the standpoint itself (if that phrase will pass!) to bother as yet with the writing of history. I may have overlooked something that would do for you; but I recall nothing more just now.

I do not know which is the best of the empirical psychologies of the 18th cent. Associationism culminates in J. Mill (Analysis)[10] and Bain; and faculty-psychology culminates, perhaps, in Kant.[11] Many of the men between Wolff and Kant are worth reading:[12] Tetens,[13] in particular, for a type of associationism; but I can't single out any preeminent man. Dessoir might help you here. James has a good chapter on association.[14] Herbart[15] and Lotze[16] are both worth reading, against faculty-psychology, with a taste of the old leaven still left in. I am afraid you will have to read historically; I know of no other way.

(2) Nor can I help you to an adequate work, later than James, on the "mental functions." Stout's Analytic Psychology[17] is ranked high, and is functional; but it is probably too abstract for you. You might look at his smaller Manual, and see if the system suits your needs. This appeared in 1899; the A.P. in 1896. Judd and Angell[18] have recently written smaller text-books of a functional sort. But "functional psychology" exists for the most part in magazine articles, which are also for the most part controversial in character. I suppose Baldwin's books[19] wouldn't do for you? I myself sought earnestly, a few years ago, to find a functional psychology, but I confess that I don't know what it means. I do not either recall anything in French or German that would meet your requirements. Possibly Meumann's Intelligenz & Wille[20] might serve to start your reading; but you will have to read a whole lot, and to pick up the functional things as you go, and to systematise them for yourself. You might add Thorndike's Elements[21] to Judd and Angell.

(3) I hadn't meant to to defend my own book; but you have, I think, gone astray on various points where I can bring myself nearer to you. So I will give a minute to it.

"Madman" is not my term. It is the term used by a supposed

contemptuous objector (p. 30), and is in fact the word always used by the urgers of such objection. I used it once only, after its introduction by the objector on p. 30, and then simply to meet the objector on his own ground (35). In my own person I speak always of disorder, derangement, abnormal, insane, &c.

I never speak of a "method" of analysis. Analysis is, for me, something to do; i.e., it is part of a problem. When we talk of methods of analysis in chemistry, &c., we mean always, I think, means or methods whereby the problem of analysis is solved. Analytical methods are not a special class of methods, but any methods whereby analysis can be done. I believe you will find my usage consistent here.

In referring to Mach and Avenarius I was not, of course, referring to their doctrine of economy of thought (which is not a scientific principle, if we may take the 19th century as our standard for science), but to the distinction of dependent and independent experience.[22] This is straight Avenarius, and Mach has given in his adhesion, and said that he was feeling earlier toward the same position.

There is, again of course, a metaphysics of parallelism, as there is also a logic or epistemology of parallelism. I have never dreamed of denying that. But I am concerned to keep psychology, as science, clear either of metaphysics or of functional logic (epistemology). For psychology, parallelism is a body of observed facts, generalised to the rank of a working hypothesis at large: precisely like the law of the conservation of energy in physics. It is quite compatible with metaphysical monism, whether taken as materialism or as spiritualism.

I do not believe at all in "psychological functions" or "mental functions," but only in organismic (if there is such a word), i.e. in human, whole-man functions. So I can't be expected to discuss them, or to base my exposition on them[23]. Some men believe still in the substantial mind, many men believe in the unconscious mind; they would write their psychologies upon those assumptions; I cannot see evidence for either, and so I cannot write a psychology of function. Psychophysics may or may not be functional, just as biology (of the cell, e.g.) may or may not be functional: there is a cell-mechanics and a cell-teleology. I have no objection, as I have said before, to a functional psychophysics or as you call it a psychobiology.

The subject matter of psychology is defined in my book without reference to consciousness. In two words, it is dependent experience.[24]

You say that my introduction is inadequate because the students ought to know, as well if not by preference, the "relation to a functional setting." The relation of what? If you mean "of mind," I do not think that there is any, and you can hardly expect me to teach what I do not believe. You lay a curious stress all through your letter on the duty of the teacher, as if I were not a teacher as well as yourself, or as if I had not the normal sense of responsibility to my students. I have an elective class of over 260 men, using this book this term, and I take them with all the responsibility that I have in me; that is what I am paid to do. You can't really expect that I shall instruct them in things that I deliberately believe to be erroneous? But you can't either believe that I read off my book to them. The book is the printed guide to what I think is true; behind the book stands the lecturer, trying to give an idea of what modern psychology is, whether it is right or wrong. I am not there to convert or to proselytise; any more than I am there to preach what I take to be false doctrine. I say in effect: Here is what people are thinking; I myself have concluded as in the book; take your choice. Always in the syllabuses and examination questions there are notes and alternative questions on the specific "functional" views that are in vogue at the time; and I do not mark a man down because he disagrees with me. But I can't print, and the publishers wouldn't, extra pages of controversial matter; my introduction gives the situation as I have thought it out. If there is a better or clearer presentation in the same compass, people will buy that and not buy me; securus judicat orbis.[25] — To be concrete; you would find my students, at the end of the term, quite familiar with Jung's complexes, and with my own tentative interpretation of their psychology. Why not?

You say again that the distinction of dependent and independent experience is not easily assimilable. Well, last year I exempted (mark of 85% on average of two prelims.) over 70% of a class of 230 odd; and in the final I had to condition only 3 of the rest. That looks to me like assimilation. I should say it depended on the teacher.

The use of "experience" on p. 12, line 24 is identical with previous use. You may write "dependent" and "independent" for mental and physical.

As regards the range of the various sciences you have missed p. 5 top. I say that the aim is to cover the whole of experience; science must be taken in that way if it is to succeed; it is you now who are laying down a priori boundaries. But I say explicitly that the different sciences can't all go the whole distance over experience. They stop where they must. Physics, e.g., can't deal with mind, since mind is not a form of energy, and can't be included in the machine.

I spoke of the advantages of language because that was my theme. Why should I speak of what is not relevant to my section? The disadvantages of language come in when one begins experimental work; they have been duly set forth by Kuelpe in his Outlines[26] and also by myself in the Exp. Psych.[27] I am showing why we do in fact rely upon language; you say in objection that language may prove a broken reed. So if I said that a train got me to N.Y. in 7 hours, you might say in objection that it wastes 40% of the available energy of the coal. To avoid criticism of that sort one would have to write a cyclopedia.

You see a transition from common-sense to science; i.e. from estimation of values to reverence for fact. I do not. Have I not a right to express my opinion? If you can prove me wrong by showing the transition, well and good; I will gladly acclaim you. But my reading of history whether of science in particular or of human thought in general leads me to my own view. Since I have acquired this view by honest work, why call it names? And in general: you speak as if I had some foregone bias, and had shaped the world to this bias in my Introduction. No doubt we are all biassed; but I have at least attempted impartiality; I have seriously considered and tried all sorts of views, and have come out to this one. Why is it not respectable, as one man's honest effort to reach clearness? If it doesn't satisfy you, you won't accept it; but then you must surely recognise the fact that, at bottom, you yourself are also biassed; I am not the only prejudiced person in the universe. Yet all that you offer in exchange is the assurance that "the problem can be solved easily enough to the satisfaction of clearer thought and so as to make the feeling of puzzle unnecessary." Well, solve it! Plato said that thought began in puzzle; and your kindergarten avoidance of it does not allure me. But go ahead and solve it, — only don't use words like "function," first, without saying whether you mean teleology or mathematics, and don't use words of mind that imply that mind is energetic, secondly, when that is the very thing that I can't grant. Any problem can be solved if you are at liberty to shape the terms to your own solution. At any rate let us have the evidence that mind is energetic.

All of your questions about parallelism are, as a curious fact, answered fairly explicitly in the Introduction. The puzzle- questions arising out of interaction (questions whose puzzle is unnecessary, because following from logical error) are questions actually raised in discussion by students, not made up by me.

The duration which is an instrument of analysis is, of course, not independent but dependent duration, not physical but mental time. You can't analyse mind by body. On the other hand, that mind itself is both temporal and spatial seems to me to be perfectly clear, and my students appear to understand it.

The paranoia-instance was given me some years ago by Kraepelin;[28] the others were suggested by the Med. Supt. of one of our State Hospitals.[29] I have been forced to appeal to men of standing in their work for these things, because the many books I have read on psychiatry don't go into psychology at all. It is very likely that the instances are wrong, but the wrongness is not of my making, — I follow what authorities I can find. Your criticism here is, I think, especially ungenerous; you have jumped to the conclusion that I have lightly speculated in a foreign field, which is your own specialty; while in fact I have read as widely as my time allowed, and have always been interested in the subject — you may remember that I suggested to Bentley[30] the writing of a book on the mental processes of the insane mind. I should have liked, e.g., to print a word about hysteria; but I find that you are all cut up into schools, at daggers drawn, and I have not the competence to decide between you. I supposed that my instances were all right, as they came from psychiatrists of some responsibility; if they are not, I shall be only too glad to change them. But how am I to find out? And is it fair to dismiss them with the expert's sneer?

Psychology is, I hold, strictly a descriptive science. I do not think that there is anything in my writing anywhere that controverts this position; at any rate, I have held it for twenty years. You can get out of it only by mental causation (substantial mind) or by the unconscious. But we may make explanations of mental processes by giving their invariable conditions on the side of physics; that indeed is the only explanatory principle possible, so far as I can see. And I see no contradiction in the two statements. Pure psychology is descriptive, and in the nature of the case must remain so : to get explanation, you must transfer to the other side, to independent experience. As to what psychology or neurology I use, I use what is given in the standard books; but I use it strictly, i.e. causally, — I discard altogether any teleological excursus in my text-books, and I discard also all the psychological intermixture in terms of old-fashioned psychological systems, of which one finds a vast deal. What is left is not a great deal; but that is the fault of physiology and simply the misfortune of psychology. I think I like personally the work of von Kries[31] best of any. I am not at all inclined to the enlargement of physiology by purely constructive work; indeed, I protest against that in my Preface. So, then, to explain my mental facts I simply wait upon the progress of a causal physiology. We have, unfortunately, no adequate account of the working of eye or ear or skin as yet; the physiological accounts are provisional and in part contradictory, as are even the historical (especially with regard to the ear); but it is, I hope, only a matter of time when physiology will know its nervous system in causal terms. In the meanwhile, my psychology does not fall apart; fact is fact and stays fact (p. 38 bottom); and my business primarily and personally is not body but mind. Physiology can't upset my findings; I am content to go on finding, and to wait the leisure of physiology for their explanation.

You will find, I believe, as a matter of fact, that the biologists themselves are mechanistic as a rule. Since our correspondence began, I have sought and found proof of this which rather surprises me. It seems to be only a certain school of "psychologists" that is coquetting with teleology. I am relieved to have made this discovery, even if there are salient exceptions unknown to me; it narrows the fight, and gives the "pure psychologist" welcome allies.

In conclusion, I must apologise for having said that you did not care to analyse your "psychobiological" or "dynamic unit." I read "unit" in the sense of "element," "unit of scientific construction," — as the gross biologist speaks of the "cell" as his "unit," or as the systematic zoologist takes the single living animal as his unit. I took it to be the last term of your particular analysis, behind which you would not care to go, but which you worked with as given in your explanations and syntheses. I have re-read your letter, and must confess that I still should so interpret it, without your present express declaration to the contrary. As I understand you now, you admit "complex units," and you mean by the phrase simply "given situations," "presented gross observations." Thus "consciousness" (in my definition) might be called by you a "unit" for my psychologising. My mistake is perhaps pardonable, since I am accustomed to work from the simple to the complex, wherever possible; so that to tackle outright a complex like a total consciousness would appeal to me rather as the goal of my training than as the normal mode of psychological procedure. I said this, indeed, in my St. Louis address.[32] But if you mean by unit simply "given situation," "circumscribed situation of the particular patient," "total causistical datum," then of course I understand that you must analyse. And I have no objection to your finding a common denominator in biology; I have repeated in these letters that a psychophysics (as I call it) is the sphere of your work as I see that work. I should, however, still uphold causality (what you call mechanistic science) as against teleology. Teleology can't explain any natural phenomenon (and biology is a natural science), since the identity in it is an identity of human purpose; whereas in causation the identity is an identity of mechanical energy, cause equals effect energetically. But we are here back again at our original point of difference. You see things humanly, purposively; I try to see things with myself so far as possible left out. I must think that my way is the way of 19th century science, and I don't believe that teleology can ever furnish a principle of scientific explanation. But the future must decide.

Yours,
E. B. Titchener

1. Titchener is responding to 5M, 7M, and 8M.

2. Max Dessoir, *Geschichte der neuren deutschen Psychologie* (1894).

3. Richard Sommer, *Grundzüge einer Geschichte der deutschen Psychologie und Aesthetik von Wolf-Baumgarten bis Kant-Schiller* (1892).

4. James Ward, "Associationism," *Encyclopedia Brittanica*, 9th ed. (1885), 10th ed. (1902), 11th ed. (1908). See E. B. Titchener, "The Psychology of the New Brittanica," *American Journal of Psychology* 23 (1912): 37–58.

5. J. B. Meyer, *Kants Psychologie* (1870).

6. The reference is to Wilhelm Wundt's, *Grundzüge der physiologischen Psychologie*, which appeared in several editions. Volume 1 of the sixth edition appeared in 1908, volume 2 in 1910, and volume 3 in 1911.

7. James Mark Baldwin, ed., *Dictionary of Philosophy and Psychology*, 3 vols. (1901).

8. D. Braunschweiger, *Die Lehre von der Aufmerksamkeit in der Psychologie des 18. Jahrhunderts* (1899).

9. Oswald Külpe (1862–1915), a student of Wundt, inaugurated a positivist reorientation of psychology that decisively influenced Titchener's intellectual development. On this point see especially Kurt Danziger, "The Positivist Repudiation of Wundt," *Journal of the History of the Behavioral Sciences* 15 (1979): 205–30.

10. James Mill, *Analysis of the Phenomena of the Human Mind* (1869).

11. Immanuel Kant (1724–1804).

12. Christian Wolff (1679–1754), German philosopher, follower of Leibniz.

13. Johann Nicholas Tetens, *Philosophischen Versuchen ueber die menschliche Natur and ihre Entwickelung* (1777).

14. William James, "Association," in *Principles of Psychology* (Cambridge: Harvard University Press, 1983), 519–69.

15. Johann Friedrich Herbart (1776–1841), author of *Lehrbuch zur Psychologie* (1816) and *Psychologie als Wissenschaft, Neu Gegrundet auf Erfahrung, Metaphysik und Mathematik* (1824–25).

16. Rudolph Hermann Lotze (1817–1881), author of *Medicinische Psychologie oder Physiologie der Seele* (1852) among other works.

17. George Frederick Stout (1860–1944), author of *Analytic Psychology* (1896) and *A Manual of Psychology* (1899).

18. James Rowland Angell, *Psychology. An Introductory Study of the Structure and Functions of Human Consciousness* (1904).

19. James Mark Baldwin, *Handbook of Psychology: Senses and Intellect* (1889); *Handbook of Psychology: Feeling and Will* (1891); *Elements of Psychology* (1893); *The Story of the Mind* (1898).

20. Ernst Meumann, *Intelligenz und Wille* (1908).

21. Edward Lee Thorndike, *The Elements of Psychology* (1905).

22. Meyer's marginal note "philos. not psy."

23. Meyer's marginal note "That is just what I would like you to discuss."

24. Titchener's statement is as follows: "We have defined mind as the sum-total of human experience considered as dependent upon the experiencing person. We have said, further, that the phrase, 'experiencing person' means the living body, the organised individual; and we have hinted that, for psychological purposes, the living body may be reduced to the nervous system and its attachments. Mind thus becomes the sum-total of human experience considered as dependent upon a nervous system. And since human experience is always process, occurrence, and the dependent aspect of human experience is its mental aspect, we may say, more shortly, that mind is the sum-total of mental processes" (*Textbook*, 16).

25. Securus judicat orbis = in its security the world judges.

26. Oswald Külpe, *Outlines of Psychology*, trans. E. B. Titchener (New York: Macmillan, 1895), abbreviated from Külpe's *Grundriss der Psychologie* (1893). See especially 13–16.

27. Titchener, *Experimental Psychology*, 4 vols.

28. Emil Kraepelin (1856–1926), a student of Wundt, became a noted psychiatrist first at Heidelberg then in Munich. Kraepelin's diagnostic differentiation between dementia praecox (renamed schizophrenia by Eugen Bleuler in 1911) and manic depressive syndrome introduced a major clarification in psychiatry. Kraepelin opposed the efforts of Freud and others to explain mental illness in psychodynamic terms, remaining committed instead to an organic approach in psychiatry.

29. Possibly Charles G. Wagner, medical superintendent at Binghamton State Hospital in Binghamton, N.Y. Around the turn of the century, Wagner lectured on psychopathology to Titchener's class at Cornell.

30. Madison Bentley (1870–1955), a student of Titchener at Cornell. In 1907 Bentley proposed studying psychopathology with Meyer, but the arrangement fell through. Bentley later became a member of the faculty of Cornell, was at the University of Illinois between 1912 and 1928, and finally succeeded Titchener as head of the department at Cornell after the latter's death.

31. Johannes von Kries (1853–1928), a friend of Titchener at Leipzig, later known for his work on the physiology of vision. For an example of a physiological

position Titchener could agree with, see his *Die materiellen Grundlagen der Bewusstseinserscheinungen* (Feiburg im Breisgau, 1898).

32. E. B. Titchener, "The Problems of Experimental Psychology," *American Journal of Psychology*, 16 (1905): 208–224. The paper was delivered at the International Congress of Arts and Science, the St. Louis World's Fair, September 1904.

10 T
[Postcard]

October 18, 1909

Reviews of Judd have appeared in all the leading journals; but I do not think that they have been anything more than the usual half-hearted notices. I seem to remember that MIND[1] and the EDUCATIONAL REVIEW[2] both had decentish reviews; but I will ask Whipple,[3] who will know more about it than I do, and who may be able to indicate some single notice of theoretical consequence.

E. B. T.

1. H. J. W. [Henry J. Watt], review of Judd's *Psychology: General Introduction*, in *Mind: A Quarterly Review of Psychology and Philosophy* 17 (July 1908): 420–22.

2. J. Carleton Bell, review of Judd's *Psychology: General Introduction*, in *Educational Review* 34 (November 1907): 416–21.

3. Guy Montrose Whipple (1876–1941), student of Titchener at Cornell and later professor of education at Cornell. He is best known for his *Manual of Mental and Physical Tests* (1910). See Frank S. Freeman, "A Note on E. B. Titchener and G. M. Whipple," *Journal of the History of the Behavioral Sciences* 20 (1984): 177–79.

11 T

October 20, 1909

Dear Meyer,

I have just recd. & read Jennings' paper on Comparative Psych. in Amer. Nat., xliii., Oct., 1909.[1] Jennings is reviewing Bohn's Naissance de l'Intelligence, 1909,[2] and remarks, p. 620:

> "The reviewer (Jennings) finds especially sympathetic the section on the uselessness of instinct as an analytic concept; the emphasis on the fact that all adaptation or 'finality' is a problem, not a solution;" etc., etc.

Here is so welcome a confirmation of my own critique of your position that I make haste to record it. I do not think that your "instinctive reaction" will serve the purposes of scientific analysis; I do not think that the teleological principle can ever replace the causal as a means of scientific explanation. I have said this, in my various letters; and I said, in the last, that I thought the biologists agreed with me. Here is evidence from one biologist: or, if you count Bohn, from two.

Yours,
E. B. Titchener

Whipple knows of no salient review of Judd. He himself reviewed the book in the Psychol. Bulletin.[3]

1. H. S. Jennings, "Comparative Psychology," *American Naturalist* 43 (October 1909): 619–33.
2. Georges Bohn, *La Naissance de l'Intelligence* (Paris, 1909).
3. G. M. Whipple, "Judd's Psychology," *The Psychological Bulletin* 5 (1908): 114–19.

12 M

October 23, 1909

Dear Professor Titchener:

Thanks for your letters. With regard to the indications of literature you corroborate what I have found myself. I have just remembered the review of Judd by Watt[1] as probably the most searching that I came across, but the specific issue of considering psychology from the functional point of view is subordinated even there and not really discussed. You can of course choose the attitude that psychology shall be strictly a descriptive science and qualify it by saying that "pure psychology" is necessarily only descriptive, and that any attempt at explanation (which might also be an obligatory purpose of science for others) has to come from what you call neurology or what I call biology. After all, it will be best to let every body have the psychology he wants and the definition he longs for. In your own definition in Baldwin's Dictionary, if I am not mistaken, you specify scientific psychology as "modern psychology" in its experimental and physiological aspects, and that, no doubt, would include "psychophysics." As far as I can see, the main constructive point on which our discussion might have turned, would be what kind of psychophysics would be most satisfactory, and what samples would appear most productive. With regard to teleology, I hardly know what to say concerning your assurance that you would still uphold causality against it and that teleology cannot explain, etc. I am afraid that I must have been very hasty and careless in my expressions to elicit such a statement as if I need it especially. I might have left out the word "teleological" to save this misunderstanding. I am sure that biology has to work /also/ with compounds which can only be understood through comparisons with accomplished standards or reactions, and I feel that the student ought to be trained in doing that accurately and critically, beside learning to manipulate the supposed "elements." This implies a certain type of legitimate "teleology," /as it/ makes it necessary to know in what sense "purpose" can alone be used in science. As to my seeing things humanly and purposively and your trying to see them with yourself so far as possible left out — I do claim that it is well to learn to do both correctly and critically, and I feel that, for that reason, I do the introspecting with less self-sufficiency than one must do who not only limits his own problems but those of the students to the matters in which non-introspective material and the fundamental conditions of mental activity can /just/ as well be left to the remote future under the cover of psychological parallelism. Both functional neurology and psychology such as I meet with are bound to present fields in which common principles must be worked for, and I feel sure that that cannot be done merely with "elements" but rather with the principle of integration and function (which is the only kind of teleology I have in mind).

Your quotation from Jennings may or may not touch the issue. As a matter of fact what I am after is a readjustment of the formulation of the problem and I know that Jennings agrees with me on that, and that Bohn would probably do so too. There is absolutely no question of the teleological principle being used to replace the causal as a means of scientific explanation.

Through the emphasis on psychophysical parallelism, an accidental and scientifically subordinate fact is given a misleading position which is apt to create difficulties in the formulation of the functional conception of our mental life. To limit psychology to introspection without adequate care to train the student of psychology in the study of the functional conditions is of course convenient, gives a clean-cut working field and saves one from embarrassing questions of fact; many of the questions avoided or made impossible by the split, are, however, not embarrassing and are extremely important. There is to say the least, a /fair/ possibility that "pure psychology" might profitably be assigned a position within the functional picture of living man or the biological unit, but necessarily with subordination of the introspector to broader problems in which the psychology is only an incident. This, of course, is an ideal of applied psychology, but to my mind also an ideal of psychology of which any naturalist or scientist might be proud.

With regard to the responsibility towards students, I do not doubt in the least that your course is well attended and that under your training the results of your examinations leave nothing to be desired; but I remember clearly that you admitted that for your own type and standard of psychology you can find but very few students in your classes. Under these circumstances it is essential that as many as possible should at least learn to see the various problems, and that, as you say, you leave to the course and omit from the book. Since I have only the book I naturally judged it from what it offers itself. I frankly express my admiration for the presentation of the definite topics as far as they go, but I feel decidedly critical with regard to the chapter which should give the settings and at least should characterize — or dispose of — the functional attitude. I feel tempted to speak of a pharisaical attitude to balance the "kindergarten avoidance of puzzle." It is not the dread of puzzle but /it is/ the habit of puzzling and of creating useless puzzles (which one might spare one's self to the advantage of science as well as of purposive work) that I am opposed to. I suppose when it comes to the consideration of "mental time" and "mental space" the ultimate standards will have to be the objective time and space; what it means to call that "physical time" I do not see. You do make the fact of difference plain, but you create a science à la Goethe's Farbenlehre.

As I see things, psychology is larger than your favorite field of work. You impress me as claiming that yours is all the psychology there is, and that what I am talking about may ultimately become a problem of psychology but isn't to-day. I can see the justification of this attitude as a personal and doctrinal one. At the same time there are undoubtedly fields which can to-day be formulated as problems of psychology, which the doctrinal psychology working with elements does not reach. On this ground a great deal of organic chemistry might be ruled out because it does not as yet work with sufficiently definite entities to reduce them to chemical formulas. The way to get there is to give them /at least/ the same chance as the simpler objects of chemical inquiry, and to shape the principles of chemical inquiry so as to also comprise the more difficult problems. Then, of course, there ultimately comes a point where the chemical problems are replaced by biological reactions as is the case with the present serum work, and it is this type of biological methods that works necessarily with adaptations and adjustments that we must also learn to use within the more complex fields of dynamic psychology. Would you then say with regard to that that whatever is dynamic is outside of psychology? Our study of the conditions of the psychological developments shows that some of them are non-mental, and others cannot be expressed in any other way but in terms of mental reactions. The Jung complexes do indeed offer a very interesting opportunity on which to show how you deal with the dynamic features, and nothing would be more welcome than to have the formulation of that issue from you or one of your men.

If you limit psychology to introspective material by definitions, you naturally exclude all dynamic features. If you make objective observation obligatory as well, you restore psychology to a discipline which can also attempt the task of explanation.

This is again a rather long-drawn reply but I hope I have made myself sufficiently clear this time to avoid covering up the issues by the teleological windmill.

Very sincerely yours,
Adolf Meyer

1. See 10T, 1 n.

13 T

October 26, 1909.

Dear Professor Meyer,

Again I cannot but admire your good-humour and patience; but again I cannot see that we have got appreciably nearer together. We seem to be speaking different languages; or at any rate our emphases are so different that statements get distorted in reception. Here goes, however, for a final try at understanding!

(1) I did not define "Psychology" in the Dict., but only Experimental and Physiological Psychology. I defined these as objectively as possible, giving historical data in both cases. But the definition that I give in my Textbook comports, so far as I know, with what I said in the Dict.

I expressly make, in the Textbook and elsewhere, "explanation" an integral part of the problem of psychology. I have recourse however not to neurology or biology (these are both your terms), but always to physiology. — The relation of psychophysics to psychology is expressly stated in the Dict. definitions, and also worked out in my work on Exp. Psych. — I do not "choose the attitude" that mind is, in terms of mind, describable only; I find that to be the fact. As a matter of fact, if I had created the universe, I should have tried to make things otherwise; but I have to take the facts as I find them.

(2) Either you admit teleological reference as a principle of explanation in natural science (biology), or you do not. Many men do, nowadays; I cannot follow them.

I know of no other modes of explanation than causality (conditioning) and teleology (utility). I do not understand that you propose any third mode. In so far as you admit teleology, I must differ from you.

(3) I do not know what you mean by "mental activity" and "dynamic psychology." You do not define. If by the latter phrase you mean "a psychology worked out in terms of energy," or a "psychology which explains present consciousness by (or from) the purpose or intention of previous consciousness," then of course I do not accept a dynamic psychology. I cannot find a mental causation, and I cannot accept a teleological principle of explanation.

But you may mean something different, and I might then be able to accept the phrase all right. In general I cannot be sure that your phrases are assimilated. You say "biology has to work with compounds": but compounds of what? I don't know. And you speak of "comparisons with accomplished standards or reactions" (italics yours). But what in the world is an "accomplished standard"? And is the standard here identical with the "reaction"? I misinterpreted your idea of the "dynamic unit" the other day, and I am a little afraid to interpret these new phrases; but honestly I am not sure of their meaning.

How do my students "manipulate the supposed elements"? This again is Greek to me. An element is what you find by analysis, and is always liable to revision if you can further refine your analysis. In so far, of course, an accepted element is only "supposed," and in so far as you force analysis further you do "manipulate" — not the elements, truly, but the gross material. Is this what you mean? If it is, isn't the procedure legitimate? You seem to be ridiculing it; but I must think that analysis is the primary problem of all science.

(4) My physiological "future" is surely no more remote than your

own, — unless by reason of the fact, which is quite probable, that your knowledge exceeds mine; but that would be only a personal accident. I use all the physiology I know, as soon as I know it. And I read everything that promises to bear on my work, as soon as I hear of it. I find, unfortunately, more speculation than experimental work; but you are, I suppose, in the same box. Indeed, I think that you show yourself to be, — because you still use such phrases as "instinctive reactions," which you surely would not use if you had their neurological equivalent in exact terms.

(5) You make a distinction between introspection and inspection (as methods) which I cannot find.

(6) What is the "functional conception of our mental life"? Where shall I find it? To my thinking, it is organic life that has functions predicable of it, not "mental life." What, in fact, is "mental life"? Apart, I mean, from its popular conversational meaning?

(7) You say that "many of the questions avoided or made impossible by the split (sc. of mind and body) are not embarrassing and are extremely important." What are these questions?

I ask these questions because, it seems to me, you have been attacking a formulated position of mine, without offering me anything in exchange more definite than "instinctive reaction" and "accomplished standard" and "dynamic unit" and so forth. I do anyhow get to facts after my Introduction; and these facts my "functional" friends do me the honour to accept — with or without acknowledgment. But you have not yet got to the concrete at all in your letters.

(8) You say that I "impress you as claiming that mine is all the psychology there is." You can hardly have read much of my published work, surely; I might refer you to my Outline, 1902, 22, fine print.[1] And I think that, in all justice, you ought to read that and other similar passages. — I must also remind you that you began this correspondence. Nothing is further from my thoughts than to claim anything or to convert anybody. You asked for my opinions, and it seemed only courteous and friendly to give them. Disagree with me all you like: but do not, in all conscience, make me assume a position which is not mine because you happen to disagree. I have said throughout, besides what I have said in print, that your work and Freud's and Jung's is all right; and that you, all of you, get into hot water only when you try to upset established psychological principles or to substitute an outworn psychology for modern psychology. If and in so far as you do these things, you must expect either to be criticised or to be let alone. If and in so far as you better and extend

psychological knowledge, all psychologists will welcome you.

My "favourite field of work" is very much smaller even than my Textbook-field; and I should be sorry to think that a book of those dimensions exhausted psychology. I have, on the contrary, in print and in conversation, said repeatedly that it would take half a dozen professors adequately to cover the field of modern psychology; and I have said that, just as no one nowadays can with honesty call himself a "physicist," implying that he covers the whole ground, so is it with psychology. How could you have got any other idea? Verily we are speaking different tongues.

(9) You ask what kind of psychophysics would be most "satisfactory," and what samples would appear most "productive." I should reply that truth is truth, whether satisfactory or the reverse, whether immediately productive or immediately barren; and that I am after truth. All that this means is that, in my personal work, I am not guided either by satisfaction (results are often personally very unsatisfactory!) or by promise of production; I try to find out what is there, what the facts are, and I leave their application to others who are better able to use them.

(10) True enough, I find the psychological temperament rare among my students. But, oh! what a misuse of that statement you make! Surely, before concluding against my "type of psychology," you should make the enquiry a little bit comparative! Does anybody at all find the temperament common? Not at Columbia: Cattell[2] wrote to me the other day that it seemed impossible to make a psychologist out of the average undergraduate: and his interests are — are they not — "functional"? As a matter of fact, I hold my big class, interest it, and turn it out with some leaven of psychological attitude; so that, ten years afterwards, I have had letters from old members, thanking me for what they learned and indicating their use of it. And do not my pupils speak for me? I have now, in university or college work, — I leave out Normal Schools, — Pillsbury, Washburn, Bentley, Gamble, Stevens, Ferree, Hayes, Coffin, Pyle, Bagley, Baird, Geissler, Nakashima, Hunter, Whipple, Murray: four others — Winger, Squire, Irons, Hamlin have died or married[3]: is that a bad record for 17 years, with the department to build up from the ground, and with an ever increasing load of undergraduate work? If I were to add Normal Schools, and the people who have taken minors only with me, the list could be considerably lengthened. Of course I get but few to become psychologists. Will you tell me, though, who gets more? Did James, for instance ? Does Stanley Hall[4]? Or Sanford? Or Jas-

trow[5]? Or /did/ Ladd[6]? I believe that the psychological temperament is rare, just as the physical is: Nichols[7] here gets very few graduates. There is no money in pure science; and nobody goes into pure science, as a profession, unless he happens to have the love of it irrevocably in him. I was urged, in England, to take my medical degree, because I could then live, and could do my own work by the side. I preferred expatriation. /But/, so far from expecting to find many men willing to become psychologists, I am often surprised at the tenacity of those whom I have inspired with the love of mind, in holding on to subordinate and poorly paid places when they might make a good income outside by other means.

Well, I can't make myself any clearer. Even on "time" we split. I see no place for the use of "subjective" and "objective" in science, psychological or other. I mean by physical time the time of the cgs system, which is a physical system. I mean by psychological time the time of dependent experience, as indicated in my Textbook. Both of these times are scientific; I do not see that the one is more subjective than the other, or the more objective. Both are facts. You say that an hour is very short, or that it had 60 minutes, according as you are talking psychology or physics; both statements are true.

I will leave the parting word to you. Would you like, also, to have your letters returned? I think that I have them all; and if you would like to have them for purposes or [*sic*, of] publication or any other purpose I could send them to you.

Yours sincerely,
E. B. Titchener

1. Titchener, *Outline*, (New York: Macmillan, 1899), 2d ed. Titchener's date of 1902 is puzzling since the two editions of this book are 1897 and 1899 with several reprints of the second edition appearing but none between 1901 and 1905.

2. James McKeen Cattell (1860–1944), professor of psychology at Columbia University and editor of several scientific journals. Cattell, a leader in the rise of psychology as an experimental science, was best known as a member of the Columbia functionalists and for his work in the field of mental testing.

3. Walter Bowers Pillsbury, Ph.D., 1896; Margaret Floy Washburn, Ph.D., 1894; Isaac Madison Bentley, Ph.D., 1896; Eleanor Acheson McColloch Gamble, Ph.D., 1898; Herman Campbell Stevens, Ph.D., 1905; Clarence Errol Ferree, Ph.D., 1910; Samuel Perkins Hayes, Ph.D., 1906; Joseph Herschel Coffin, Ph.D., 1908; William Henry Pyle, Ph.D., 1909; William Chandler Bagley, Ph.D., 1900; John Wallace Baird, Ph.D., 1902; Ludwig Reinhold Geissler, Ph.D., 1909; Taizo Nakashima, Ph.D., 1909; Hunter?; Guy Montrose Whipple, 1900; Elsie Murray, Ph.D., 1907; Winger?; Carrie Ransom Squire, Ph.D., 1901;

Irons?; Alice Julia Hamlin, Ph.D., 1896. Titchener left off one student, Margaret Everitt Schallenberger, whose Ph.D. dated from 1902. It is interesting to note Titchener's equation between marriage and death in the case of his female students: the comparison was apt since most of his female graduate students ceased their careers on marriage.

4. G. Stanley Hall (1842–1924), then president of Clark University, was best known as founder of the American Psychological Association, founder and editor of the *American Journal of Psychology* and the *Pedagogical Seminary*. He was closely linked with the child study movement in America and was responsible for inviting Freud, Jung, and Ferenzci to the Clark conference of 1909.

5. Joseph Jastrow (1863–1944), professor of psychology at the University of Wisconsin 1888–1927, was the first to obtain a doctorate of psychology in the United States, under G. Stanley Hall at Johns Hopkins University.

6. George Trumbull Ladd (1842–1921) of Yale University from 1881 to 1905, was one of the first generation of American psychologists. The psychological laboratory at Yale was one of the earliest in the United States.

7. Edward L. Nichols (1842–1921) was professor of physics at Cornell University from 1887 to 1919.

14 M

October 30, 1909

Dear Professor Titchener:—

Well then — here is my parting word: Thanks for the interesting experience with your outspoken and non-compromising spirit. I admit a certain disappointment over the fact that we have been moving in a circle and that it was not possible to single out any specific issue that might have caught some light from the one or the other. Perhaps some day when you will discuss the Jung-complexes and the effect on the association experiment, I shall feel that you are discussing matters which will allow me an insight into the broader validity of your position. In the meantime we shall go on serenely with our respective presentations of the things we meet and have to get square with, and I hope that others may find the common ground which you consider impossible.

Pardon the persistent intrusion upon your time. Do not bother about my letters. My secretary makes a carbon-copy as with all my correspondence. Publication would hardly have a sense, as the matter was discussed too informally and in a way too personally on my part at least.

Very truly yours,
Adolf Meyer

The Correspondence of 1918

15 M [M 1][1]

March 18, 1918

My dear Titchener:

In the very interesting study of Boring and Luce on appetite[2] I meet with a formulation which seems to go a long way towards bridging over the chasm that seemed to gap between you and me in 1909: "Appetite can be adequately described only as a food-seeking attitude or meaning, a reaching-out-after-food." Would you be good enough to refer me to a good discussion of your viewpoint concerning attitude and "meaning" as used there which might readily be a possible common link between views which I still consider capable of much more profitable friendly relations than you seem to entertain? Or would you favor me with a brief exposition ad hominem of what you would offhand think of the possibility of including the psychologically interesting facts in the same broad field of objective data and problems?

Believe me

Very truly yours,
Adolf Meyer

1. In his May 9, 1918 letter (31M) Meyer began referring back to earlier letters in the 1918 series, which he numbered, with some gaps which we have closed, from the first in that series through 38T. He used his initial followed by the number in the series to refer to his own letters, and Titchener's initial followed by the number in the series to refer to Titchener's letters. For clarity, we have indicated Meyer's numbering in brackets at the top of each letter; in the body of the text, letters identified by Meyer's numbering system are also identified by our own.

2. E. G. Boring and Amy Luce, "The Psychological Basis of Appetite," *American Journal of Psychology* 28 (1917): 443–53. This article was number 36 of a series entitled "Minor Studies from the Psychological Laboratory of Cornell University. Communicated by E. B. Titchener and H. Weld."

16 T [T 1]

March 24, 1918

Dear Meyer,

I am heartily glad to make another attempt, and appreciate your friendliness in inviting me to do so. I will put things dogmatically in order to be brief.

I. GENERAL

(1) We may read the world-of-experience teleologically, for our sakes (for the sake of the progress of mankind, the alleviation of suffering, &c.), in terms of Means and End.
We may read the world-of-experience also existentially, for its sake (with a view to transcription of the given), in terms of Covariation (popularly phrased as "cause and effect").

(2) Bodies of knowledge held together by a single End are Technologies.
Bodies of knowledge unified by singleness of Point-of-view over against existence are Sciences.

(3) The unit of subject-matter of a technology is a Meaning.[1] The unit of subject-matter of a science is a Fact.

(4) It is often held that a Technology is correlated with a Science, directly, as an "applied science." In reality, the relation is far more complicated. Every technology draws upon more than one science, and draws also upon sources that are non-scientific. The relation is also fluid; so that no formula of relationship, of a general kind, can be laid down.

(5) The man of science who is progressive is continually availing himself of technological inventions; and the technologist who is progressive is continually having recourse to various sciences. Neither field of occupation is more "worthy" than the other, since both are essential.

(6) Since, however, men of different "temperament" are attracted to the two fields of occupation, there is likely to be mutual distrust. To the technologist the man of science is likely to appear narrow and pedantic, to the man of science the technologist is likely to appear superficial and overconfident.

(7) The ideal thing is to recognise clearly the logical distinction between the two fields of occupation, and at the same time to recognise their equal claim upon civilisation.

(8) It should further be borne in mind, both by man of science and by technologist, that there are other theoretical disciplines (namely

the value-disciplines) besides the sciences. The man of science will then see that technology has other theoretical sources to draw upon, and the technologist will see that the narrowness of science (in this particular respect of the neglect of values) is part and parcel of the conception of science and is therefore inevitable.

II. SPECIAL

(1) In speaking of "applied psychology" we are likely to think of the post-psychological "applications" of the psychological system: of medical, legal, vocational, etc. psychology.

(2) There was, however, a pre-psychological technology, of a very general sort, wherein that which was later known as psychology was involved in the sense of I (4).

(3) To be concrete — long before there was any "psychology" in the scientific sense, our forefathers "used" their "minds": "used" them for the "understanding" of their surroundings, including other men, and "used" them for making themselves "intelligible" to other men.

This single End of mutual understanding and mutual intelligibility gave rise to a vast technology, a sort of Art of Living, to which we may give the name of Common Sense.

(4) Many of the technological terms of this Common Sense were found later, when a scientific psychology appeared, to carry a psychological reference. Among them were the designations of certain "bodily" states, appetites, derangements, etc.: Hunger, Thirst, Appetite, Nausea, Giddiness, Micturation, etc., etc.

(5) Since these terms carried a psychological reference (or appeared to do so), psychology was bound to take hold of them. Recognising that they were technological terms in the sense of I (4), psychology had none the less to ask if their analysis would reveal psychological Facts (and if so, what Facts) in the sense of I (3). Such investigation does not prejudice either their total technological status, or their concomitant scientific investigation by other sciences (physiology, biology).

(6) The psychological investigation of Hunger reveals a constant and persistent factor of psychological Fact. Hunger, then, is not only a technological Meaning, but it is also a definite psychological Fact (and, of course, a definite physiological Fact too).

(7) The psychological investigation of Appetite reveals no constant and persistent factor of psychological Fact. Appetite, then, is a

technological Meaning which is not correlated with a definite psychological Fact. If there is a definite scientific correlation, the terms of that relation are probably biological, in the wide sense: it is at any rate doubtful if they are physiologically constant.

(8) It follows, therefore, that, within this particular group of terms, the "psychological reference" of the great ultimate technology of Common Sense is not to be accepted without special examination.

(9) This conclusion is important:

(a) within psychology. For while we have long ago learned to discount the overt "psychology" of Common Sense — while we have discarded the common-sense notions of Mind, Soul, Spirit; and also of such lesser terms as Memory, Imagination, Reason — we have been too little critical with regard to these common-sense terms of "psychological reference."

(b) as regards the relation of science to technology. For we see that technology may convey a suggestion of scientific relationship which strict examination fails to confirm.

(c) within technology (though I speak on this point with diffidence). For we see that if a Meaning is to be dealt with by way of guidance, avoidance, arousal, control, etc., the fact-reference of that meaning (in cases like those under consideration) does not indicate the true point of attack.

These statements cover, I think, the general and special points raised in your letter. I have had time only to skim your enclosed pamphlet — for which many thanks! — but I gather that the point on which we differ most is that you regard the Science of Biology as teleological ("reactive and constructive adaptation," etc.).[2] My opinion is that, so soon as teleology comes in, it is good-bye to Science! I have no objection in the world to teleological interpretations; I object only to their being confused with, and offered as, the existential descriptions of Science.

Yours sincerely,
E. B. Titchener

1. Meyer's marginal note, "(or trick?)"

2. Titchener refers to a passage in Meyer's paper "Objective Psychology or Psychobiology with Subordination of the Medically Useless Contrast of Mental and Physical" (1915), *CP*, 3:38–43, which Meyer had enclosed in 15M. The passage is as follows: "[The] realm of objective and determinable facts of the individual as a person constitute what we as physicians need to know as psychol-

ogy. The science dealing with these facts I call psychobiology. . . . Its facts are behavior in the widest sense of reactive and constructive adaptation of the completely integrated organism" (*CP*, 3:40). In this paper, Meyer made it clear that he did not endorse Watson's radical behaviorism, but included mental experience in his definition of behavior. Titchener comments on Meyer's paper in detail in 24T.

17 M [M 2]

March 29, 1918

Dear Titchener:—

I appreciate your prompt and helpful response. In order to make clear any apparent or real difference of view-point, I make the following running comments.

Ad. I. GENERAL. (1) In view of the fact that propaganda is something readily distinguished from calm and sober work for the establishment of fact, I should give the problem of covariation — or, as I prefer to say, the reduction of the observed data to terms of strictly controllable experiments — the fundamental and real rank, and teleological issues might or might not come out in the individual choice of interests but without any effect on the status and the rules of the game of the fundamental issue.

In other words it is not the use or uselessness but quality that characterizes the qualification of any inquiry as scientific.

(2) Bodies of knowledge held together by certain special methods or practical aims may be called technologies. These technologies may serve scientific as well as not strictly scientific problems.

The characterization of sciences does not satisfy my scientific conscience. It is not exclusively singleness of point of view that is essential and it would be directly wrong to make too much of the "point of view," but the postulate of reduction of systematized facts to the standards of critically controlled experimentation or calculation seems to me more fundamental and yet more pragmatically plastic. The point of view alone may suggest wrongly the specificity of a science. The point of view may be arbitrary although incidentally it might also single out the same group of facts such as would demand the recognition as a specific "science" with a specific system and specific methods — the type of thing I call a group or level or unit of integration.

(3) When you say that the unit of subject-matter of a technology is a "meaning," the term meaning evidently receives a connotation

rather unusual and calling for definition or explanation. I should rather think of a method and its specific application: that each deal with "fact" is a primary and fundamental urgent postulate.

(4) I subscribe to, also (5) — consideration of "worthiness" naturally is irrelevant.

(6) There is perhaps less distrust than disappointment. (To me distrust is, by the way, a more important problem — what I in my search for formulation speak of as an impure affect, the characteristic center of many reaction tendencies of psychopathology. Could you suggest any formulation of this "technological" concept?)

(7) The distinction lies in the character of the systematizations.

When we come to the special points, I am willing to accept the paragraphs 1–4 as a very helpful characterization of the available terminology as applied by more or less critical common-sense to facts or suppositions.

(5) Instead of turning my interest to these topics as "terms" with "references" to various sciences, I should feel inclined to think of components which do or do not constitute workable facts of definite sciences.

(6) I suppose it is here that the difficulty begins to touch the original inquiry concerning "meaning." The first condition for any concern is that we actually deal with facts of which a record can be made. The second issue is whether the facts can or cannot be demonstrated to be of a type actually open to the inquiry with the methods and data of certain systems of fact characterized preferably by methods of inquiry rather than "point of view." In the case at hand we would ask: Are there any characteristic specific and workable data of the type of psychological data? There, of course, you may emphasize the view-point in order to help to define the type of fact; and on this point we probably still are at variance, and may remain so without making discussion impossible. I should prefer a characterization and formulation which would not call for absolute change of point of view; I therefore characterize as psychobiological (a term stolen or at least differently used by Dunlap[1]) a group of facts which you prefer to divide according to the principles of parallelism, but which I prefer to treat as objective reactions of totally integrated individuals or organisms as opposed to reactions of partly integrated organs and parts on the one hand and mere data or problems of logic on the other. Whether we agree on calling "psychological" facts what you single out or on my conception of objective psychobiological data, I can subscribe to your (5) and (6), only in (6) I should substitute as my topic of interest

"more or less unanalyzed group of facts," covered by the term hunger for what you call a "technological meaning."

(7) Appetite, then, figures as an empirically specified group of facts without a definite and obligatory specific psychological component in the sense in which you define your domain of psychology. It is here that my looser and more provisional grouping of facts as psychobiologically or not psychobiologically integrated does justice to what you intimate by "probably biological," and I should always be willing to analyze it as far as would be necessary to do justice to the demands of experimentation and interpretation in terms of "the conditions under which it arises, the form of the reaction, the probable effects and the range and conditions of experimental modifiability" — the fundamental question of biological and perhaps even broadly scientific inquiry. I would not, however, look for absolute measures or standards.

In (8) I should look for "the strictly psychological component" rather than the psychological reference.

With regard to (9), I evidently claim that it is advisable to recognize a formulation of "mentation and behavior" in terms of overt plus implicit and more purely implicit reactions because there are not physiologists who would do justice to the "sets" and "reaction tendencies" which you would rather relegate to some one else because you prefer to limit your systematization and inquiries to the data of psychology, which, in addition, you require to be viewed from your different "point of view." And even if the proper physiologist should come along — you would not call Max Meyer[2] or Watson[3] a physiologist such as we need for this? — we should probably both agree that that physiologist should have the very best psychological training as well, before he ventures on a substitution of physiological facts in the (technological?) psychobiological facts and problems.

On (b) I naturally quite agree. The "relatively unanalyzed facts or groups of facts" of critical common-sense must not be considered analyzed when treated to a kind of logical analysis but must be given a definite systematic analysis lege artis of the specific sciences — best tested by reduction to terms of controllable experiment.

(c) shows me the difficulty with this concept of meaning.

I had watched the various usages of the term "meaning" in your writings, but could not be quite sure.

In Boring and Luce's articles (p. 452) I find the sentence: Appetite can be adequately described only as a food seeking attitude or meaning, a reaching-out-after-food. I see now how you might use "meaning" as a psychologizing equivalent of the more definitely and broadly biological concept "attitude." As you may see from my reprint, I want to make it possible for my students to work with critical common-sense and that in a biological setting and formulation. Your formulation of meaning psychologically regarded as context appeals to me. As soon as you emphasize the "set" and the "purely" physiological terms I should, however, tend to fall back upon biology and speak of attitudes and reaction tendencies, and we are naturally most concerned with those for which we have no other terms but the psychological or psychobiological ones.

I can readily see that in your psychology you want to limit yourself to the concrete process or psychological happening or activity without including the lasting organization. As psychobiology I treat the organization actually in action and as capable of action. The distance between us is one not merely determined by utilitarianism, but by differences in the philosophical critique and the type of data we work with. As far as I am concerned I always feel it is a responsibility to understand the contrary-minded and I also like to get my standpoint into such formulation that the possibly contrary-minded can understand me. In these days of brutal struggles, one likes to turn to the constructive types of friendly "war-fare" or debate and as such I most sincerely value your kindness in answering my inquiry.

Very truly yours,
Adolf Meyer

P.S.

Just one word with regard to "teleological." I am as stubborn with the demand for limitation to "facts" in my conception of reactive and constructive adaptation as any legitimate definition of science can demand. Speaking in these terms implies the responsibility of furnishing the facts or guarding against disregard of the facts which constitute the necessarily broader settings of a biological "experiment" and at the same time the negation of loose speculation. The demands of science for existential descriptions may be somewhat more difficult to control and to attain in biology, but they are as necessary an implication of my formulation as of any other. We may often deal with preliminary formulation, which neither poses as explanation nor as anything else but formulation. Call it "task" or "aufgabe," or tendency; the fact of settings calling for formulation is a problem which you may not have to consider so much owing to the definition of your science, but which can and must be scientifically and rigorously handled. In the reading of my article it will therefore be quite essential to approach me not with vague distrust but with frank and open demands and criticism if I should err in the problems or formulations. I assure you that I am determined to eliminate mysticism and looseness; but I trust critical common-sense more than dogmatism. It is to me almost like a difference of faith in democracy and faith in ordained guidance.

1. Knight Dunlap (1875–1949), psychologist at Johns Hopkins from 1906 to 1936, in 1912 published a book entitled *Psychobiology* and in 1917 founded a journal with the same title. Although he attacked introspection as held by his contemporaries and later claimed credit for behaviorism, Dunlap retained consciousness in his psychology. In 1916, when the arts and science campus of Johns Hopkins relocated uptown, Dunlap established his laboratory at Homewood, while John Broadus Watson on Meyer's invitation moved his laboratory to the Phipps Clinic. As a result, Hopkins effectively had two separate departments of psychology. Meyer was unsympathetic to Dunlap's work, which he regarded as narrow and academic.

2. Max Frederick Meyer (1873–1967), German-American psychologist, between 1901 and 1929 professor of experimental psychology at the University of Missouri. In his *The Fundamental Laws of Human Behavior* (Boston: The Gorham Press, 1911), Meyer put forward views similar to Watson's behaviorist theories.

3. John Broadus Watson (1878–1958), professor of psychology at Johns Hopkins from 1908 to 1920, in 1913 launched the behaviorist movement in American psychology.

18 T [T 2]

April 2, 1918

Dear Meyer,

It promises to be some little time before I can get seriously to work at your letter and paper. I therefore send this, as a possible interim contribution to the discussion.

Some time ago I was talking with Ned Holt[1] at Cambridge; and in the course of the conversation he said: "At any rate, Titchener, this (and he thumped the arm of his chair with his fist) is a FACT!" I replied in effect as follows:

No: it is a meaning, the meaning of "Ned Holt thumping the arm of a chair." No science can deal with that! And the factors of it are also meanings; no science can deal with "Ned Holt" or with "thumping" or with "chair." If you want to make it fact, you must translate, out of the language of meaning, into the language of some science. — I can give you, up to the limits of my knowledge, a rendering in terms of psychological fact, and a rendering in terms of biological fact (biology proper, physiology, anatomy), and a rendering in terms of physical fact (physics, chemistry, physical chemistry). I daresay that the value-people could give you similar renderings in terms of values. But neither the fact-renderings nor (I suppose) the value-renderings would have anything to say about you and your thumping and your chair. The fact-renderings would be simply the statements of fact that you find in the scientific text-books, made specific by a further statement of the conditions under which these particular fact-renderings were obtained. The meaning — "Ned Holt thumping the arm of a chair" — is a common-sense rendering of a situation which, as fact, enters the field of view of many sciences, and must be reported by each one of them as that particular science sees it.

I think that this instance may help to clear up my distinction of Fact and Meaning. My impression is that you would agree with Holt that his behavior was a bit of fact, and that it lies within your science of psychobiology. If we really differ here, we differ radically.

The instance may also clear up my "parallelism." I am just as parallelistic over against physics-biology as I am over against biology-psychology. Just as I take the subject-matter of psychology to be a dependent variable of the organism, so do I take the subject-matter of biology to be a dependent variable of the environment. Hence I think mechanism and vitalism to be mistaken issues. For even if physics and chemistry should prove altogether adequate to the "organism," they would prove to be so only from the point of view of physics and chemistry; as soon as one changed over, to the point of view of biology, one would see those physical and chemical facts "in a new light," namely, in the biological. Wherever one can take a new standpoint over against existence, one has a new science; and since the sciences are differentiated by point of view, their renderings of experience must be "parallel," in the sense that they lie side by side and cannot meet or fuse. Whether Philosophy can ever go behind the differentiation and bring together Facts and Values and Meanings — which have arisen from a common matrix — into a transcendent unity, I don't know.

Well, this may help or it may not! I send it for what it may be worth.

Yours sincerely,
E.B. Titchener

1. Edwin B. Holt (1873–1946), psychologist and member of the neo-realist movement, author (with Walter T. Marvin, William Pepperrell Montague, Ralph Barton Perry, Walter B. Pitkin, and Edward Gleason Spaulding) of *The New Realism* (1912), *The Concept of Consciousness* (1914), and *The Freudian Wish and Its Place in Ethics* (1915). Holt was at Harvard University from 1901 to 1918 and at Princeton from 1926 to 1936. The conversation with Titchener probably occurred during the Harvard meeting of Titchener's Society of Experimentalists in 1917.

19 M [M 3]

April 6, 1918

My dear Titchener,

Your letter of April 2 does indeed give me an application of your principle, but also some fear that we might disagree — to my mind unnecessarily; because I am quite frank to say that I do not care whether you decline to accept my pursuits as science, as long as you might give some of the problems your human interest, with some light on the possible relations to the science as you see it.

When you call Ned Holt's thump a meaning, you evidently deviate from all usage of the term known to me. It is a fact with a meaning (or with more or less meaning) and it may even be that the meaning of it is of greater importance than the fact itself. Now, of course you say: There you are with your "importance"; "there is no such thing in my science." This is why I say I may have to appeal to your plain human interest. You say we deal with a common-sense rendering of a situation. That is what always forms my starting point /and what I try to come back to by making my common-sense "trained and critical c–s."/ Now this fact is supposed to enter "the field of view of many sciences and must be reported by each one of them as that particular science sees it." Take the attitude of distrust which marks the fundamental incapacity of a still young woman whom I am just now trying to guide from a fatal ruin of her life in the form of paranoia. She is unable to take for granted that the difference of opinion occurring between her and her environment could possibly deserve anything but the interpretation of damnable malice and injustice. What "sciences" can profitably view such a problem and the question how this very keen and bright human being might be so modified as to bestow the benefit of doubt or, even better, a benevolent confidence and faith in reasonably good intention on the part of the otherwise sadly misjudged environment.

The thump might of course be studied qua neuro-physiological process and would as such be fairly uninteresting. Even in its broader setting it may be hardly more than an emphasis working favorably as a stimulus of attention. This would characterize the psychobiological position. The distrust in my patient is a psychobiological misfit, applied from a deplorably complex relation to a half-insane father during her childhood and further development because she yielded to the marriage to a man whom she had really not cared for. These are psychobiological problems as I see them. Now I claim for this term a position which need not be confused with your view of psychology. It is a dependent variable of the organism which I do not expect to be able to do justice to without involving the environment in the explanation and in the shaping of the therapeutic experiment.

I fully agree with the fact that the data covered by biology can but insufficiently be viewed by physics or chemistry. We have, to see them all properly, to view them "in a new light," namely, in the biological. This is what I imply by a special "type of integration"; only I put the emphasis upon the nature of the facts requiring "the new light" and not so much upon our taking the "new standpoint over against existence." It is these facts that force the new viewpoint, and that interest me and not the fact that I or somebody else has waked up to the need and possibility of a "new science." It is not so important that the sciences are differentiated by points of view; but it is very important that there are combinations of facts which demand specific viewpoints because they are made up of combinations from which our capacity of experience would slip off unless we had methods and viewpoints fit to cope with the set of facts.

The term "parallel" seems unfortunate. Equally justified and dealing with a consistent mass of facts — that is my assumption and scientific "faith"; but the most striking feature of the different integrative groups or levels, as I have called them, is that each entity or group — such as the various groups in physics, and chemistry, and physiology, etc. subdivide into different types of units which are as little analogous and parallel as can be;— hence the raison d'être of the fact that the different combinations of facts are distinguished into specific sciences. This makes clear that I mark the distinction of physics and biology, and biology and psychology, although I am inclined to look upon psychology and its facts as part of the domain of biology, as long as I have no working acquaintance with spooks such as McDougall[1] seems to bow to.

Science is a single-minded pursuit of facts and their connection not for the sake of this or that application, but for their bearing in a system of reactions and relations which constitute laws and standard facts. What constitutes such a system is naturally open to a process of evolution and selection. It ought not to be considered dogmatically. Obviously the matter included, the methods employed, and the logical problems involved tend to make up the distinctions and the connections.

Neither your scheme nor mine will ever be universally accepted (unless we appeal to the feudal dei gratia or the Teuton Absolute in contrast to the democratic principles of pragmatic appeal through simplicity of the scheme, its naturalness, its fruitfulness, its life-value). I only know of solidarity and reasonable consistency and maximal dependability in a world of more or less orderly relativity.

Philosophy may as far as I can see have less difficulty in going behind the differentiations than it may seem. But that is not as near the center of our discussions. The questions would be, Who deals with "the facts" and "the values" and the "meanings" involved? Is it possible to follow common sense in its tendency not to split fact, value and meaning? Where could we find a reasonably good treatment of "meanings"?

After you answer these questions, it will be my turn to wait for your questions which you might formulate so as to force me to face the issues which would appear essential to you for any common ground. I simply cannot see why we should not be able to find some common ground from which further discussion would become helpful. I may agree with Holt that his behavior was a bit of fact, and may assume that distrust exists and works as I see it, and you probably do too. The question is whether qua problem of modifiability, i.e., of experimentation, you call the problem one of any workable science /or of a combination/. Say that "psychobiology" used in such a sense is not a "science"; that will not offend me, although I define science differently; but tell me how you would put your shoulder to the wheel with such a problem and what you would call the performance. To me it is a problem with vital reality. It is the problem of "winning the war" carried into the struggle for human health and ability to live. You are right in saying that science has nothing to do with that. /But/ is that really so /in the end/? Whoever has done something by force of training and point of view would at least not have done it without the "science." And if there is anything like it, I should like to have it and I try to develop it. At the same time I want to be sure that I do not mix up things for those who do devote themselves to method for method's sake and to science for science' sake. Each Technology does well to keep in touch with the pertinent sciences and to respect /their/ spheres.

I suppose this is the hour when President Wilson begins his talk.[2] How much more effective would it have been to develop a policy of preparedness, and work for a democracy with a firm conviction and integral feature of solidarity, when the danger and necessity of war became clear! I hope the scales will turn in time.

Very sincerely yours,
Adolf Meyer

1. William McDougall (1871–1938), British-American psychologist, in 1918 was Wilde reader in mental philosophy at Oxford University. McDougall was best known for his *Introduction to Social Psychology* (1908) in which he described human behavior in terms of a large number of instincts. Influenced by Hans Driesch, McDougall subsequently developed a purposive or "hormic" psychology in opposition to Watson's behaviorism. McDougall's explanation of collective behavior in his *Group Mind* (1920) was discussed by Freud in his *Group Psychology and the Analysis of the Ego* (1921). Meyer's disapproving reference is to McDougall's support for psychic research and the study of the occult.

2. Woodrow Wilson was speaking at Baltimore on the occasion of the first anniversary of the declaration of war on Germany and the beginning of the third war bond campaign.

20 T [T 3]

April 11, 1918

Dear Meyer,

I think we can get within talking distance of each other, if we don't broaden too much. This last letter leaves me distinctly cheerful.

(1) What sciences can help in the matter of your patient? — I should say that (a) psychology could. Psychology could do for this sort of case just what Külpe tried to do for Seelenblindheit (Psychologie und Medizin, 1912, 62 ff).[1] The trouble is that such work takes a lot of time, and that the psychologist has his own work to do and so doesn't get round to it. Külpe did the thing once in a lifetime, and did it then only as an incident in the campaign he was waging for the academic status of psychology. The psychiatrists, on the other hand, don't know their psychology — haven't time for it — and are likely to look on such programmes as Külpe's with impatience and lack of comprehension. My remedy would be that you attach to your clinics a man like Boring,[2] who has had thorough psychological training, and

give such a man the precise duty of psychologising typical cases. Slow work, no doubt, but I see no other way. Boring would then be a link, say, between yourself and myself, in communication with us both, literally a bridge between the two kinds of activity. His psychology might leaven you (I speak frankly!) and his problems with you might lead me this way and that further than I should otherwise go. I have always urged that this sort of middleman should be recognised by institutions — but it is not easy to find the right type of man and not easy to persuade the institutions that he is wanted when found.

I should say (b) that neurology ought to help. I don't know how far neurology has got in the matter of functional differences, apart from structure. If, as I guess, it has not got far, then I think that is again the fault of the pre-occupation of the physiologist, as he is at present placed and burdened. You want your physiological middleman as you want your psychological.

These sciences, then, would be your assistants, laying their hypotheses and their found facts before you. YOU would still be necessary: not only for the coordination of the scientific contributions, but also to HANDLE the case, — in the light of every blessed thing, common-sense or technical or scientific, empirical or speculative, personal or impersonal, that your knowledge could compass or your experience approve or your insight suggest.

(2) Treatment of meanings. — The beginning of Münsterberg's Grundzüge der Psychologie, 1900, i., gives you the thing in a determinate epistemological setting.[3] (You need not swallow the epistemology!) See, e.g., the sentence about existence on p. 56. — In my Commemorative Volume Weld[4] has a technical paper on a certain class of (intellectual) meanings; you might skim that for method, though the details will hardly interest you. — In my thinking facts don't "have" meanings; it is of the essence of a fact to be existential only. Popular meanings (telephones, steamships) are mixed medleys of fact and meaning: facts pure are the data of science; meanings pure are the data of the value-disciplines. Technology takes the popular attitude, but clarifies and systematises, and so makes its mixtures (in your phrase) dependable. But all this is only scaffolding, and our terms don't matter so long as we understand each other. — No more time!

Yours sincerely,
E. B. Titchener

1. Oswald Külpe, *Physiologie und Medizin* (1912).

2. Edwin G. Boring (1886–1968), student of Titchener and at the time of this letter, instructor in psychology at Cornell. Titchener allowed Boring to lecture on abnormal psychology and even to offer courses on the topic (see 22T). Boring's interest in abnormal psychology dated from his graduate student days. In the summer of 1912 he worked with Shephard Ivory Franz (1874– 1933) at the Government Hospital for the Insane at Washington, D.C. and published articles on dementia praecox. See Boring, *Psychologist at Large* (New York: Basic Books, 1961), 26.

3. Hugo Münsterberg, *Grundzüge der Psychologie* (Leipzig: Johann Ambrosias Barth, 1900), i.

4. H. Weld, "Meaning and Process as Distinguished by the Reaction Method," in *Studies in Psychology: Contributed by Colleagues and Former Students of Edward Bradford Titchener*, ed. L. N. Wilson (Worcester, Mass.: L. N. Wilson, 1917), 181–208.

21 M [M 4]

April 17, 1918

My dear Titchener:

Your letter of April 11, 1918, gives me the strictly orthodox rendering of the sciences probably more readily applicable in the problem of Seelenblindheit, one naturally very different from such a problem as distrust. I know Külpe's attempt. I had hoped to have a chance to discuss with him the point of view detailed in my Bulletin reviews, especially those of 1912 (p. 129–145), and those of 1907 (Misconceptions of Moebius, p. 170–179).[1] The suggestion concerning a middleman naturally would interest me greatly. I have, in this spirit, put our laboratory at Watson's disposal,[2] and I am convinced that in such a procedure there is a welcome chance for leaven in every direction. The above mentioned discussions should serve as a background for what I discuss in the paper sent you. May I look for your discussion?

Very sincerely yours,
Adolf Meyer

1. Meyer, "Pathopsychology and Psychopathology" (1912), *CP*, 2:640–53; "Misconceptions at the Bottom of *Hoplessness of All Psychology*" (1907), *CP*, 2:573–80.

2. In 1916, Meyer invited Watson to move his laboratory to the Phipps Clinic. Since Watson was looking for ways to apply his behaviorist theories to the human subject, he accepted, and there began the series of experiments on children that culminated in 1919 in his experiment showing that it was possible to condition a child to a phobia.

22 T [T 4]

April 19, 1918

Dear Meyer,

Yes, I will get to your paper as soon as I possibly can. Meantime I will try to hammer this present argument out. There seems to be a demon that tries to twist us away from each other!

I grant that there is a tremendous difference between Seelenblindheit and your case. My point was only that psychology CAN HELP in such problems as you deal with. I instanced Külpe (a single psychologist) because he (for another major purpose in a single case) did come to close quarters with a problem of the same order or genus as your own; did point out, from his psychological standpoint, lacunae in previous work; and did offer (in vain, as he complains) to handle a concrete case in the light of his programme. What happened in this one instance might, I contended, be made to happen, within measure and degree, all along the line. But if it is to happen, there must be institutional recognition of its value.

For the psychologists have no time (there is one chair of psychology here, e.g., for half-a-dozen of physics, to say nothing of chemistry and physical chemistry!); they have no money (I usually have to supplement my grant, even with the modest laboratory I have, out of my private purse; and Harvard is worse off still); and they have any number of scientific problems of their own, which call both for time and for money. So that, as things are, they are not in a position to help. — Further, it is relatively of little use to keep doors open, so long as the men who enter the doors are full of their own problems and careers and interests. I have held my own doors open to psychiatrists and psychopathologists, and even got the authorities to provide a course in psychiatry; and they called Wagner of Binghamton; and the visitors whom I entertain have been more concerned to tell me of their plans than to learn of mine. Very naturally! — So that, if the CAN HELP is to be come a DOES HELP, then you men who have foundations and funds must SALARY a man trained in psychology who also has leanings in your direction and aptitudes for your kind of work.

For the last two years I have allowed Boring, who made the request, to give courses in the psychology of the abnormal. That has meant that every single member of my small staff, from myself down to the junior assistant, has had to take more routine work and to give up some of his research-time: so pressed are we by the demands of students for regular course-instruction. We all took it cheerfully, partly to give Boring his "chance," and partly because we recognised the objective importance of his subject. But that is the condition that we are in, and I suppose it is the same everywhere.

Now I submit, in all friendliness, that to call all this tangle of effort and restriction, and the convictions born out of the tangle, a "strictly orthodox rendering of the sciences," doesn't take us much further! The question is whether my proposal would work; and everything that I know of psychology at first-hand and of your problems at second and third hand makes me think it would. I find it difficult to get a couple of clear days to digest your paper; but a psychologist who could live with you, day in and day out, would be digesting all the time. At first there would be friction and some mutual annoyance, I daresay; but I believe that in the end there would be very great advantage. I have used Boring as an illustration only: but isn't my "rendering" fairly fertile, after all, if it turns him into his interest in the abnormal and encourages that, and turns a man like Whipple into the educational interest, and a woman like Miss Washburn[1] into the animal interest, and so on? Not that I am bothering about myself; it is the concrete proposal that I want to make clear and to vindicate.

Yours sincerely,
E.B. Titchener

1. Margaret Washburn (1871–1939), student of Titchener and author of *The Animal Mind* (New York: Macmialln, 1907), 2d. ed. 1917.

23 M [M 5]

April 20, 1918

My dear Titchener:

Just a word in reply to your letter of April 19. I fully understand your attitude and should be only too delighted to find a possibility of getting Boring to come here, but unfortunately we too have no foundation and funds and have to supply many things out of our own pocket. I had hoped that in view of the service he has rendered with regard to the Head theories,[1] it might be possible to secure Boring on some terms. Of course, there will be discussion, but I do not think that it would be likely to take the form of annoyance or would be more than the wholesome friction which I think we all need in order to get a purchase in our efforts. I certainly appreciate your looking for some time to go over the papers mentioned and shall value what you may have to say. Much may appear objectionable to you, but I shall appreciate your culling out from it what you can accept and recognize as a move toward middle ground /and formulate questions which will put me on my mettle/.

Believe me

Very sincerely yours,
Adolf Meyer

1. E. G. Boring, "Cutaneous Sensation after Nerve-Division," *Quarterly Journal of Experimental Physiology and Cognate Medical Sciences* 10 (1916): 1–95.

24 T [T 5]

April 22, 1918

Dear Meyer,

I was able yesterday to tackle your paper.[1] I enclose my comments: first, a running commentary; then a sort of summary of impressions; finally some appended notes on your letters. I had to work at pressure, and if I have expressed myself too sharply or too dogmatically, I can only ask you to pardon me. I stick to the sense of what I have said, but it may very well be that in the hurry that I could not escape I have phrased things badly, — more polemically or more stringently than was right.

I take your general attitude to be something like this: "I too believe in the dignity of science, and wish to keep free of final causes. But I am faced by the concrete situations; I want to understand them; and science gives me only generalities. I want to understand these situations in order that I may ameliorate them; and the orthodox sciences give me no help. Yet the task is worth while. So I face the organism as a whole; and by way of biological concepts such as reaction, adaptation, integration, trend and tendency, level of development, I am able to rationalise my situations, to bring them under control. I do not ignore psychology, either. So far as I see mental activities entering into my situations, I take account of them. My whole outlook is factual and objective; I take the human situations as I find them. Unless then you mean to dogmatise about what science must be and must not be, why isn't my procedure (controlled as it is by experiment) as much scientific as anybody else's?"

All these pleas I hope I have taken account of, by way of frank recognition or of equally frank criticism, in the following pages. The two principal temperamental differences that I find between us are these. (1) You seem to me to be present-day-minded, while I seem to myself to be historically-minded. I cannot see science except historically, and I cannot help respecting the older generations even if I think them quite wrong. I believe, e.g., that Aristotle has done us more intellectual harm than any other single man; yet I never read him without admiration. You, if you believed about him what I do, would turn your back on him in a sentence. (2) You are[2] interested in the individual, in his life-history and prospects and improvement and so forth. I am not. I am interested in the individual only as a unit in a certain orderly distribution for which I want to get the equation. My interest is therefore in statistics and the resulting law.

I don't suppose we shall ever transcend these differences, but I hope that some good may have come out of the effort at mutual understanding.

Yours sincerely,
E. B. Titchener

TITLE. — I do not, of course, differentiate Mental and Physical as different classes of "objects" or different "kinds of things." I differentiate (although I realise that this formula is not transparent without systematic explication) not psychisch and physisch, but psychologisch and physikalisch.

I may make the remark here, at the outset, that I think you are a little inclined to stress terminology when it is used only for teaching-purposes, as if it had a connotation other than that which the text-book exposition gives it. In teaching youngsters, one has to begin from what they already have some familiarity with; and the stuff that they are familiar with is a watery Descartes. I have always consistently fought that, though I usually start out with it so as to get a starting-point. You seem a little inclined to pitch upon words, instead of taking the sense of the whole exposition. No doubt we all do![3]

P.3 § 2. Applicability to the needs of common sense or of technology is the very last thing that science should think of. See Mach, Principien der Wärmlehre, 1896, 449 last §.,[4] for a summary statement with which I am absolutely in agreement.[5]

P.4 § 1. You should of course, have found no metaphysics, solid or liquid. What you did find, by your own statement, was the watered Cartesianism that Wundt summarises in Essays (Aufg. d. exper.

Psych.), 1906, 190 middle. That is what we all start out with, and it is also (unfortunately) what a good many teachers do not transcend. I make no defence of incompetent psychological teachers; there are too many of them.

P. 4 § 3 and p. 5 § 1. (1) If you look at a thing "biologically," I shd. say you could see nothing but the biological. Psychological for me = existential experience regarded as logically dependent on the nervous system (or its biological equivalent); biological for me = existential experience regarded as logically dependent on the environment (C, H, O, as Henderson's[6] reduction makes it). If you can include my psychological under your own biological, I shd. think the physico-chemist might come and say — I can include your biological under my physico-chemical. So we should all melt away into physical chemistry! I firmly believe, on the contrary, that Physics, Biology and Psychology are three coordinate ways of reading the existential universe, and that if you take up the attitude of any one of them you eo ipso do not take up the attitude of either of the others. (2) I have always said the psychological experience is shareable. Just in so far as the biologically "normal" approaches the physically "general," just in so far does the shareability of psychological experience approach the shareability of physical. But it approaches even more closely. For the "abnormal" can oftentimes be reproduced, by scientific method, for the normal; I can put myself e.g. in a colour-blind environment, and so share the psychological experience of the colour-blind. Psychology does not study my anger, my hope, my expectation, my will, but it studies existential experience regarded as logically dependent upon the nervous system, i.e., upon a "normal" or "generalised" nervous system with a certain margin of differentiation. (3) All through these §§ you seem to have in mind the crudest sort of introjectionism.[7] "Mind" for me is a function of the individual, in the sense that mind = subject-matter of psychology = existential experience regarded as a logical function of the biological individual (which latter reduces to nervous system, as environment reduces to C, H, O). I don't know any other "mind." (4) Consciousness, by which I take to mean awareness, has to my thinking no part or lot in any kind of science whatsoever. A "knower" is presupposed by all sciences, and enters into none. (5) Everything psychological is, of course, as observable and as objective as anything in natural history. But you don't say how "activity" can be observed. I don't think it can. I think you can observe only facts.[8] And activity is an interpretation of facts. When you talk of "activity of the stomach" as observable, I should say you have made two interpretations: you have first identified your stomach (by a number of observed facts) and you have then dubbed it active (as an inference again from a number of observed facts). Having identified, and having named, you can of course interpret all in a moment (as if you observed), and say offhand "Here is stomachic activity." But if there were no logical inferences to be necessarily added to observation of facts, science would be as easy as taking dictation, instead of being the immensely difficult and complicated thing it is. (6) You end up with a fling at "traditional" philosophy and psychology. One need not go far to make a similar fling at "traditional" psychiatry! Why not take the modern views that have emerged and are emerging out of the traditional? I cannot see the good of pounding away in a destructive spirit at what no competent psychologist or philosopher would dream of standing for. I believe that it is again (as I said at the start) mainly a matter of terms. Every science is conservative in the matter of terms, and keeps putting new wine into the old bottles: does not physics still hang on to "force"? although I suppose no genuine physicist thinks force. Well, as the terms stick, the outsider is likely to miss the new matter that they label. You speak (p. 4 top) of Fechner's parallelism as if that could stand for such present-day parallelism as that of Wundt or Avenarius or Ebbinghaus! You might just as well (or just as ill) have said Spinoza's parallelism.

P. 5 {S} 2. I always object to "psychology for medical students" as I object to "English for engineers" or "physiology for students of agriculture"![9] If the fundamentals, the expositions of principle, are needed at all, then I think they are needed as they are; these technological students should have the best there is going. So far, the war-demands have borne me out. Yerkes[10] and Haggerty[11] and Goddard,[12] and just now Dunlap,[13] apply to me for men trained in psychology, pure and simple; such men take the lead of the more specially trained men who might have been expected to step into the technical jobs offhand. So if I were lecturing to medical students, I should give them straight psychology as an introductory course, the best psychology I knew, and not try to adapt my psychology to their specialty. Here, I am afraid, there is a real difference between us.[14] And for that matter both of us could claim great names, I imagine, as representing a like difference.

P. 6 {S} 1. If you ask yourself what you mean by "introspection," I believe you will find that your definition involves again the worst sort of introjectionism. Introspection for me = observation of existential experience regarded as logically dependent upon the nervous system. It is the primitive and universal scientific method, — I mean observation is: and it is identical in psychology, biology, physics. I have set this forth in various places, more or less definitely as I have grown to it; and in the preface to my last book I say that the term /introspection/ is going.[15] Psychology can get along with "observation" and so avoid the misunderstandings that the old bottle persists in raising.

You asked me to read sympathetically, and with an eye to the whole. But I am bothered, all through, by your language. You speak here of FACTS; and in the next breath of assets, resources, going wrong, being modified for the better: one and all terms of VALUE! You can estimate and state an asset; how can you observe it? If I could think that these and like terms were only metaphorical, I should still be troubled to translate them back into scientific terms; but they seem to me, in reality, to be of the very woof of your thinking; your "science" seems to me to imply values at every step.

You seem, I think, to use "observe" in a very wide sense, as more or less = vorfinden.[16] You then "find" all sorts of things about you, much in the sense of Avenarius' positivism. (He, it is true did not find values, but he found valuations.)[17] But the main criticism that has told against Avenarius' Kritik is precisely that you do not "vorfinden" facts and values (or valuations) in the same way, in the same attitude; you shift your attitude, you change your standpoint, as you see now one and now the other. Empiriocriticism breaks down, in other words, just because it has no theory of values. — This may not apply, and you may resent the name of positivist; but I am trying to get your doctrine whole.[18]

Pp. 6–8. This detailed programme I do not need to comment on, since what I should say is implicit in what has been said. I note only that I know nothing of "degrees of consciousness" (p. 7).

Pp. 8–9. Here our difference shows. I regard mathematics as included in logic; and I do not regard logic, history, philosophy, religion as sciences. I know three representative sciences:

Physics = science of existential experience regarded as interdependent;

Biology = " " " " [19]dependent on environment;

Psychology = " " " "

[20]dependent on
nervous system.

All dependences are logical or functional; and physics is logically prior to biology, biology logically prior to psychology. Perhaps you mean by Science what the Germans usually mean by Wissenschaft, while I mean by it the stricter thing that the British make it? (Cf. Merz.)[21] That would account for a tendency to division between us, though it would not account for the actual division as it is given.

Pp. 10–11. I do not find anything for further comment in the Summary. I do, of course, believe in the "clinical psychologist" very heartily, if you mean by him a man of Boring's type attached to a psychopathic hospital.

I have read the paper three times; and the general impression it leaves is that of an eminently practical attitude and practical interest. The underlying theory seems to me to be undoubtedly positivistic, though I should suppose that you had less interest in theory than in the practical moulding of behaviour that the theory warrants; still the theory shows through. As a result of the practical interest, I think you use terms somewhat loosely, making them do duty in your sense without regarding their implications and limitations: such terms are "science," "fact," "observe." As another result of this practical interest, I think you are rather impatient with theoretical science, especially with psychology, your account of which strikes me at times almost as a caricature. I think also that your use of teleological terms in biological reference ("constructive adaptation" e.g.) may be misleading. But indeed I miss all through the definitions of your technical terms, which you could not of course give in a brief paper but which you undoubtedly give in your courses.

I agree that mental and physical are not genera. I agree that for practical handling of men the facts of biology and the facts of psychology shd. be combined, and the organism taken as a whole. I agree that for such practical handling values must be taken full account of. I agree that under these conditions new terms, new units of thought, must be struck out, — even if one finds it difficult to make them logically clear; one must make the venture. I agree that, when these new units have been solidified into something like a system and tested by application, the resulting body of knowledge may be of immense value to medical students. I agree that the name is of little moment, though I should prefer (using bio- in the Aristotelian sense) to call it biotechnics rather than psychobiology.

I reserve, however, the rights of the theoretical sciences, — physics, biology, psychology, — all of which describe existential experience from different points of view. The method of science I take to be observation, and the correlate of observation I take to be fact; the system of science I build up from facts and logic (including mathematics). Science I think has nothing whatever to do with values; so that its description of the world is partial. For that reason, if for no other, I bar philosophy from science altogether: the sciences are compatible with any form of philosophy.[22]

So that for me your psychobiology is both more and less than psychology. More, because it has to do with values (assets, resources, rights and wrongs, betters and worses): less, because it selects from the total system of psychology only such facts and laws as it can use for its own ends.[23] I do not agree, therefore, that in teaching psychobiology you are giving your medical students psychology. Aside from this, I have no quarrel with its conception whatsoever: psychology and psychobiology may go on peacefully side by side, and if there is a middleman ought to help each other: though there are a good many points of detail in its doctrine that I shd. probably criticise — just as you would doubtless criticise points of detail in any system of biology or physics that you happened to study.

APPENDIX I.

(1) I heartily agree that any classification of knowledges — yours or mine or anybody's — is provisional and relative to the era in which its author lives. For that very reason I prefer historical continuity and slow development to anything revolutionary and catastrophic. I think that Descartes' res cogitans and res extensa, and Spinoza's parallelism, did magnificent service in their day; and I think also that this service is incorporated in the history of thought, in such wise that we can never again lapse back into pre-Cartesian and pre-Spinozistic thinking. I am neither Cartesian dualist nor Spinozistic parallelist, but I am very glad to have been able to see these men's problems in their way, and to have built up my own scientific views on the basis of a forced criticism of them.

We stand on the shoulders of the past; and the future will stand on our shoulders. We criticise the past as acutely as we can, and the future will criticise us as acutely as it can. What I can't understand in you is your contempt for outgrown doctrines; it is almost as if you denied to their authors the common human power of thought. So James' savage contempt of Fechner and Ward's of Spencer are to me quite unintelligible. I suppose there is hardly a page of Spencer's voluminous writings that I should not find criticisable; but why on that account should I despise him? There is very little of Fechner that I do not directly traverse (as I have done, of course, in print); but I have acknowledged and feel the highest respect for his work.

I have further the personal belief (which you may not share) that any question which at any time has seriously engaged human thought is likely to be a real question and to reappear (with change of form and of context) at later periods. We say that such-and-such is a dead issue, only to find that there is a lively growth, some distance off, from the same root. For this reason also I am disinclined to break with the past.

II.

(2) Perhaps if I schematise my ideas of Science and Technology the relevant arguments will be clearer:

	Science	*Technology*
Problem	Description	Attainment of end
Method	Observation	Explication
Data	Facts	Meanings
Scope	Existential universe	Means to end
Attitude	Impartial	Selective
Ground of distinction	Point of view	Nature of end

By "end" I mean such things as preventive medicine, sanitary engineering, improvement of agriculture, etc.

Common to science and technology is the whole of logical method (including mathematics, the planning of experiments, everything that is given in the large Logics under "scientific methodology").

Interplay between the two is guaranteed in various ways. Thus science may lead to a technological device (Helmholtz' Augenspiegel)[24]; the scientific text-book is a technological performance; science needs lots of technological things (photography, e.g.); the technologist may need scientific knowledge at some stage in the attainment of his end, and may find that science can't give it him, — then he does the scientific work for himself, or suggests its doing to a man of science, etc.; a technological device may suggest scientific problems (aeroplane); and so on. Each is necessary to the other, if steady progress is to be made in either. But they are through and through different, and naturally make appeal to different temperaments. The man of science is always in the great minority.

III.

(3) There are many points in your letter of commentary which show something like agreement. One point of remaining difference I think I can perhaps smooth over. I greatly prefer Biology to Physiology (as the preceding letter has shown) in matters of general definition. I was brought up to biology, with physiology only as a special branch of it. But when I began to lecture over here I found that my students knew nothing of biology, but did know something of physiology. Even now I think that to most American students of psychology the word Biology is nebulous — vaguely suggesting evolution and heredity — and far less concrete than Physiology. But I welcome the biology part of your psychobiology, and in my last book I have myself sought to utilise and emphasize the "biological" as distinct from the more narrowly physiological organism.

It seems to me that in practically every chapter of the "traditional" psychology — in perception, in association, in emotion, in will, in instinct — we run up against biological, as distinct from strictly physiological factors.

(But just as I regard physics and chemistry as differentiations within a single point of view, so of course also do I regard biology and physiology as such differentiations. I take the names Physics and Biology a potiori [sic, posteriori?]: physics covers physics proper and chemistry and physical chemistry, and Biology in my definition covers physiology and anatomy and cytology and so on, as well as biology in the narrower sense.)

1. In the notes appended to this letter, Titchener responds in detail to Meyer's paper "Objective Psychology or Psychobiology with Subordination of the Medically Useless Contrast of Mental and Physical" (1915) a reprint of which Meyer had enclosed in his letter of 18 March 1918 (15M). (Cf. 16T.) Note that the reprint of Meyer's paper has its own pagination, beginning on page 1.

2. Meyer's note, "[also]".

3. Meyer's marginal note, "Yet it is remarkable how my formulation goes to the spot? Or wants to?"

4. The passage from Mach to which Titchener refers is as follows: "The investigator strives for knowledge of a field of facts; it is all the same to him *what* he finds. The technician strives for a definite purpose; he leaves everything alone which does not seem subservient to his ends. Because of this, the thought of the technician is more one-sided and narrower. It is similar to that of a geometrician who seeks the solution of a problem of construction. Yet the technician, when examining his resources, is often an investigator; an investigator, when pursuing definite aims, is often a technician. The investigator strives for the removal of an intellectual discomfort; he seeks a *releasing thought*. The technician wishes to overcome a practical discomfort; he seeks a *releasing construction*. Any other

distinction between discovery and invention can scarcely be made" (Ernst Mach, *Die Principien der Wärmlehre* [Leipzig: J. A. Barth, 1896]; trans. P. E. B. Jourdain and A. E. Heath as *Principles of the Theory of Heat* [Boston: D. Reidel, 1986], 407).

5. Meyer's marginal note, "But why repudiate critical common sense? [pertinent?].

6. Lawrence Joseph Henderson (1878-1942), professor of biochemistry at Harvard University. In his *The Fitness of the Environment* (1913) and *The Order of Nature* (1917), he concluded that the "fit" between the properties of matter and energy and those of the physicochemical environment could not be explained in mechanistic terms but must be due to a kind of order or "teleology" in nature. Partly under the influence of the Italian sociologist Vilfredo Pareto, Henderson extended his organismic, holistic approach to the study of physical systems to the analysis of society.

7. Introjection was the term used by Richard Avenarius for the tendency to attribute mental experience to other people when such mental experiences are not given in one's own direct experience.

8. Meyer's marginal note, "Inference is not excluded from science!"

9. Meyer's marginal note, "?"

10. Robert M. Yerkes (1876–1956), psychologist at Yale, during World War I was in charge of psychological testing for the United States Army.

11. Melvin E. Haggerty (1875–?), at the time psychologist at the University of Minnesota. He was heavily involved in educational psychology and psychological testing.

12. Henry H. Goddard (1866–1957), at the time director of psychological research, Training School, Vineland, N.J., and author of *Feeblemindedness: Its Causes and Consequences* (1914).

13. At the time of this letter, Knight Dunlap was in the division of psychology of the United States Army air medical services.

14. Meyer's marginal note, "?"

15. E. B. Titchener, *A Beginner's Psychology* (New York: Macmillan, 1915), 19, 22.

16. Vorfinden = found, given.

17. Danziger has noted that in introducing his concept of existential experience into psychology, Titchener diverged from Avenarius, who took phenomenal experience as his starting-point and accordingly included the experience of value in psychology (Kurt Danziger, "The Positivist Repudiation of Wundt," 77 n.).

18. Meyer's marginal note, "why."

19. Meyer here adds the word "Logically."

20. Meyer here adds the word "Logically."

21. John Theodore Merz, *A History of European Thought in the Nineteenth Century*, 4 vols. (1904–1912).

22. Meyer's marginal note, "?"

23. Meyer's marginal note, "?"

24. The reference is to Helmholtz's invention of the ophthalmoscope.

25 M [M 6]

April 24, 1918

My dear Titchener:

Just a line off the bat after a rapid reading of your very much appreciated letter. I really do not see how we could have swelled the differences to any such proportion as actually prevailed, as soon as we look at the facts in a broad way. It seems to me that your letter makes many of the differences much less glaring. Off-hand I would say that I am probably more elastic with regard to my conception of the inter-relations of science and technology, and also with regard to the position of the theory of values. If I feel that I have to include certain things which others can study from the point of view of values, I still believe that I keep on an impartial scientific basis. Probably the only /and quite subsidiary/ point on which I have to ask a serious question is that of "How do you formulate that which I designate as degrees of consciousness?"; the facts that I point to will show that we evidently do not mean the same thing when we speak of consciousness. To me is [*sic*, it] is the mode and extent of hanging together of the functions of the parts, which varies in sleep and different waking states and pathological conditions.

In what I have written I may not have given evidence of appreciation of the historical attitude. As a matter of fact, I enjoy the historical aspects as keenly as any one can and I do respect historical background, and if I do not mention it often the reason is that my type of memory and my conscience about my accuracy do not favor discussing historical facts extensively. I rather leave it to those who have the time to do it well.

Once more my thanks. I shall give your letter a careful reading and discuss it in my next letter and I hope in a way that will help toward further differentiation of the landmarks and common ground.

Believe me

Very truly yours,
Adolf Meyer

26 M [M 7]

April 25, 1918

My dear Titchener:—

I greatly enjoyed the reading of your letter of April 22nd, 1918 because I see more and more possibility of common ground.

Your summary of my general attitude is essentially fair. All through, of course, you tend to err in two directions: that of assigning to me essentially and exclusively /practical/ melioristic ambitions, and on the other that of /insisting unduly on my /being loose in theory and definition, historical background etc. But let us take the practical view that I make you but relatively responsible because I evidently have not published my views with sufficiently clear exposés of the general background — which I have no special name for. You speak of what you see as "positivism." I speak of it as "critical common-sense." The main point is what the performance in reality deals with and performs. On the historical problem I have already expressed myself in this morning's note. I have enough history for my working purposes, but not in a form in which I would want to pose as historian. I am interested and practically familiar with your references.

When, on page 2 of the letter, you say "You are interested in the individual etc. . . . I am not —" I wish you had said "You are interested in the individual as well as in the generic fact etc.," because I am not blind and insensitive to what may come from your statistical approach.

The "orthodox sciences" do not worry me "because they do not help"; I only regret that they have to be so exclusive and straight-laced as to call "inference" and "values" an unconditional breach of the rules of their game. Your reference to Mach led me to pick up the interesting Wärmlehre — of which I have only the 1900 edition, so that I cannot be sure of the identification of your reference. Like Avenarius, Mach emphasizes the economic or economizing aspect of science. Is that too much like valuation? It is not so much the "rationalizing" as such that I extol as the reduction of the data to terms of experiments and to system; a free system to be sure; but as good a system as facts will permit.

When you speak on "page 1 of the current comment" of the applicability to the needs of common-sense or of technology being the very last thing that science should think of, you state what I too would subscribe to. But I am turning the proposition around. I claim that common-sense can have a better relation to science than it is given credit for and that critical common-sense is a formulation truer to nature /& logic/ and safer as a method than any type of "science" which leaves the doors wide open for the utterly uncritical notions in fields that the "scientist" is not responsible for, owing to some definition of his field. (See Mach's chapter on "Der Sinn für das Wunderbare.")

Whether we all start with anything worth calling Cartesianism is questionable to me. I don't remember having held it. Wundt's attitude was a disappointment to me when I looked for light in his essays in the middle eighties. I must have been very close to my present view-point even then. And so were the early Hebrews and poor Aristotle with all his "sins" and many more mortal mortals.

A great difficulty arises from the fact that you have to "look" at things "biologically," where I /simply/ "see" biological things or facts. There is the fundamental difference. In other words the difference is due to epistemological assumptions /or regulations/ on your part where I am satisfied with an epistemologically naive scheme. Where I speak of accepting a "frankly biological view—," I mean accepting the facts as biological facts, i.e. data recognized as belonging to a group requiring certain presuppositions and methods and precautions in our study, different from those required by the physical and the chemical groups of facts. In other words, the difference lies in the facts and methods and not in any special attitude of mine, so that, as I put it in our earlier correspondence, I do not have to pan-biologize the whole world, whereas it is true a much wider scope is open to physics and chemistry, without there being any need of physics and chemistry swallowing up biology or any liklihood of their making it unnecessary. When I see a biological fact, I can study it with the biological methods or with the methods of physics and chemistry and any other approach that may be applicable. The fact remains the same. Henderson's formula does not reduce the fact but certain mystery-seeking or mystery-breeding assumptions, to terms of C,H,O. My concept of integration keeps the data and their formulations on an objective basis, with essentially one fundamental epistemological starting point, which you are quite right to compare with the "vorfinden," although I have to /take account of/ my behavior towards the "Vorgefundene."[1] It is therefore not the student who has to switch from attitude to attitude; there is a difference of material and a difference of the methods, accessible to one and the same student with a unitary view-point of wanting to know and knowing how.

Sub (3) on page 2, you say I seem to have in mind the crudest sort of introjectionism. Do you mean that I ascribe it to others or that I indulge in it myself? A fuller discussion of the concept of integration and its application to psychology would show that we cannot differ fundamentally.

As to (4), "consciousness," I repeat what I said in this morning's note: consciousness is the form and extent of hanging together, and not "awareness" à la Dunlap,[2] and I should like to know what term you use for the different types and degrees, sleep, waking, etc. We might speak of it as different ranges of attention but it is a broader problem than that of attention.

Your scruples about including activity among the observable facts and your calling "activity" an "interpretation of facts" are probably referable to the epistemological difference. You seem to make a distinction between fact and datum, and to exclude inference or "comprehensive" understanding of "compounds," simultaneous or successive or serial.

The fling at "traditional philosophy and psychology" is not meant to be absolutely damning or disrespectful. And after all the terms, as I said, are apt to go a long way to suggest definitions. I might have spoken of the parallelisms. I can see their relative justification, but I consider them at best as truisms favoring undesirable inferences and suggesting a call for "shifting the point of view" where we have a difference of facts.

Your criticism of "psychology for medical students" touches something on which no doubt we are fundamentally agreed. The practical and blunt statement might suggest what you take issue with; but I did not mean to emphasize more than the fact that in the end nobody has all the psychology there is, and nobody can offer all; some selection and grouping will occur and the nearer it comes /to/ the best psychology one has to offer the better for all concerned.

Your taking issue with my blunt use of the term introspection after the valiant efforts at discussion of the term of late years touches more my bad manners than what I had in mind. We both seem to be fundamentally much more closely in accord than I had supposed even after reading that remark in your preface.

Now of course my language and the unblushing assumption that some matters which others look upon sub specie of values are to me plainly objective facts — these are possible obstacles and causes for complaints which I must accept as a fault of my innate pragmatism.

My vorfinden is not quite as elaborately epistemologically conditioned as that of Avenarius. And yet what I accept as what we might call compounds of facts where you speak of "values," is not mentioned for "value's" sake, but because it is an objective fact — an equation or an experiment compared with another without any moral or other indignation and accepted in cold blood. Is the trial and error formula necessarily a "valuation?" This objectivity is a necessary part of my "critical common-sense." When I do bring in actual valuations I do not, however, have to shift my whole ground and yet I know when I am doing it.

Your grouping of the sciences is clear, but as I said, on an elaborate epistemological basis where mine is practically on the naive basis but, of course, also not altogether unsophisticated but critical. I do include logic with mathematics under a "theory of relations."

I appreciate what you say on page 6 but believe that the preeminently practical appearance which conceals the actually preeminent theoretical interest is possible only through the intrinsic oneness of standpoint in facing the various sets and groupings of facts and methods of work. And it is this that I wish to impart to my students and fellow workers. It is not impatience with the sciences /nor with the workers,/ but possibly impatience with some of their guardians. And as to the definitions — I am often satisfied with what a term suggests and perhaps for this reason expose myself in other connections /by/ making too much ado about the terms of others when loosely used by them. I shall try to offer some definitions; indeed I should like to have a list of vexatious terms put up to me for such an effort at a personal glossary. It would naturally call for an extensive confession of principles. My "teleological" terms might be misleading, but not any more than that the acceptance of the term "biology" might expose one to being taken for a fullfledged old-time vitalist working with a divine spark in the background. We can, I think, run the risk and let the suspicious get over their suspicions.

The points on which we are in agreement (page 6 of your criticism) make me feel that we are in accord on very essential points. I might even have a leaning towards substituting biotechnics for psychobiology. I have often felt peeved at the fact that "anthropology" has been usurped too exclusively for the physical and ethnological issues. Fortunately we can always fall back on "behavior and mentation" or "behavior," applicable to animals and men. But I do believe that any use of "psychobiology" which anteceded that of Dunlap should have precluded his using the term as he does. Yet there again, after all, I am not such a stickler about terms. We evidently are in accord on the principles of the system of science being built up from facts and logic. That the sciences may be compatible with any form of philosophy is however a very conditioned truth. The science may; but it may not save the scientist from serious foolishness.

"Psychobiology" is more than what you include in "psychology" — hence my choice of a non-committal term. It is not less in principle, but necessarily so by accident — about in the same sense as that nobody "has" all there is of psychology; and no course can cover all. Yet for medical students and for public lectures or a rigid course nothing but one's best should be offered.

With regard to the Appendix I, I repeat that I am sorry — in a way — you see I am really very bad — for the unbridled tongue or pen. I do not mean to be disrespectful towards history. I suppose my own trend is a revival of "dead" issues.

The table of page II is quite helpful. Somehow I should include under science both as problem and as method not only description and observation but experimentation and construction as well as analysis.

I still feel that technology is a servant of science as well as of its own "purposes." The scope may be the existential universe, if one cannot find any limits /to one's zeal and enthusiasm of method/, but in reality it is concerned with whatever presents the pertinent facts. The attitude also is impartial, even if experiment and construction and analysis, and formation and testing of hypothesis is involved, and it is selective to the extent to which common-sense and pertinence call for discrimination. At least we have to say that of one's work or one's version of "the" science.

The ground of distinction lies in the type of facts and methods while the point of view is essentially unitary with me — pluralistic with a fundamental confidence in consistency, as I put it in one of my old Bulletin reviews.[3] The "end" does not belong to technology alone. The end of science is systematization of facts established with all the critical methods at one's disposal. Not only the logic is common to science and technology, but many procedures and methods which are more than logic.

All this interplay you do full justice to. Your "through and through different" to me is largely a "practical difference" of the extent of accuracy and systematization and interest in "principle" vs "application"; /the application as such is unessential./

Your approval of the term "biology" is I think very well founded. After all the student "catches on" very quickly. Even some of your Cornell pupils seem to have a very strong leaning in this direction although a few at least try to remain faithful to the definition of dependence on the nervous system, until they consider the possible role of the internal secretions etc.

Your last parenthesis expresses in your way what I cover with the concept of integration and its groups or levels.

I don't know whether with this off-hand discussion I am not undoing again some of the much appreciated finding of common ground. I do not think so. The differences may become clearer but also, I hope less radical as far as the pursuit of scientific interest and work is concerned. It is, I am quite sure now, an essentially epistemological one at bottom, determining differences of "point of view" — rather radical in a way, but not altogether mutually unintelligible, or calling for mutual condemnation. This would be quite foreign to me, no matter how bad my language may sound at times.

It is queer how these war times force one — at least me — to take even one's philosophical status critically and earnestly. I turn against unnecessary misunderstandings. While there is one enemy who behaved so archaically that he has to be dealt with with archaic methods, there still is a world which he has not englobed, and I hope that we shall emerge from the ultimate victory with fresh impulses and fresh devotion to the great call for better fellowship among the fellow-workers and more intense love for more and more "systematized experience" as well as technological skill. My Swiss blood looks for a democracy with a better appreciation of solidarity. This seems to pervade my nature — down or up to my way of looking at the sciences.

Sincerely yours,
Adolf Meyer

1. Vorgefundene = that which was given.

2. Meyer seems to be referring to Knight Dunlap, "The Results of a Questionary on Psychological Terminology," *The Johns Hopkins University Circular*, No. 5 (1916): 3–55, a survey of 125 senior American psychologists concerning their use of various terms in psychology, in which Meyer but not Titchener participated. Based on the results of the survey, which demonstrated widespread inconsistencies in the use of certain basic concepts, Dunlap suggested that the term "consciousness" be defined as "awareness," a suggestion with which Meyer did not agree. Dunlap's investigation led to the appointment of a committee on terminology by the American Psychological Association. Cf. 28M, 2 n.

3. The reference is to Meyer's "Misconceptions at the Bottom of *Hopelessness of All Psychology*" (1907).

27 T [T 6]

April 29, 1918

Dear Meyer,

I too welcome the chance of mutual understanding. If we can make out where and how we differ, the differences themselves will probably be seen to follow from differences in presupposition, practically inevitable in the present stage of the division of labour, and therefore neither ultimately irreconcilable nor mere matters of personal prejudice.

One such difference that seems to stand out now is that you take your epistemology (critical common sense) into the bosom of your scientific thinking, whereas I push epistemology back out of the way of science altogether. Critical common sense is precisely, as I see it, a positivistic epistemology. (A good deal more, no doubt, but certainly that.) It seeks to understand, to begreifen. Whereas I set epistemology so far back that I seem to be able to say: Science is compatible with any epistemology, and is committed to none. I honestly do not know what my own epistemology is. No one of the theories that I have read seems to answer just the questions that I want answered. But I seem to see clearly enough that the Knower, or Understander, or Positor, is presupposed by all sciences (physics, biology, psychology) and is presupposed by all in the same way. So far as science goes, therefore, I have an external constant which doesn't matter.

The problem of science, sensu stricto, I take to be description and not understanding. But the system of science, science made available for the generation, holds its facts together by logic. Mach's economy holds, I believe, of this systematic logic. For science it is indifferent whether the description be given in a page of words, or in a single compact mathematical formula; and, as Mach says, the "economical" varies in fact with the public addressed; sometimes verbal logic is understood when mathematical is not, and then the verbal is the economical. So the rule that generalised descriptions (what perhaps you would call integrations) are to be given in the "simplest possible terms" is a logical ideal, an ideal of the systematic presentation of science — with a touch on it, sometimes, of an aesthetic ideal also, — and with a touch, again if a textbook is in question, of a technological ideal; according as it means, just "simplest possible," or "prettily simple" or "so simple that students of this particular training can understand."

All this, I am afraid, seems to you like hairsplitting. To me it is clarity —,so far as in my own thinking I have been able to attain clarity. I find in the history of science an imperative need of strict usage, strict definition, strict delimitation of the universe of discourse. Controversies and philosophical vagaries seem to me to spring in the main from lack of this rigour. I began my thought-life (I was near enough to the men to do it) as a Darwinian-Spencerian; I took my Oxford "first" as a Spencerian! As I have worked and worked at science, and at the history of science, Science itself has become more and more "limited" for me; I have learned that it can't be science without these limitations of science; I have learned that if scientific work is to stand, it must be done within these limitations. (When I say "I have learned," I mean that this is the lesson that my work has taught me; it is personal only.) No one is more modest than I as to the range and claims of science; no one is more confident than I of the surety (and social value) of science if its limitations are respected. Astronomy is the type — because society has permitted the astronomer to follow his own strict path; the study of the stars is so "wonderful" to the public, that no pressure is exerted from them. Physics and chemistry come next: partly because atoms and molecules are also so "wonderful" and strike the public imagination, and partly also because the "results" of these two sciences are so obviously, almost blatantly useful. Biology is very mixed; there is scant public esteem for physiological experiment, and the doctrine of evolution was as much disliked as liked: so biology has wasted time in barren controversies (mechanism and vitalism, e.g.) and in trying to square itself with the public; it has had nothing of the serenity of astronomy. Poor psychology, with its immense load of philosophical tradition, has wobbled worse than biology. Everybody has thought that, because he could "use his mind," he could psychologise; physics has forced its analogy, and biology has forced its, upon psychology; and the outcome is a dreadfully unscientific mess. Wundt is, I take it, the very first large figure in the history of thought who is temperamentally psychological. I thought I saw this as long ago as 1888, and I have confirmed my opinion again and again. I believe that Wundt's generalisations are mostly wrong; I do not at the moment recall any one of the larger ones that I accept today — though I have in my time swallowed most of them; but I still affirm that Wundt's instinct is psychological, even where it leads him astray (under the influence of tradition, training, milieu, controversy); and he still seems to me to be the one man among the "philosophers" of whom this can be said. That is his importance: not the special things he teaches.

April 30, 1918

So much I wrote last night; and I was evidently tired, as I rambled and became reminiscent! But let it stand. The points are:–

You take up a positivistic attitude into your science. The advantage is that you can be understood by the general public (up to a point, of course), that you have no need for my fine distinctions within your subject-matter, and you are nearer to practice than I am.

The disadvantage is that you are open to all the standard criticisms that have been urged against positivistic or "common sense" theories of knowledge. You have a perfect right to be "common-sense." Another man might have equal right (that of serious conviction) to be an absolute idealist in his scientific work. But you can't avoid the inconvenience that critical common sense is a determinate philosophical position, co-ordinate with other positions, and open to considered and formulated objections. Lovejoy,[1] with his idea of a sort of philosophic ledger, would be able to tell you offhand what these objections are: I have mentioned two or three in previous letters.

My advantage is that I root in the history of science itself, that my positions are compatible with all and any theories of knowledge, that all my "sciences" are of a piece, systematically coherent. My disadvantages are that the philosophers never forgive the thinker who refuses to think philosophically, — they forgive the poet, but never the thoughtful man of science, — and that the general public is entirely indifferent to pure science, which it either tolerates (astronomy) or ignores (witness the treatment /in/ the "histories" of science so-called!).

Now a digression! It may be that science, as I conceive science, is as Mach believes an instrument of survival, or as Münsterberg believes a sort of trick of the teleological world-mind to help itself toward its ends. (In so far as this is what Mach means by "economy" I am willing to let him believe it.) I don't know, and I very heartily don't care. I am concerned with what science IS, and not with what part it is called upon to play by the scheming of a Cosmic Principle or a Divine Mind. I don't suppose that (in the present connection) you care either; but you refer to Mach's Wunderbar and to his economy — and both of those things (tho' the latter in part only) go beyond our present argument. Let the philosophers speculate as they will: they can swallow me whole, if they want to.

A second and derivative difference between us is that you find OBJECTS of different sorts before you, while I do not. You find OBJECTS which offer themselves for biological consideration, which are in fact biological objects, biological Sachen or Tatbestände.[2] I find only the great tissue of Experience, which I can contemplate

I. analytically	
(1) as values	Axiology
(2) as facts	Science
II. synthetically	Philosophy

Under Science I find the three subordinate points of view which I have characterised in full in previous letters.

So I find no separate classes of objects at all. Only aspects of Experience. And when I charge you with introjectionism, I do so because you appear to postulate or to find "mental" objects (states, activities, operations) that form a class apart from your biological and physical objects. Thus a "sensation" for me (would that I could get people to see this!) is psychological and not psychical: it exists only in the subject-matter of psychology, in the field of view of the psychologist; it is not a "something" in the world alongside of planes and screws and cats and men; I know nothing of all these "objects" — though common sense, of course, has made them and takes them therefore for granted. The "sensation" is thus not in the brain, not in the sensible world, not in my "inner" experience, — it is nowhere save in the purview of psychology, in that field of existential regard of experience which is the subject-matter of psychology. — And whether, again, Experience is metaphysically one or many, singular or plural, I don't know or care within science. Science describes the whole existential field from all possible points of view. It has nothing more to do — it is not concerned with "reality" as it is not concerned either with the subsistence of values.

Here, I really think, is the beginning and end of our differences! You — critical common sense, with its various kinds of objects; I — existential experience, with its various aspects. You claim Science as your mistress; I claim her as mine. Securus jubicabit orbis terrarum![3] Meanwhile, if we see (as I said) where we differ, the battle of mutual understanding is more than half won.

Now a few notes.

(1) Wundt's account of watered Cartesianism is this: "That the substances of this world divide into Minds and Bodies; that Minds are unspatial and Bodies extended in space; that Minds obey the laws of thought and Bodies the laws of mechanics; that Minds are free and Bodies subject to a blind causality; and that nevertheless these different sorts of things are at times bound up with one another and can act

upon one another: who is there among the public untrained in philosophy that would not subscribe to these—statements?" (I omit the qualifications at the end.) This seems to me to be a somewhat clarified account of the common stock of ideas that all our students bring into the class-room; it is also what we ourselves were brought up, by implication, to believe. It is therefore the point of departure for the teaching of psychology.

(2) I did not know that you held Wundt's notion of relative synthesis as = degree of consciousness. For me the difference between sleep and waking is a difference simply of existential description, attributive (qualities, times, etc.) and correlative (range, succession, etc.). Any cognitive difference would be ultrascientific, and any diagnostic difference would be technological. Poor man, you'll say, — how he handicaps himself! Yes — and now think how much we know descriptively about the dream! Just a few tables of frequencies and a few individual pictures. I could keep a laboratory busy doing nothing else than "observing dreams." And that surely must someday be done, whatever else is done in addition.

I doubt if degree of Cs = relative synthesis will find general understanding today. Cs is a dreadfully slippery term. But you are wholly within your rights to use it in that sense.

(3) Trial and error is a logical method. It therefore belongs to scientific methodology, and not to science is [*sic*, in] the sense of facts-got-by-observation. Experiment, again, is to me simply observation guided by logic; what you do scientifically in experiment is to observe; you plan your experiment, plan for your observing, by logic.

(4) Most men "of science" are plunged into work of teaching before they have had time to think, and are occupied by teaching all their lives. Also the profession, as it stands now, attracts a good many weaklings. I hold no brief for incompetence, in myself or others. This country needs and would gain by a school of solid and well-based Criticism. As Sanford has recently said, America has been content with "good enough for America" and has too often excused sloppy intellectual work on the ground of the physical "pioneering." I have criticised savagely in my time. If I am more tolerant now (I don't know; I am not "inside of me") it is because of the immense difficulty I have found in getting my own constructive work understood. People ascribe to me the beliefs and views of 20 years ago — and even those are as a rule imperfectly given! I agree with all my heart that there is too much "serious foolishness" abroad. Perhaps I am a little tired, and let it all go by too easily. My men sometimes say to me: You ought

really to reply to so-and-so — he'll think he has the better of us. My tendency is to reply: No, I am moving steadily towards a real system, and after all these years I have the right to sit back from controversy and do my construction; so-and-so will be dead by next month's issues of the magazines. Perhaps I am wrong, and perhaps a manifesto of polemical nature every other year would be good! What critical hay couldn't one make of a lot of Southard's writings!

But I am well under way with the prolegomena volume of my big system of psychology,[4] and that work seems more important. It goes very slowly, and is very exhausting; especially as it is continually cut across by the war. All the same it seems a duty to go on with it. Publishers will look askance at it— and the public will not understand it; but I shall have got it done all same.

I have had to give only odd times to these letters, and have probably put things mixedly and repetitiously. It seems to me that we have now got pretty near the bottom of our differences. If any special points are still unclear, please ask about them. I think I see (as well as a man of different temperament can) what you are after. I hope I have made you see, to a like extent, what my position is. I have sought in the history of science for the essence of science, and I have tried to formulate it clearly under all heads — subject-matter, method, problem, scope, etc. The essence I think I have got, after long years of doubt; the formulation of it is, necessarily, coloured by time and space and personality.

Yours sincerely,
E. B. Titchener

1. Arthur Oncken Lovejoy (1873–1962), professor of philosophy at John Hopkins University from 1910 to 1938, expounded his epistemological dualism in his *Revolt Against Dualism: An Inquiry Concerning the Existence of Ideas* (1930). He was one of the organizers of the American Association of University Professors, for the defense of academic freedom, and, with Philip Wiener, in 1940 founded the *Journal of the History of Ideas.*

2. Sachen = thing; Tatsbestande = matters of fact.

3. Securus jubicabit orbis terrarum! = in its security the earth will judge.

4. Titchener's magnum opus was never finished. The chapters being prepared at the time of these letters were published posthumously as *Systematic Psychology: Prolegomena*, ed. H. P. Weld (New York: Macmillan, 1929).

28 M [M 8]

May 2, 1918

My dear Titchener:—

You touch my idiotic spot or my obduracy on two points — in what you have to say about the "objects" (which term I use in a logical sense, not as necessarily designating "things," but functions or relations as well, i.e. data of observation and experience) and about the "epistemology." You may be able to pigeon-hole my "epistemological" standpoint or view-point; (which I doubt, because I am as little aware of having seen the same pattern in any previous brand of "positivism" as you can find one generally labelled identical with your view-points). Let us drop the term and say simply "/points of view/." You distinguish the "purviews" of physics and chemistry, and biology and psychology and say science describes the whole existential field from all possible points of view (actually limited by you to three). You /justly/ say sensation is "nowhere" save in the purview of psychology, in that field of existential regard of experience, which is the subject matter of psychology. You say science is not concerned with "reality," as it is not concerned either with the subsistence of values (I should say its consistency between facts and formulations). You say sensation is "psychological" and not psychical (which I accept as a logical distinction worth minding). You know nothing of "all these objects" etc.

Let me try to take up a few of these points to see how I can deal with them. Should I assume that you do not want to study certain "objects" of this world for psychological manifestations, i.e. special modes of behavior recognized as special because we need special methods for their experimental "manipulation" and description of their behavior? Your "point of view" is made to be the distinctive feature. Now is this not a qualification of your "knower?" I take the known for granted without prescribing anything special to him or her or to its working, except the obligation to be critically alert toward consistency or inconsistencies in the world of experimental data.

You mention "sensation." To me sensation is a psychobiological reaction and therefore not an "object," except /in/ the logical sense of "object of study, observation, etc." I know that in the occurrence of sensation the definite parts of a definite psychobiologically integrated organism or individual are involved, including the "brain," including the sensible world, including inner experiences, if you wish to mention /them all/; but the questions as to "where" the sensation is has no special sense and is not asked except with a disregard for one's logic. The sensation is a reaction which we can describe for various features, quality, intensity, duration, clearness —; you can view its relation to other psychobiological reactions (such as the "relative synthesis" and subsequent memory etc.) and to the situation (stimulus and reagent). But I admit that after I had thought I had your view-point, I am disconcerted by the sentence about the purview of psychology, "that field of existential regard of experience which is the subject-matter of psychology" — that which elsewhere you define as dependent on the nervous system. In the first place there are many nervous functions and facts dependent on the nervous system and ways of looking at them which have nothing to do with this field of experience. And therefore it is necessary to specify. Yerkes does make a world of psychics and considers himself endorsed by you. You evidently prefer a world of neutral "tissue of experience," exactly as I do. My "science" does not predicate as to the one or many, but deals with as many units as the facts call for in the descriptive formulation. In the second place you say "science" describes the whole existential field from all possible points of view. Mine does that; but you seem to limit it in a way which evidently slips from one's understanding so readily that one who believes he has tried honestly to follow the modifications, and your relation to the standpoint of others, still risks doing you injustice.

Lovejoy has had a "whack" at my conceptions but his regrettable physiological indigestion seems to have englobed this feature of his digestive capacity.[1] Unfortunately he is abroad just now. He takes great delight in pigeon-holing me offhand, but the old holes after all are not quite suitable habitats and that largely because he does not digest the meaning of integration. As to my bringing an epistemology into my science — I do not know any attempt at scientific formulation which does not present epistemological features. I am clear enough concerning mine to be able to say that it avoids many objectionable features of those which I know of; but as epistemological structure it does not condition my experience. It is the other way around. And that is I suppose what you feel about your own.

Your question from Wundt again shows me clearly that I never was even a potential Cartesian. And I truly believe I am not a unique specimen.

As to trial and error — it is a method. But there is also a body of fact representing the basis for the method, back of what suggested the combination as a definitely applicable method.

The relative synthesis or degree of consciousness presents not only the specific structural facts but especially the various types of aggregates of facts intelligible as lawful parts of definite sets of conditions.

It is the possibility of taking in broader sets of conditions that distinguishes my "psychobiology" from your determined limitations to elements and their synthesis.

Your sympathy for a call for critique quite appeals to me. But for that it is necessary to get some standards. These, in psychology, had best be taken by showing exactly the type of work men of various view-points are likely to undertake with a reasonably well defined part or instance of existential experience. I suggested to Warren that the terminological discussions should be cancelled until we might agree on some standard facts to be discussed.[2] I have tried to find such "equivalents" in various works. You describe a situation in your text page 471.[3] McDougall describes a few. Could we agree on a few well chosen fundamental situations which would serve as readily reproducable [sic] starting points or standards on which to observe what the various workers are doing, what they speak about etc.?

There would I think be a wonderful gain. Would you cooperate in an effort to select a few such "standard starting points" — as I say readily reproduced, if possible for a demonstration in a class before any discussion of any of the topics of psychological science starts?

The situations should not be chosen as narrowly as in the ideal experiment, ideal for the structuralist; but so that the behaviorist would not have any difficulty to satisfy the conditions needed from his point of view.

With a few standard situations we should soon be able to understand what the various workers take as their facts and as their viewpoint, procedure etc.

Don't you feel that here we are making another definite step toward greater clearness not only for our own discussion, but, I really believe, for a general scientific discussion of the problems which concern us?

I am very glad to hear that you are at work on a comprehensive presentation or system. You are quite right that that is more worth while than polemics or discussion of ephemeral character. Public discussions are rarely as helpful as personal efforts to clear up points and to reach common ground. One is apt to think of the observers of the combat and to lose sight of the aims. The attention to /the/ constructive aim of clearness is what makes me appreciate greatly your helpfulness and patience.

Just one more question. Where do you feel you have expressed most definitely the distinctive features of the point of view of psychology as contrasted with that of other sciences? I should like to be sure that I do not misconstrue your /present/ position.

Yours sincerely,
Adolf Meyer

1. In 1916, in an exchange of letters with Meyer, the philosopher Arthur Lovejoy accused Meyer of holding to a version of psychophysical dualism and consequently of being a parallelist or an interactionist. The correspondence is in The Adolf Meyer Papers, The Alan Mason Chesney Medical Archives, The Johns Hopkins Medical Institutions.

2. Howard Crosby Warren (1867–1934), psychologist at Princeton University from 1890 to 1934, was editor of the *Psychological Review* from 1901 to 1934 and editor of the *Psychological Bulletin* from 1904 to 1934. Meyer's reference seems to be to the investigation then in progress of the committee on terminology of the American Psychological Association. Cf. 26M, 2 n.

3. On p. 471 of his *Textbook*, Titchener describes a situation in which someone sitting at his desk hears the sound of a car crashing outside the window, followed by a shrill scream.

29 T [T 7]

May 4, 1918

Dear Meyer,

(1) Your point about "where my points-of-view belong" is a good one. I have thought a lot on the question, and my tentative answer is that they belong, not to epistemology, but to methodology. I triangulate the existential field, it is true (though of course I admit within this triangulation every possible science that is going today); and I do so, I think, because one can regard this field methodologically in three ways that do not seem to be reducible any one to any others. If biology can be reduced to physical chemistry, — or if, conversely, a fourth, fifth . . . methodological variation can be introduced, — then the triangulation would change at once and accordingly. My reason for regarding any such subdivisions as methodological is twofold. (1) Experience is given without differentiation as a starting-point; I do not find different "knowings" of existence; and (2) the division matter-life-mind (which I hope we have transcended) is itself an empirical, historically justified division, free of epistemology; and therefore not epistemological when clarified for latter-day use.

I find, however, a rather curious blindness in the "literature" as regards this issue. Everybody appears to be ready to take "point of view" for granted: whereas it is clear that the term may be employed in very various contexts — scientifically methodological, axiologically methodological, epistemological, ontological, &c.

(2) Do not, nevertheless, be misled by the figure of "field" and "triangulation." You attribute to me a definition of the subject-matter of psychology as "that which . . . [is] dependent on the nervous system." Not at all! That would be to slip back into the belief in separate objects or genera. I define the s.-m. of psychology as "all existential experience regarded as dependent on the nervous system," that is, as exist. exp. ueberhaupt[1] taken from the point-of-view of this dependence. I know nothing which, as object, — as thing, function, relation, datum, experience in the concrete, — is set apart for psychology, is intrinsically psychical.[2] I know of nothing, on the other hand, whether in heaven or earth or the waters under the earth, that cannot be regarded from the psychological point-of-view, and so transformed from its given appearance-to-common-sense into subject-matter of psychology.

(3) So of course I want to "study certain 'objects' of this world for psychological manifestations." I want to study all the objects of this common-sense world from the standpoint of psychology. Or more exactly (since science deals with the general) I want to study all classes of such objects, not every single object. I don't want, however, to play favourites; I want to study all impartially. If I am ever forced to select, that is at the hest of secondary motives, — the preparation of my students, the history of psychology itself, imperative practical needs. In so far as I give way to these secondary motives, I am human, allzu menschlich![3] — but I derogate from science.

(4) In your objection about the various sorts of dependence on the nervous system, don't you forget my table of logical priorities? Physics (in the large sense) is logically prior to biology (in the large sense), and biology is logically prior to psychology. All biological dependencies are therefore (logically) out of the way before psychology begins.

In so far, I should say, as there are energetic interdependencies in the N. S. or between it and other things, we are talking physics (physics, chemistry, physical chemistry). In so far as there are environmental dependencies, we are talking biology. In so far as there are dependencies of the third logical order, we are talking psychology. All this I put briefly, because I think your objection is answered at once by reference to my table.

(5) I don't really "prefer" any kind of world. I have striven

through several that I have had to give up. I have finally fallen back on the "given" world of everyday common-sense, and have tried to see how the so-different world of Science could have come out of it, how it is related to it, and so on. I think I see my way now; and I am the more inclined to confidence because I think I can also see how other ways have been struck out, and where they lead to. For the past 10 years I have been moving, at first very slowly and now with some speed, towards what insight I have got; and the motto has been forced on me, for Science: Entbehren sollst Du![4] Limit, limit, limit! — and be clear, clear, clear! But I very certainly did not "prefer" all this; my bias was towards a largely-phrased Darwinism.

(6) The difference between Yerkes and myself is shown, technically, by his acceptance of mental causality. No system which includes that can be anywhere near mine! I do not in the least blame you for missing this point, because there is no reason why you should bother about us; but now that I call your attention to it, you will surely see at once what the implications are. Yerkes himself has discussed the matter with me,[5] and I think (I am not sure, but I think) that he knows the gulf that separates us. But Yerkes has not thought deeply about systematic psychology. It was a great thing that a man of his leanings should think about it as much as he did. He is far nearer to Wundt than he is to me, or than I am to Wundt.

(7) Words are slippery, again! You say your science, like mine, "describes the whole existential field from all possible points of view." But for me the words "describe" and "existential" are correlative. One can describe /(for me)/ only what one can observe, and one can observe only existence; one certainly can't describe functions and relations! And existence is the mode of being of observable facts, and not that of values; they and functions and relations have other modes of being. I think you make existential = given: wherewith I should again say (at the risk of offense) that you betray your positivism. Facts are about the very last things to be "given." They have to be got, by observation, and usually by observation under logical control, — by experiment. Moreover, they are thus got always within a certain science; they do not, after they have been found, lie about in loose and detached and universally valid form; they always have on them the presupposition of a determinate science.

It is here that we seem to touch the heart of your "integration." It is probably true that I don't properly understand it. But you seem to me to think it possible to write a situational formula in terms, say, of relation, function, scientific fact, bits of everyday experience, common-sense interpretations, and so forth, — as if you were writing a formula within physics in terms of time, space and mass. You seem to take such logical objects as relation, scientific fact, everyday meaning, and to put them on the same level of direct observation; and when you have set them all together in proportion and order, you seem to claim to have "described" the situation. All these things seem to enter, on the same level, into your "description." Is this a caricature? It is my old difficulty: you seem able to "describe" a situation in terms of assets, resources, relations, functions, as if these things were (so to say) interchangeable with, could be mixed in with, could "integrate" with, "facts" of biology or psychology. Everything "given," in other words, seems to be as good matter for integrating as everything physical is within physics, everything biological within biology, &c. I can see very well how such synthesis should be possible for practical purposes; but I understand you to claim much more than that, to make a scientific claim.

So I think you owe it to me to show your method. How do you integrate? What procedures do you follow, and what reductions (to get a common denominator) do you undertake? You have said various things against my method, which I have set forth with definition on definition, as the stages of argument came up: but I think you owe me a positive characterisation of your procedure.

(8) The presupposition of the method of trial and error is, I should say, not a "body of fact" but rather a body of implication. The method is a way of explicating what is implied. What else can a logical method be? — But you may mean by trial and error something different from my own idea of it, and I may not have caught your point. We can hardly differ on the point of logic.

(9) I see two difficulties in the way of pedagogy by Situations — I mean, general education in the matter of the sciences. (1) A situation is a horribly complicated thing, and would need a very great deal of talk or print. (2) A situation is essentially a biological thing, and it would be especially difficult to physicise it.

I have sometimes taken as starter a thing like the Müller-Lyer figure.[6] We have there (1) /physically/ two linear distances which, as measured by cm., are equal within the margin of error of the measuring-rod. We have (2) psychologically two visual space-perceptions which are unequal. We have (3) for common sense two black lines on white paper which look different but are really equal. — The instance can be worked out in some little detail in a quarter of an hour, and one has the advantage of actual demonstration. I do not find, however, that such illustrations "carry" well. They are enjoyed, and apparently understood; but one will find in the next hour that the lesson has not bitten in; common sense gets its sway again, and one is told that "the lines are different for the mind but are really equal." There is no royal road into science, I am afraid; one just has to repeat and repeat and repeat, and illustrate and illustrate, until the scientific "set" is either proved impossible for the student in question or becomes an ingrained habit.

There is another and a more fundamental objection to such illustrations. It is that you must by hypothesis start out with some common-sensible object, — thing or situation. Your student, who is horribly sharp where you would prefer him to be blind, is all too likely to think that you have chosen the particular common-sensible object with a view to your own subject-matter. And indeed one would rather start out in psychology from the Müller-Lyer figure than, say, from a dry cell. (Just exactly as you yourself instinctively propose "situations" — though I don't get to them, apparently, till page 471!) So I myself, in using the M.-L., do add to it something like a dry cell, and do show that this object (which at first thought seems to "belong" to physics) can also be regarded psychologically and sets some psychological questions. But that makes the whole thing cumbrous and time-taking. What one ought to find is an object (thing or situation) which, for common sense itself, "belongs" as naturally to physics as to biology as to psychology. Wundt takes the tree given to common sense, and then regards it physically, botanically, psychologically: but the "psychologically" is a little forced. After you have your points of view, any illustration will do; before you have them, this fundamental difficulty is likely to crop up.

(10) You have spoken more than once of the behaviouristic "point of view" or "standpoint." In my critique of Watson[7] (which you doubtless know) I challenged him to produce one, and showed that what he had so far said was both inadequate and incoherent. I don't think that the b-ists are at all bothered about fundamentals. I think they like to do a certain sort of work (which is perfectly good work of its kind) and they like to damn what they think is psychology; but I heartily doubt if they have thought their own position through.

(11) I can't give you any better summary of the way I see things than has been done in these letters and in my recent papers and the Beginner's book. I hope to put things into some generalised form in my next volume. Meanwhile I can only ask you to be patient if the whole position seems, now and again, to "slip from under." It will

come back! But I know, both from my own experience and from that of my graduate seminary, how almost irresistible is the tendency, for some time, to read into technically used words meanings that belong to an older context than that in which they are now, by hypothesis, employed. If you are sufficiently interested to use my terms just as I define them, and to throw overboard every other meaning that association would suggest, then the position is stable.

In the matter of sensation e.g. I used the Brain of the materialists, the Sensible World of the epistemologists, and the Inner Experience of the psychologists of Psychism, to show just what I threw overboard. I am free of all that speculative cumber. Sensation for me "exists in the subject-matter of psychology"; that is, it is a logical construction whose components are aspects of existential experience observed from the psychological standpoint. It is a systematic term in psychology; and like all systematic terms it may be discarded for another term if logic finds that better. Call it a "primary attributive connex" if you like! and let the biologists keep the term "sensation" for something in their purview. I only wanted to show that I do not mean by the term what most people seem to mean by it themselves and to think that I mean by it.

Your own following definition escapes me. How can, I ask again and again, — how can a reaction have existential attributes? Is not a reaction a teleological something? If it is not, why do you call it a reaction? — the re- implies that it is an answer, a response, something therefore that either fits or misfits a question put. You deny that you have teleological leanings, and yet you use terms in this way that inevitably suggest teleology. If my position is difficult, because I cut free of the ordinary associative meanings, yours is surely no less difficult, because you do not define — except by denial — at all. If you do mean, as I have suggested above, that all that is "given" is on a par for science, is all alike and equally "existential," then that is the point of our divergence (as I put it in my last letter). But your present letter seems not to accept this.

I have written these things at various times, and have doubtless again been repetitious. I am afraid of going round in circles: as soon as things clarify a little, we come back to our starting-point. I regard science as tremendously different from common sense, almost (in certain regards) its antipodes. Common sense is to me through & through interpretative and teleological: science is descriptive and existential. The system of science is logical, and that is where the bridge comes from science to technology; but in principle the man of science might hand his facts to a logician, and let the logician do the system-making.

Keep it up, if you think we shall ever get any nearer! I am heartily in earnest in all this correspondence; but I am still disposed to think that the disjunction of my last letter hits our fundamental difference on the head.

Yours sincerely,
E. B. Titchener

1. Ueberhaupt = above all.
2. Meyer notes here, "But I do!"
3. Allzu menschlich! = All too human!
4. Entbehren sollst Du! = you must dispense with it.
5. Titchener and Yerkes corresponded on this and other issues. Their letters are in the Yerkes Papers, Sterling Medical Library, Yale University and the Cornell Archives, Cornell University.
6. The Müller-Lyer figure is reproduced in Figure 1, page 20.
7. E. B. Titchener, "On 'Psychology as the Behaviorist Views It,'" *Proceedings of the American Philosophical Society* 53 (1914): 1–17.

30 M [M 9]

May 7, 1918

My dear Titchener:—

I had an interesting experience this week which I feel you will sympathize with. A Dr. Osnato[1] undertakes to balance my views on "dementia praecox" and Southard's.

I have for many years advocated a biological-functional rather than pathological-anatomical conception of disease. This Osnato interprets /me/ as assuming that dementia praecox is a "functional psychosis" and that "therefore it occurs independently of any pathological changes in the body, including the brain." He then gives an apparent summary of my division of activities into mental and non-mental, marred by such a statement as "the non-nervous functions would include the various activities at physiological and psycho-chemical levels." "Meyer seems to believe . . . that the important factors in the production of all types of psychoses, excepting the organic, are not the secondary submental or non-mental changes, but the primary disorders of consciousness." He makes me "follow Freud and Jung." He finds certain statements "exasperatingly vague" and claims that I "dismiss" the neuropathological evidence; while he speaks of "pathological" evidence when he means anatomical and histological evidences etc. etc.

All this comes from the inability to accept the fundamental conceptions; a functional interpretation can be made of the most "organic" process. "Pathology" deals with function as well as structure.

Osnato's kindly admonition that I ought to acquire and show a knowledge of normal anatomy, both gross and histological, is certainly praiseworthy and I have made several efforts on my part to do something along that line. He gives me the compliment of very clear vision in assuming that mental disorders in the main are to be viewed from the psychobiological or psychodynamic, the metabolic and the structural viewpoint, but claims that I immediately proceed to forget in the discussion of dementia praecox all except the "collisions of functions with incidental disorders of the organic balance of these functions" — he is unable to see the physiological, physio-chemical and organic structural implications seriously.

I suppose one never should expose oneself to misinterpretations of this kind. The only way to avoid it is to take definite cases and facts and to discuss them from one end to the other as a fullfledged demonstration of one's vocabulary before one takes up a general discussion exactly as I proposed in my last letter with regard to the prototypes of fact from which to start in our more specialized problem. To consider that writers would consider it fair to suspend judgment until they would have read the essential contributions of a worker whom they undertake to criticize will undoubtedly become a habit among us in due time. I probably have been unwise in putting most of the fundamental discussions in the Psychological Bulletin and the Journal of Psychology which are not within the reach of physicians. Hence the frequent accusations of my being a reflector of Freud and Jung, and a man disregarding my /actual/ pet fields of comparative, normal and experimental anatomy and histology of the nervous system and autopsy-studies.

The points illustrate what you say of psychologically considered vs "psychic" facts. Our language is a crude tool.

Yours sincerely,
Adolf Meyer

1. Michael Osnato (1883–1952), New York neurologist, published "A Critical Review of the Pathogenesis of Dementia Praecox," *Neurological Bulletin* 1 (1918): 106–18.

31 M [M 10]

May 9, 1918

My dear Titchener:—

Your letter of May 4th reached me just before a discussion of the relation of overt and implicit psychobiological activity, and of the matter mentioned in the discussion of Dr. Osnato. I am really grateful because I think some points become better defined:

(1) brings us very much nearer together. I also feel that it is method that determines the pursuits, and not an epistemotology of some ultraerudite and overspiritualized or oversystematized Husserl type.[1] I accept the known and various groups of facts brought out by various methods.

(2) I realize that you want all existential experience approached psychologically, biologically and physically. We are in accord on this point /but since this distinction is one mainly of methods, the result should be an orderly side by side, not 3 totally different bodies of facts./ I go further and ask for the dependence on this or that person or genus of animal and that is where a "separate object" looms up with me. I compare facts from case to case, from man to man etc.; it is not the, but a nervous system or individual. I can conceive of the nervous system and human or animal individual /for the broadest issues and the system,/ but always study specific individuals and am willing to limit myself so as to be free of "astral" or other uncontrolled detachable products of introjections and ejects which Yerkes seems to provide for. I can see quite clearly my leaning towards objectivation, and it is there we /seem to/ diverge strongly. The reason is, however, fundamental on two counts: first for descriptive reasons already mentioned, viz. that I consider /the/ facts conditioned by specific individuals or genera and call them their "functions"; and secondly because I have to consider causal relations. Both for explanation and causal interpretation you are willing to refer to biology (or physiology and anatomy) as the "set" of the nervous system (with which I should include the sense organs and muscles and visceral mechanisms and their functions and the situation with its "stimuli"), because if we do not attend to them nobody will do it for us — hence the unitary treatment of what to me forms a unitary problem, psychobiology.

I was and am, of course, fully aware of the fact that Yerkes digresses from most parallelists by accepting "mental" causality. He treats you and Münsterberg alike on this point; and it is my "need" of "mental" or some sort of causation or causal consideration in "suggestion" and all through my "understanding" of conditions, that make me work with broader "units" or "combinations" fit for causal inquiries. /(Please forgive the terms "need" and "understanding" and "fit.")/

Now (/your letter/7) /(marked T7)/ [29T],[2] I do not get the point why we do not describe "functions" and "relations" as "facts." The distinction between the mode of being, of observable facts and "values," and existential, as opposed to "given," and why the positivistic streak should be objectionable — these are points to which I do not seem to react enough.

/My fundamental tenet is/ to study impartially, but I naturally am limited to /relatively/ definite problems.

The table of logical priorities does what I evidently objectivate /or recognize as given in fact/ in terms of integrative groups or entities or levels. At the same time I look upon biology /as the broadest field/ as embracing the psychology which is defined by the psychological methods, and the logic of the field is allowed to figure as a collateral problem, like a Hülfswissenschaft,[3] /i.e. part of the method of dealing with it./

(3) The "preferring" of any kind of world of course implies a free sense of the term, very much as when I speak of "nature's experiment" and of trial and error complexes. We can take it on faith that I do not mean to inject any naive options and purposes.

You consider the integration /as/ part of my method, where I consider it objectively as a condition of the facts to which I apply the method. I want to try and illustrate both the concept and the method.

Of course the first question is whether we recognize simple and compound facts, or even more definitely whether we recognize objects and situations as facts. Somehow some passages of your earlier letters make me still uncertain whether there might be some "epistemological" flaw in the matter. Take chemistry. Does or shall chemistry consider the substances with which it works, or haughtily claim that is [*sic*, it] is only concerned with the number recorded on the scale and the denominator of the mass in terms of the elements present?

It is a serious question to my mind whether it is not essential to recognize the call for independent objects to be studied as the "forces they are," partly to do justice to common-sense and to the pragmatic cohesions implied in such a plan and the logical simplicity ensuing from it. We have tended to get away from it and to talk disparagingly of the positivism involved because systematic attempts had been made to make the positivism of this type an all-embracing system and to claim that there was nothing else to be considered. By a process of overcompensation the other extreme has been attempted, the elimination of objects and a pure functionalism. The two have to work together. (I wonder if Lovejoy wants to hit this with his frequent claim that I want to eat the cake and have?)

Notes on Letter T7 (May 4th) [29T]

In T7 page 1/2 you say you "know of nothing which as object, — as thing, function, relation datum, experience in the concrete — is set apart for psychology, is intrinsically psychical." I suppose this is where my "positivism" comes in. All I can say in its favor is that it is not so absolute that it would have to exclude seeing anything else from a psychological point-of-view, or so absolute that my positivism would have to exclude psychology as we know it through you and those of similar view- point. I am willing to use current and critically safe psychologizing descriptions and terms and all the data which most psychologists single out as the data of their science. I do, however, use the terms so as to include the entire function or process, including situation and individual reaction, overt and implicit. I may use one sweeping term for what counts or is necessary for definition, and /for/ safety against error in experimental formulation, and <u>may</u> emphasize parts of function or process or may point to parts of the body and parts of situation specifically implicated. I certainly consider what I am talking about as "<u>there</u>" to whoever wants to, and can, study it as I do. In this sense data of science must always be objective, and potentially independent objects; and not all classes of possible objects in the existential world of experience are equally pertinent and obligatory for our consideration qua psychology. In a similar way I objectivate the logical priorities in terms of level of factual /and/ not merely methodological <u>objective integrations</u>, for the same reason that a fact of scientific experience must be accessible to any competent observer, with differences according to individual view-point but with recognition of the objective existence of the common topic or object of experience.

Your having finally fallen back on the "given" world of everyday common-sense is exactly what has been my <u>natural</u> trend and fate; only the world of science that comes from it is not so fundamentally different with me. Not by "preference" either in the sense of "unconditional choice" — but as far as preference comes from my type of logic and intellectual feeling and discrimination. You have excluded so much that I am afraid you have displaced yourself beyond what I consider obligatory for a /"natural/ science," a dynamic conception. Hence the elimination of causality and its relegation to the neurologist and physiologist and biologist who will make the best job of it if he knows how to formulate the psychobiological data before he begins to neurologize, physiologize and biologize. Where "essentially psychological" situations are assumed (with the implication that there are no absolutely psychological situations except in logic or abstract relations) and dynamic problems call for consideration, do you /separate/ psychology and its account of the facts? I do not, but consider the psychological facts of a specific type of integrations— /i.e. compounds of facts of a lower order forming a new system./

You say you "certainly cannot describe functions and relations." I take existential as equivalent to given = possible object of experience. This is part of my "neo-positivism," if I have to call it such, of my viewpoint of the world of more or less critical common-sense and of my scrupulously critical common-sense-science. You also admit the experiment, but as a show-case rather than as a test of "behavior," in the active play of causes and effects.

When you discuss my integration, you put a very liberal medley of "logical objects" "on my level of direct observation." /I have to/ let it pass, in terms of assets, resources, relations and functions /until I/ see what is "facts" of biology or psychology. The "integration" is /seen in the/ intrinsic consistency, notwithstanding the difference of denominators /subdivisions/ in the facts of the various levels (physics, chemistry, biology etc.) I may have to describe, and reduce to terms of dynamic experiments and formulations, situations and reaction complexes which go beyond our grasp of detail /of one level/ and beyond what we can prove /within it/; but that is the very job of science, to reduce more and more to terms of verified experiments /with due recognition of the different denominators./ It is not I who integrates, except in the sense of my recognizing the biological denominator of the psychobiological attitude and processes or reactions or actions. What then is my procedure?

The Müller-Lyer figure gives a more or less static example, in its way as static as the fact of the blind-spot or the facts in colorblindness, but evidently not anatomically conditioned, but much more probably connected with some laws of the role of motility and recognition of relations in spatial fusion /a point for hypothesis to be tried out by sets of experiments/. I can formulate a description of the facts; to go beyond into what you call the understanding or explanation, or what I call objectively the reduction to the essential factors of an experiment, is a matter of experimentation such as we all would arrange according to our grasp on methods and facts.

As to trial and error — it is a method; but it is also a fact in the maze experiments etc., i.e. an inevitable feature when we try to sum up the series of events which forms the unit of experiment.

Your instance illustrates what I give my students in connection with an anecdote concerning my late colleague Mall.[4] A candidate for examination in anatomy was waiting for him. Mall came in and skipped once or twice and asked: What muscles did I use? The skipping can be described psychobiologically — as type or part of what type of psychobiological activity, how acquired, with what "meaning?" i.e. requiring what setting to be intelligible or taking place with necessity? Or physiologically (with activation of what neuro-muscular functional processes) or anatomically (what muscles and parts involved?)

Perhaps (ad T7 p.6, 10) I should have said the "behavioristic standpoint" — with its various limitations and breadths. I might be called a behaviorist who does not damn psychology.

Now the examples in your own writings. The formulations I found most liberal are in your articles in the Int. Encyclopedia.[5] /But/ I shall read the Beginner's book once more.

When you say "If you are sufficiently interested" etc. (p. 7), you touch me with a /genuine feeling of/ <u>obligation</u> which I have to fulfil [*sic*] before I want to criticise or claim that I understand you. The difficulty must not be underrated. To do that for every coworker or writer is not easy. Such a formulation as sensation "is a logical construction whose components are aspects of existential experience observed from the psychological standpoint," might readily floor one and rouse comments which would not strike the essential or "primary attributive connex." To me it is discriminative and orientative <u>presentative activity</u> with the obligatory help of the sense organs, and I have to meet the function <u>and</u> the "content" — that which can also be "remembered." It almost <u>looks</u> as if we were both equally far from what the average mortal might think of first. /But which is closer?/

What you say of action and reaction and teleological leanings all shows the mutual difficulties. I may figure as a ridiculous optimist in failing to see in all these differences matters of keen interest rather than sources of hopelessness. But I really feel at heart that we are getting nearer a mutual understanding and that is /what/ we /both/ expect. "Nearer" does not necessitate absolute identity of views —

but more common ground than I at least had been led to expect and often intimated in discussions. We evidently come now to the discussion of how to dispose of the problems mentioned, of the problem of causal or dynamic formulation.

The feeling that /I/ might be getting into soliloquizing prompt my conscience to look over some of the ground covered:

The starting point of our discussion was Boring's statement: "Appetite can be adequately described only as a food-seeking attitude or meaning, a reaching-out-after food."

It is my task to so describe situations and attitudes, that I can see in them modifiable experiments, i.e. groupings of conditions, out of which certain reasonably definite results can be expected to arise, with the possibility of a methodical trial of modifications of the result by modifications of the factors of the experiment.

This is a reading of the world of experience in formulations which I consider fundamental in science, in terms of covariations as you put it.

Now you specify for a science the singleness of point of view over against existence, whereas I rather speak of a specific methodological approach /to facts arranged in groups of experimental formulation/ — i.e. formulating the facts and the method of approach in terms of experiments of a more or less specific kind. I see different issues, relations or processes involved in /sets of/ physical, chemical, broadly biological, physiological or psychological experiments. The characteristic issues make up what constitutes the science; objects, facts and relations are involved, more or less characteristic of each type of experiment. In this sense we cannot help recognizing not only methods of any given science but bodies of facts (objects, processes etc.).

A science merely of descriptive material without natural history events or processes, without fullfledged experimental situations, without causes and effects, conditions and results, to my mind is a merely descriptive or a logical function, not a fundamental science. A natural science as opposed to logic necessarily includes the formulation and working with experimental situations, /or the formulation of the facts in experimental terms./

According to T1 p.3, (5) [16T], common-sense entities carrying a psychological reference, are bound to be taken hold of by psychologists. Psychology would analyze them for what psychological facts /or factors/ they would reveal. Such a psychological fact is revealed in hunger; but not in appetite. What then is the psychological fact? Is it anything that can be said to behave in any specific way in terms of an experiment (— /the/ only safe and fullfledged element of what I call science)? We should study psychological references for facts capable of serving in /or being expressed by/ a methodologically characteristic experiment. How do we discount the overt "psychology" of common-sense? Could I get examples?

Reactive and constructive adaptation is characteristic of the prototype of biological experimentation, and it is so of that of psychobiological experiment as I see it.

In my letter of March 29th [17M] I tried to eliminate from the discussion the teleological and technological categories as not fundamental. The experimental formulation as the principle of any science and the fact that one deals with objective facts of a characteristic type of integration or unit formation makes the specific science.

My tendency to objectivation comes out in M2 p.4, (6) & (7) & (8) [17M]. My reason for the objectivation and the obliteration of several of your divisions including the parallelism are given in my reply to (9) M2 p.5. I do not share the appreciation of the term "meaning" as a substitute for the generally biological objective fact "attitude."

In this first reply (M2) I should have emphasized the demand for a formula dealing with events, processes etc. as the essential criterion of a "natural science" of to-day.

In T2 p.1, [18T] you give an example of a psychobiological act — which enters the field of view of many sciences, and must be reported by each one of them as that particular science sees it. I should say psychobiology views this "fact" in the light of an experimental situation which would with reasonable certainty lead to this result or imply this result.

When you then speak of parallelism existing between physics and biology and biology and psychology, you mark the relationship between my (objective) levels or types of integration. /Parallelism thus is an expression for a type of discontinuity in systems of facts which my concept of integration expresses in a positive way./

You then proceed (T2 p.2) to speak of subject matters of psychology and biology as dependent variables of the organism and of the environment respectively. Somehow there seems to me to be a flaw in this distinction. It cannot be carried out in a thorough-going manner, and especially so because you refuse consideration to the processes.

And with regard to the adequacy of the various types of description for the various degrees and types of integration, we should simply say that physics and chemistry do not approach the possibility of expressing economically and intelligibly, i.e. scientifically, facts which are simply and specifically expressed in terms of the pertinent level of integration with its special methodological approach. It is here (M3, p. 3 and 4) [19M] that I give my concept of integration and I ask the question why not obliterate the "parallelism" — and why not make one person responsible for the "facts," "values" and "meanings" when one deals with a clearly enough specified field? That such a person hits upon formulating a "psychobiology" should not do any harm to the more favored who can choose their problems to suit their system.

In T3 [20T], you attempted to show how my patient's attitude of distrust or Holt's act could be treated by psychology and neurology. My synthetic product or perhaps /rather/ my recognition of a special type of integration would nevertheless have to be on the spot, because according to you psychology does not deal in terms of cause and effect, whereas that sort of formulation (presentation in terms of conditions and results or cause and effects and their modifiability) constitutes my problem — quite objectively, without any humanitarian feature being involved of necessity. And here we simply run up against the inevitable part of objective teleological formulation.

On this point I have found the psychologist helpful in description, but only if he is willing to tackle situations as well as details. And that presupposes the dynamic formulation. The psychology obtained from you gives me the feeling of security that we deal with indicators of facts, real natural history facts, not matters of logical gymnastics of the older psychological types. But I admit my tendency to positivism. And in my position I go all the length that may be needed to do justice to the problems as I find them.

P.S.

In order to do justice to the correspondence, I have gone over the letters yesterday, numbering them M, 1–9 and T 1–7, so as to be able to refer to them correctly. I feel that we have made great strides towards mutually acceptable ground and mutual understanding and I begin to see more clearly what points to single out as most helpful in the discussion.

I suppose none is more fundamental than the placing of the scientific formula as most of the biological workers see it: 1) the reduction of facts to terms of a dependable experiment or series of experiments; 2) the subordination of description and the descriptive definition to the "behavioristic" definition, that of what a thing or fact does, that which it is as a factor. This is the first group of points.

The second group of points turns on the role of the method and of the type of fact one works with and the extent to which one emphasizes the limitation of occurrence and objectivation and the applicability of certain characteristic methods.

What is it that gives you something like an anaphylactic reaction when these two groups of issues come up? And what makes me cling to both groups? I suppose it is clearness and simplicity of definition and problems on your part and an experimental attitude on mine; cognition vs action? Can we say that either deserves the exclusive recognition? Cognition to me is orientative activity, activity is the broad formula in biology and in all the dynamic sciences as opposed to the logical descriptive sciences and formulations. We deal with formulations in terms of static descriptive logic and in terms of the logic of behavior, /of the experiment,/ the questions what and how and when — under what conditions?

The most important issue seems to be, What can be accepted as "fact?" To me it may be a logical descriptive /formulation/ or an actualistic formulation /in terms of/ data which can enter the experiment. I am willing to accept /even/ highly complex units, beside the simple units such as relation, activity, etc. which seem to suggest some impropriety to your formulations.

Do these contrasts touch vital points or would you recast the questions and contrasts?

In the mean time I hope to read your Beginner's Psychology again. I note the summary statement on p. 18,[6] and wonder whether I shall get examples of the working out of these problems, or how my formulation would meet them. I also remember the discussion of the brain-habit p. 117, your emphasis of context and my inference that that expressed my call for sufficiently broad units to command the context. And since nobody is interested in these pertinent physiological processes, I have to formulate them myself and add them to my psychobiological program in terms of action complexes, record of past behavior and systematic biography.

I am afraid this tripple [*sic*] installment of discussion should be recast. A few marginal notes will mark the order and points.

It is a great satisfaction to have the helpful stimulus for clarification of the positions. I shall try to furnish more positive definitions. Perhaps these jottings contain a few.

Very truly yours,
Adolf Meyer

1. Edmund Husserl (1859–1938), German philosopher, in an attempt to overcome mind-body dualism in the early part of the century, introduced a transcendental phenomenological approach in psychology. Meyer briefly touched on Husserl's views in his review, "Pathopsychology and Psychopathology" (1912), *CP*, 2:640–53.

2. At this point in the correspondence Meyer began referring back to earlier letters in the 1918 series, which he numbered, with some gaps which we have closed, from the first in that series through 38T. He used his initial followed by the number in the series to refer to his own letters, and Titchener's initial followed by the number in the series to refer to Titchener's letters. To aid the reader, references to Meyer's numbering system are followed by references to our own.

3. Hülfwissenschaft = auxiliary science.

4. Franklin P. Mall (1862–1917), first professor of anatomy at the Johns Hopkins Medical Institutions.

5. Meyer refers to Titchener's several articles on psychology in *The New International Encyclopedia*, 2d ed., ed. by F. M. Colby and T. Williams (New York: Dodd, Mead, and Co., 1914–17).

6. Titchener's summary statement reads: "In fine, then, the problem of human psychology is threefold: to analyse mental phenomena into their elements, to discover the laws of mental connection and to work out in detail and under all its phases the correlation of mind with the nervous system" (*Beginner's Psychology*, 18).

32 T [T 8]

May 13, 1918

Dear Meyer,

There is a lot of detail here! But I think we are getting somewhere, and I will try to stick to fundamentals.

(1) I can't of course see anything in the distinction of "static" and "dynamic." The distinction comes from the older Newtonian physics; and if I remember aright, Tait[1] persuaded Kelvin[2] to give up the term "dynamics" in the Treatise. In the older physics (and it may be today for purposes of the elementary physical instruction; though I doubt that) the distinction was (and may still be) useful. But it is essentially a physical (interdependent) distinction, without sense in biology proper or in psychology proper. A great deal of harm is done, I think, by

this transference of terms from one universe to another: witness the transfer of "evolution" from biology to all sorts of other places. If you mean something quite special by dynamic, then give me your definition! I don't think you have the right to use an old-time physics-word, out of its context historical and other, and to assume that we shall all understand it. (I believe I said this in my critique of Watson; I have said it in print somewhere!)

(2) Experiment to me too is all-important. Experiment is, however, two-fold. It is a plan for an observation. As a plan, it is logical; as a plan-for, it is teleological; it moves so far in the logical realm of ground-and-consequence. As an observation, on the other hand, it bears directly upon fact, and is in the strictest sense therefore scientific. If we were all Copernicuses and Newtons, we might perhaps be able to observe directly, without recourse to the plan: though even Newton used experimental observation for his optical work. What science gets out of the experiment is, in any event, the Fact Observed; all the rest is detail, important only as a procedure whereby other men may get easily and accurately to the same Fact Observed; and indeed a great deal of our time is spent in so simplifying and modifying an original experimental procedure that our students and coworkers may get at the same Fact Observed more easily and more accurately than we or our predecessors have done. What are our "standard" instruments other than embodiments of logical safeguards of observation?

All this seems to follow from the pertinency of the question: WHY do we experiment? We experiment BECAUSE we can't get our facts by "unaided" observation. If we could, we should never dream of going to the trouble of experimenting. But the pertinency of WHY and BECAUSE means that logic (procedure by ground and consequence) is involved. All experimenting means that we argue and plan prior to observing.

(3) I don't explain or causally relate at all, at all! In science all the "explanation" that there is for me is the correlation of a dependent with a (logically prior) independent variable. In psychology the logically prior is biology, in biology the logically prior is physics. In physics we set up independent variables for /intra-physical/ methodological purposes, and what figures as dependent in one context figures as independent in another: we have in fact only interdependences. So if I "explain" psychology by biology, that means very simply that I take the biological as independent variable in any case where correlation is involved. I use the word "explanation" to stu-

dents just to show them that there is nothing in science like the "accounting for," "giving a reason for," which is the meaning of the word in logic. Causality I regard as mythological, — if you mean by it anything more than correlation.

Parallelism is the historical antecedent of this doctrine of correlation, and as such is preferable to interaction, which skips from one logical universe to another. But the parallelism of objects (neural things and psychical things) I take to be transcended.

(4) You can't observe a relation, I should say, because your cogbitive [*sic*, cognitive] attitude is different and less simple than in the case of facts. A relation is a meaning, and you "apprehend" (not "observe") it. So with function, use, adaptation, &c. In apprehending a relation you are already interpreting.

The basis of correlation is simply: If A changes, B changes. As soon as you devote yourself to the relation itself, instead of (or in addition to) A and B, you are interpreting. You then say: The RELATION of B to A is that of functional adaptation, or of useful application, or what not; and that is an interpretation. You "apprehend" such a relation.

(5) Chemistry will take up its special point of view, as a subordinate point of view to the general physical standpoint of interdependence, and will then have the right to consider as chemical subject-matter <u>whatever it can see</u> from that point of view. Here perhaps a further word will help clear things.

The sciences are differentiated by point of view. It is obvious, however, that when a science has described, from its point of view, for any length of time, what is visible from that point of view, — when it has done this, it will have <u>amassed</u> a special subject-matter. Thenceforward it is possible, logically, to define the science by its subject-matter, — this subject-matter being, evidently, the transcript of existential experience as made from the determined point of view, and therefore being strictly correlative with (and indicative of) the point of view. So that, if one wanted to define physics today by reference to "atoms and electrons," I should have no objection in principle: I should say: "Very well, — that means that if you regard existential experience interdependently, you come out with facts that are most economically described as atoms and electrons." I should object if it were implied that atoms and electrons are lying around in the world as objects to be picked out from the other and unlike objects of the world by the physicist who is in search of them. Because the physicist is precisely <u>not</u> in search of any particular kind of thing! — he describes whatever he can see from his physical standpoint; and what he sees turns out /(in the hypothetical case here adopted)/ to be describable as atoms and electrons. So definition by subject-matter is possible, as logically posterior to point of view; not otherwise.

So with chemistry. If your chemist finds that he sees "substances," then let him say so, and describe his substances. If he finds that the substances, which he thought he saw at first, evaporate into quantitative variations of a single substance, let him say that. We shall accept his report, as we accept that of the physicist, as being the most economically phrased description he can give of his purview. Only he certainly must not give us a statement of subject-matter which overlaps (say) the subject-matter of biology: if he does, we shall be obliged to say to him: You have left your chemical standpoint, and are mixing up two logically distinct things.

I have not raised before this issue of posterior definition by subject-matter because I feared it would complicate the issues already in debate. But perhaps now it will help. Existential experience, regarded in different ways, becomes different subject-matters as the sciences advance and their reports of existence grow in detail. But, once again, since the subject-matters thus emerging are correlative with point of view, they cannot (on the scientific level) be integrated interchangeably, item of one science with item of another; you cannot (to be extreme) compose a situation out of electron, mammal, perception — because you get to these three things only by way of the adoption of different standpoints.

So I should say you cannot have at once before you, in science, "essentially psychological situations" and "dynamic problems." If there is any such thing as an essentially psychological situation (and I can make that phrase intelligible: when e.g. I am sitting in the laboratory ready for a particular observation), then I should think it was incompatible with anything in the way of a "dynamic problem" — though I very honestly don't know what that means, unless it is a practical problem in real life. — If again I find a situation in real life which appeals to me (as psychologist) as affording, if psychologised, good lecture or text-book material, then I change it over at once from the concreteness of real life to science; and certainly there is nothing left of it that I could call dynamic; I wholly psychologise it.

(6) You ask me, as I asked you, what is your method of integration! I don't know, unless it is common sense.

Suppose I ask for the common-sense notion of a particular tree. I may be told: that it was put here on the roadside for shade, that it is an elm, that it would make 8–inch planks, that the botanists up there at the university could tell me a lot about it, that it was set out by so-and-so when he was developing the place for real estate, that it had the beetle last year and probably will have it this, and it looks ragged on one side because of the prevailing winds, that it must make the house dampish, that the householder ought to have the lower branches lopped, etc., etc. That is a common-sense "integration," — and it seems to me that yours is of the same order, except of course that you have an intermixture of various scientific knowledge which the man in the street lacks; but there is no question that you are "nearer to the average mortal" than I am! Thus, your definition of sensation seems to me to involve psychology (content), physiology (sense-organs), general biology (orientative), logic (discriminative; obligatory help), theory of knowledge (presentative activity, has to be remembered), and all of these things /seem to be/ given a common-sense colour, or set in a common-sense matrix.

(7) Many of your recent queries are, I think, old ground: though if my first replies didn't bite I am very willing to try again. Thus, I have admitted that many of the problems we take up in our laboratories are forced on us by history, by another science, etc. Among these is the question of the psychology of nausea, hunger, thirst, appetite, lust. Popular psychology distinguishes all these as psychological; that is, the traditional common-sense psychology does; and recently physiologists have been dealing with the physiology of them. Now we take them up scientifically, and we find that there is nothing constant in the subject-matter of psychology that can be called "appetite," though there is such a constant that can be called "hunger." In other words, appetite is not visible from the psychological point of view, while hunger is. We judge therefore that, in so far as appetite comes within the field of view of any science (as the physiologists tell us it does for them), it is a biological and not a psychological thing. Had the sciences been working in isolation, biology would have found appetite, psychology would not. Where is the difficulty?

The psychological "fact" of hunger is the uniformly observable pain-pressure, definitely localised, which we find whenever the organism is "hungry" in common-sense terms. There is no such /uniform/ fact observable when the organism (in the same common-sense terms) "has an appetite." We can give a psychologically descriptive reading of hunger, but not of appetite. It is precisely because common sense makes these mistakes that the "found" cannot be identified with the "existential," — meanings and values out of the question.

I pass to your postscript.

(1) You want to see "the reduction of facts to terms of a dependable experiment." I say that facts are got from experiment. Experiment is logically controlled observation; and observation is the method that bears directly upon (correlated) fact. Facts are things you have to get; not things at all that are given. Given are common-sense interpretations. Very few people can observe; and so very few people get directly acquainted with facts.

(2) You want, not to describe, but to find what a fact "does." For me a fact doesn't do and can't do anything. Only when logic transforms it into a meaning can it "do" or appear as "factor" in a complex of ground-and-consequence. As thus transformed, it can "do" a thousand things and never get exhausted; it can do not only what you want done but what all sorts of other people want done. But this doing is not science: no doing is science, nor can ever be; doing involves cause-and-effect /(or, at least, ground and consequence)/ and other logical procedures that we read into the facts. I want, not to make facts do, but to ascertain and describe them.

(3) I don't believe in types of fact or limitations of method. I believe that every science covers descriptively all of existential experience from a certain standpoint. I believe that every science uses all the logical methods that there are, though at various periods of their history special sciences may prefer special methods (I mean their representatives may): that is an accident of growth. Comparison, discrimination, induction, deduction, analogy, — whatever they may be, science as system makes use of /all/ these logical procedures.

(4) Relations and activities are not facts, and are not observable. They are inferential, interpretative. The scientific system employs them, if it wants them, — though I had hoped that "activity" was dead! It employs them, however, in its logical constructions; it does not — because it cannot — enter them as observable facts. All that science can say is: If fact A changes, fact B changes. But this is very different from saying "The relation of functional dependence of B on A is itself observable fact." That relation, if it is handled at all in the system, is handled as inference from observations.

(5) I do not see that there can be any question of "what we accept as facts." Facts are stubborn things; we dig for them, by controlled observation, and they appear. If we refuse to accept them, we simply suffer for it. If we allow our logic to suffuse, penetrate, modify, colour, contaminate them, we suffer for that. Reverence for the fact is the great lesson of science, and we have to be meticulously careful nei-

ther to add nor to abate in dealing with fact.

(6) You are right, of course, in thinking that my dominant ambition is to be clear. Muddle I take to be the great enemy of scientific as of other thinking. Provided that the same fundamental honesty in [*sic*, is] given in both cases, I had rather be clear and wrong than muddled and (so far as that comports with muddlement) right.

(7) All positivism seems to me to be muddled in that it puts /e.g./ scientific fact, literary appreciation, logical relatedness, all on the same level of immediacy for cognition, and all in the same straight line of methodological procedure. To say that all three are "given" is a triviality, if not pressed, and an error (in my view), if taken pregnantly. What I find given is the medley of common sense. Then my scheme is something like this:—

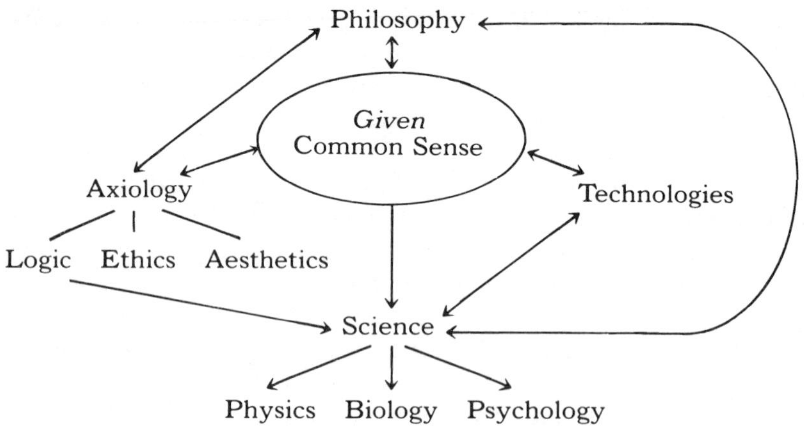

I have not the least quarrel with philosophy: on the contrary, I think that philosophy is bound someday to see that her problem is integration and method of integration, and that she has been struggling toward that problem these many centuries. I have no personal quarrel with positivism, and I should never dream of any public controversy with it; it is an entirely respectable position; only I can't accept it, because I think that, like materialism (though at a different point), it muddles. So I do not accept absolute idealism either, because although that does not muddle, it dogmatises: a lesser sin, for me, than muddle, but still a real sin.

What I have set myself to do is to study the history of what is called "science," and to see if, under all the ramifications and vagaries of this title, I could get at something essential, constant, uniform, persistent, — something that all scientific men approximate, though some blindly and blunderingly, some explicitly and clearly. I hope that now I have it. I have no idea of reform: people will still go on calling all sorts of mixed things "science," and I do not mind — it would be useless if I did, but in point of fact I don't. What I hope to do is to trace the lines of this essential core of science clearly, so that those who are interested as I am myself can use me as a preliminary guide in their own work, and be saved the trouble that I have had in getting to a clear-cut view. Primarily, however, I have worked — as I suppose we all do — for my own soul's sake and not for other people; I could not be happy if I had not made the solid effort to be clear.

I am sitting then (or trying to take my seat) at the innermost heart of science, of all science: you are working with individual cases and individual situations out towards the periphery of science, where uses and values and relations and facts intermix and the sorting has not yet been done. I don't suppose that the one task is easier than the other, or that the one result is more "valuable" than the other. A man pitches in where he sees his problem most clearly and where he feels that his powers are most available. Only we can't expect to see eye to eye, since our environments and routes have been so different!

You "find"	all experience
I "observe"	all existential experience
You "find"	different kinds of objects
I "remark"	different modes of approach to the same existential experience
You "observe"	everything given
I "observe"	only fact, and "apprehend" meaning

and so on. As you now say, I think we have got to a fair degree of mutual understanding. I can even understand, after your last letter, that the precise definitions, essential to me, which I have asked from you, might actually be a hindrance to you, and that it is more practical for you to leave yourself loose edges.

Yours sincerely,
E. B. Titchener

1. Peter Guthrie Tait (1831–1901), Scottish physicist and mathematician, was author of the well-known *Sketch of the History of Thermodynamics* (1868). Cf. n.2, below.

2. William Thomson, Lord Kelvin (1824–1907), physicist, was professor of natural philosophy at Glasgow University from 1845 until his retirement. Titchener's reference is to Kelvin's influential *Treatise on Natural Philosophy* (1867), written jointly with Peter Guthrie Tait.

33 M [M 11]

May 17, 1918

My dear Titchener,

T8 [32T] proves to be a document which goes very helpfully to the core of some of the contrasts. It brings out the differences of temperament especially with regard to the extent to which the system of facts or system of words, and the system of direct clearness and simplicity or the demand for fundamental coherence, dominates. To you the simplicity attained by your method of psychologizing tends towards a doctrine of exclusive salvation where I feel a largely collateral science is erected — one with a perspective too radically opposed to what a broader psychobiological conception may attain in time. I can agree with many of your points in principle where I diverge radically in the execution and in the choice of starting points. I feel the consistency of your scheme, /but/ I feel as consistent in mine. I find you persisting in some contrasts which I obliterate in order to obtain new lines of attack and new contrasts.

It clearly becomes my own task to state dynamic problems; to formulate what integration is in my conception. Your dissection of my formulation of sensation is especially instructive with regard to your point of view and the great difference of my psychobiological program. The question is whether I really become guilty of mixing incompatible issues, or whether I merely use references which may readily be borne in mind no matter what science or issue one may be specifically concerned with. After all, psychology, physiology and biology and logic, and a functional characteristic in the mention of which you prefer to see theory of knowledge, can almost be read from the term "psychobiology."

As to the appreciation of clearness, we also agree. But we differ somewhat on the lines along which we should suspect or actually spot "muddle." Consistency and directness is my standard of clearness and avoidance of unnecessary complications. I have always admitted the logical consistency of parallelism and its substitutions, but I also maintain it emphasizes a point of subordinate importance.

Your discussion sub 7 gives a good illustration of some concrete differences of interest. I am interested in appetites; you prefer to exclude them from your field; I am not averse to compounds and appreciate Boring's drawing the attention to the difference between hunger with its constant nucleus and appetite with its inconstancy of detail. And I am tolerant of "ground-and-consequence" relations such as you mention on p. 7 sub (2). I do not limit methods and types of facts; that comes quite automatically. Relations may or may not be fundamental psychological data; Dunlap favors them as such; others pass them by. Activities might be dead and should be, if inference and the recognition of compounds are not permitted in the logic of science.

What you say of reform on p.9 is quite true. And yet, clear contrasts will attract certain groups of followers, and stimulate new departures; many a one "sitting at the innermost heart of his science" drawing the Thing as he sees It for the God of Things as They Are!

As to the precise definitions — I really think of formulations oftener than of definitions.

Such a definition would be what figures to me as "dynamic." I contrast dynamic with logical. The one necessarily deals with energies, with functions of things; the other deals with functions of words as signs.

Experimental formulation is such an arrangement and interpretation of one's facts as will include its own test in terms of "cause and effect," "ground and consequence," or "conditions and results." Explanation in terms of such formulation does not necessarily have to go outside of one field as long as the integrated units of another level can be taken for granted. As you formulate psychology, yes; but not as I formulate psychobiology. There is no mythological causality about this.

I sincerely hope that I have not bored you with my bias and with the very hastily formulated discussions. I certainly feel I understand the evolution of your viewpoint much more clearly. I can see its logical attractiveness; and the attractiveness of the types of problems to a certain extent. You probably have not had the same desire or call to draw out the essentials of my own position. That may be due to the difference of our respective fields of concrete experience and work and also to the fact that I have /not/ formulated in print as much as I have had an opportunity to see of your own work.

With it all, I still wish I could get as many standard problems and standard situations as you see them as possible so as to saturate myself with their possibilities, and it may be that I /may/ get more of my own problems into such shape as would give them an appeal to your own human curiosity — the kind of inner drive which forces one to heed more of one type of thing or more of another in the effort to be true to one's demand for intellectual clearness and in accord with the facts. If I have not been "clear" in my formulations it may be that it has been partly due to the fact that we use similar words in two systems of thought and should always make sure that the fundamental conception (with me the equivalent of causal or conditional formulation) receives due credit. In the matter of precise definitions, for instance, I do not feel guilty of self-indulgence, but I accept the facts as they are.

I wish very much I could get your criticism of Watson.[1] He gave it to me once; but that and kindred utterances from you have often been inaccessible to me except by some favorable accident and I should appreciate a reprint if you could spare one, or a reference. I certainly am very grateful to you for the helpful spirit in which you have given me unsparingly of your time and of your thought matured under an admirable self-discipline. I wish I might some day be able to reciprocate in a measure.

Very truly yours
Adolf Meyer

1. Titchener, "On 'Psychology as the Behaviorist Views It,'" *Proceedings of the American Philosophical Society*, 53 (1914): 1–17.

34 T [T 9]

May 20, 1918

Dear Meyer,

I was a little afraid of all that detail! This is our danger-point — the point at which we agreed to differ in our previous correspondence. We have reached the point far more slowly, however, this time; and the slowness of approach may help us to get over the line on this occasion.

First, now, a general remark. Aren't you a little inclined to think that, because I cut my logical lines sharp and clear, and try to know definitely where I am in any particular research-milieu, I therefore can't take account of — or can't be interested in — what lies outside? Aren't you disposed to think that when I "relegate" (as you say) this or that item to this or that non-psychological context, I therefore wash my hands of it, as if it ceased to exist for me? So that "clear" thinking tends to become "narrow" or "exclusive" thinking? — It seems to me that you have this undercurrent in your attitude to me; and I am sure I don't blame you. Only, as a matter of fact, what I find in practice is that my drawing of logical lines opens the universe to me, and gives me an assured outlook on problems which, as an old-fashioned psychical psychologist, I really used to fight shy of, and be a little afraid of. I don't mean, of course and of course, that I know very much about anything; life is particularly short. But I do mean that, since I began to get my inductions from the history of science, I am not afraid in principle, in logic, of facing any problem that can come up. And so far from any curtailment of interest, I find that my whole range of interests widens (with understanding of the human points-of-view) — widens in an almost embarrassing way.

Of course I can see, e.g., a problem in "relations." The very last doctorate thesis, that I examined on last Saturday, is a study of the so-called "feeling of relation" in psychology.[1] The very last minor study that I sent in to the American Journal is a study of the way in which Charles Dickens chose his proper names for his novels.[2] Another doctorate thesis, just completed, shows how and why schoolmen and physicians have varied so profoundly in their estimates of the effect of practice and fatigue on the cutaneous two-point limen:[3] by deliberately adopting the common-sense, as distinct from the psychological, point of view we have been able to reconcile and logically to explain all the medley of divergent results that the technical men have been obtaining. There then is a strictly technological experiment, done in my laboratory, for the sake of clearing things up both within and without psychology. Also it was I who put Boring first on to Head's absurd cutaneous theory and later on to the organics, and every word that he published had been gone over and approved by me before the MS went to the printer; I want him next, in cooperation with the physiologists, to take up a big study of Emotion; and he is preparing (or was when he left me) — again at my suggestion — a book on the principles underlying the study of psychologically abnormal cases. So my experience has been, that the more clearly you can think the more (and the more varied) problems are you capable of tackling. Look at the range of subjects represented in my memorial volume! — from psychology of religion to blindfold chess, and from theory of comparative psychology to the problem of waking at a predetermined hour in the morning, and from the logic of meaning to mental tests of defectives. Most of those studies had been definitely suggested by me, and several had been actually supervised by me (in complete ignorance of their destination).

So far from feeling that I am hemmed in, therefore, by my logical rigour, I feel on the contrary that the position is immensely fertile. I once asked a close friend of a certain psychologist X why X had resigned his position in psychology and had gone over into education. Oh, the reply came, X ran out of problems! — Whereas my difficulty is to find enough time and enough students to carry through even a fraction of the problems that come up in every chapter of the psychological system. I have always believed in the test of Gallio [sic, Galileo] — that if a position is of God, it will prove endlessly fertile; while if it is of man, it will prove barren and tie you up in a cul-de-sac.

I don't, on the other hand, want to make converts. I think that the great majority of any generation cannot and will not think clearly, and that all one can do is to follow out one's light for oneself. To think clearly means years of worrying, and more reading than one likes to look back on. It means therefore a strong animal constitution, and what our enemies call Sitzfleiss [*sic*, Sitzfleisch].[4] Its reward is interior and not external; one keeps in touch with at most a scant half-dozen of likeminded Strebers[5] — and with them one necessarily disagrees on many points! — I have a very great respect accordingly for any man who honestly works, even if he comes out at a wide remove from me; I had very good talks with Freud, and respect him immensely, though I think his psychology is antediluvian and his constructions largely precarious; but he is a man who has worked and thought and suffered; and I have no stomach for controversy with him, — all the more as the future will finally decide as to what is good and sound in both of us.

All this, then, by way of re-orientation! I don't want you (since you are definitely interested in my ideas of Science) to confuse logical rigour with narrowness of problem-choice. I venture to say that, in the list of experimental studies published in the Bibliography at the end of my memorial volume, there is a wider range of topics than in any similar list that the country could show; and the studies made by other officers of instruction here (not published in that list) were in the great majority of cases inspired by me. So soon as I find myself running dry of problems, I will come over to you and be a psychobiologist!

Now a few words on the letter.

(1) I doubt if there are in either of our fields any "incompatible issues." Because an "issue" implies meaning, and you can integrate

meanings to any extent. It is points of view (and correlated facts) that, as simultaneous, are incompatible.

(2) Activities are, of course, "permitted in the logic of science." But as involving inference they are in the nature of the case logically posterior to fact. I have no objection to them as inferences, i.e., as post-observational, interpretative.

(3) Experiment is for you an "arrangement and interpretation of facts." For me it is a means of discovering, getting at facts. You appear to have your facts before you experiment.

(4) You define dynamic by contrast with logical. I take that to mean that dynamic and logical exhaust a certain universe, which is (so to say) divided between them. But you do not name that universe. Is it experience at large?

You say that the dynamic necessarily deals with energies. (a) Is the necessity logical? Hardly, because dynamic is contrasted with logical. Of what sort then is it? (b) Energy is a physical term. Are you not using it metaphorically, — and if so does it not call for definition?

You say that the dynamic deals necessarily with functions of things. (a) Do you mean in the sense of logical function? Hardly, again. Then in what sense do you use "function"? (b) Things is not a scientific term, but a common-sense or a philosophical term. A "thing" is not the scientific vehicle of an "energy."

You say that the logical deals with the functions of words as signs. (a) How then does it differ from a dictionary? (b) What is your reason for implying that a "word" is not a "thing?" (c) Is the word "function" used in the same sense here as before? (d) What are the words signs "of"? —

I can see what you might mean by dynamic if you have in mind the play and counterplay of motives, the push and pull of circumstances, the weighing of considerations for and against, the balancing of reasons on the one side and the other, the struggle of conflicting tendencies within a given organism and a given experience, and so on. But that is all popular and interpretative, a matter of "casuistry" (logical and ethical) in the technical sense of casuistry; worlds away from anything scientific, and patently and obviously teleological and technological! None the worse for that, if recognised as such: on the contrary, material for a careful handling with promise of positive result; wholly worthy of study. My lack of comprehension begins when you make the claim of a scientific meaning for the term "dynamic," — then I have to ask for definitions. And then your explanatory statements seem to me to bristle with points of interrogation.

Let me repeat that for me science /covers/ a very small part of the total universe of the given. If you adopt a wider definition of science, you are doing what the great majority of people do at the present day, and you are therefore far nearer the general sense of the community than I am. But, if you bother about science at all, then I think you are under obligation to give your definitions. We can either say: We are doing different things, and we can respect each other professionally; or we can say: We are aiming to do the same thing, and so must understand each other. In the latter case, — which I take to be your alternative, — definition of terms is essential.

I send very gladly a copy of my Watson paper.

Yours sincerely,
E.B. Titchener

1. Josephine Mixer Gleason, "An Experimental Study of 'Feelings of Relation'," *American Journal of Psychology* 30 (1919): 1–26.

2. E. De Laski, "The Psychological Attitude of Charles Dickens toward Surnames," *American Journal of Psychology* 29 (1918): 337–46.

3. Cora L. Friedline, "The Discrimination of Cutaneous Patterns below the Two-Point Limen," *American Journal of Psychology* 29 (1918): 400–19.

4. Sitzfleisch = perseverance; the term is normally used pejoratively.

5. Strebers (Titchener anglicizes the word) = strivers, pushers.

35 M [M 12]

May 23, 1918

My dear Titchener,

Your appeal to a spirit of fairness on my part /does/ indeed /contain/ a goodly array of points which show that definition need not paralyze human interest. It may be that at times I had a feeling of undue exclusiveness on your part, undoubtedly more owing to the conclusions of the past than owing to the present status. The question is now: Is there but one possible offshoot of the order of sciences which figures in the history of science as you see it, or would a realinement [*sic*, realignment] such as mine have any kind of chance to acquire a status?

To begin with (1) of T9 [34T] p.4. You say there is no trouble about integrating "issues" because issues are "meanings"; only points of view (and correlated facts) are compatible, as simultaneous. My conceptions deal with one point of view and one world of existential experience and various sets of integration determined by definite sets of methods and types of subdivision of the facts and relations so brought out. It then remains a question whether what mixture of entities of various realms of integration occur in any statement, are used in an incompatible way or not. Incompatible mixing can happen, to be sure; the critique obligatory in all common-sense will have to eliminate such blunders.

(2) To speak of activities as mere inferences and as post-observational is an inference from your system of definitions. I wish I could get hold of as many representatives as possible of what you call "facts" to make sure whether the exclusiveness you have created is essentially justified or mainly a resetting of the data of the "old-fashioned psychical psychologist" with as little modification of the content of your science as possible, but a liberal adoption of a number of "universes" transcending the naive parallelisms without disturbing the patterns. /We/ naturally wish to reduce your fundamental formulas to a minimum of factors. What these are and why the limit is imposed should become clear out of the facts at hand and grouped together in your systems.

I assume that just as in mechanics the concept of motion figures as the essence of kinematics, without any denial of its being open to observation, so activity can be accepted as a fundamental concept representing observable facts, although either of these "facts" can be subdivided into series of part observations which need not imply actual motion, but mere differences of position. The possibility of such reduction to geometry-like formulas is no reason why we should not also work with motion as observed and as studied in its actual process and effects.

(3) Experiment is used in two senses: you seem to use it only in the sense of "experimentation"; whereas I use it in the sense closer to the etymological form as experimentum, the accomplished trial, or its formulation. It brings out the facts and shows them in their factual and not merely logical relations.

(4) Here, of course, we might readily cross in space without intersection unless we heed the difference of the two starting points. I have the one ("objective") viewpoint towards the one existential universe and note in it facts integrated in dynamic systems beside systems which mark only logical relations consisting in functions of words or signs, in contrast to functions of things.

[(a)] In saying that the "dynamic" necessarily deals with energies (and, I add, with functions of things), the "necessity" is factual, i.e., it /simply/ does not occur otherwise; wherever I might come across energy which is not a function of a thing or things I should have to look for a new category or a new formulation. It would be easy to modify the formulation if one should dissolve the complex and try to speak of energy as such as the component out of which things are bound to consist; but I do not consider it wise to make obligatory a system of absolute energetics. If facts should point that way, I do not see that I should have to modify my statement except by qualifying "things." For the time being I am specially concerned with the inference from our present data and there are no facts in favor of assuming a psychobiological "energy" detachable from living organisms. Why cater to the yearning for telepathy and spirits?

(b) To you energy is a physical term. To me it is a fundamental term belonging to all "natural sciences" as opposed to the sciences of logic and of adynamic relations /generally/. With your parallelistic differentiation according to "viewpoints," you naturally create a system of /psychological/ processes devoid of energetic and causal connotation, and that I find the great disadvantage of your formulation, what I consider an unnecessary and complicating systematization and emphasis. I suppose that is where Pillsbury[1] and his "functional" concept diverges from you.

Now when we come to functions of things, we face the term function in the sense in which biology and physiology uses it and in which "action" is a more specific and autonomous equivalent. And "thing" is used in the sense of the unit of matter under question, in this case evidently a unit capable of a function.

And "logical" refers to functions of words as signs or to signs of a systematized kind practically or actually constituting that which constitutes logic in our experience.

(a) A dictionary has no concern for the system which has the specification "logic." (b) A word may be a thing if handed to you in metal or on a paper; but that is evidently (i.e. readily seen with critical common sense) not the sense in which the term is used. No system of expression unless it be created ad hoc can be used without that "critical common sense." To use a drastic phrase, no system can be considered fool-proof. Hence why not cultivate the critical common sense quite frankly? (c) Function evidently is used here in the somewhat broader but not essentially different sense of dependence. In logic (and mathematics) dependence of a controllable kind is spoken of as function, and the dependence occurring in biology as "function" is a more than logical, viz. a dynamic function. The apparent shifting of the sense is conditioned purely by the facts at hand, without any change of "viewpoint," and without any call for specific definition after the fundamental principle of my formulation (one viewpoint, one existential universe and various systems of facts) is stated. (d) What words are "signs" of — is similarly determined by the "context" and the facts at hand, the situation. Grammatical construction answers part of the question and where, as so often in English, the reference like the gender of person must be inferred, the topic of discussion creates the explanatory and determining setting.

The casuistry which you collect for the illustration of "dynamic" refers only to very complex types; to my mind, all "processes" (to use your word in the Beginner's Psychology) are dynamic as opposed to the static concept of mere disposition or organization (or mechanism, which has become unduly popular). Here, of course, I am bound to be met by the suspicion of non-permissible teleology, where I frankly accept teleological formulation in scientific statements: in the "formulation in terms of an experiment"; that it may refer to technological issues is possible and logical in my system of presentation, because technology is not a fundamental category of fact and data, but really an issue of application.

You evidently are forced to say that my formulations are incompatible with science as you see it. And yet, would it not be possible to /consider it as/ "science as Meyer formulates /it/." Neither your formulation nor mine is generally accepted or perhaps even generally acceptable. The question is: Are the two intelligible and consistent, and which one is used in a specific presentation or discussion?

Am I coming nearer definition? If not, go for me. I shall not resent any amount of questioning of my position and shall honestly try to get the "common foundations" from which we may ultimately find ourselves diverging — each in his way: each willing to accept the judgment of trial, and asking primarily for clearness and consistency. I admit the radical break with a past (and present) which I can respect but after all, steer clear from.

Many thanks for your helpful questions.

Sincerely yours,
Adolf Meyer

1. Walter Bowers Pillsbury (1872–1960), a student of Titchener at Cornell, was professor of psychology, University of Michigan from 1897 to 1942. Best known for his book *L'Attention* (1906; English translation 1908). Meyer's reference is to Pillsbury's *A Psychology of Reasoning* (1910) in which he argued that thinking is a function which is performed only when there is some definite

occasion. Pillsbury's account of the reasoning process was analogous to that of Dewey in the latter's *Studies in Logical Theory* (1903) and *How We Think* (1910).

36 T [T 10]

May 25, 1918

Dear Meyer,

A thought has just occurred to me as illuminating, after the reading of your present letter. Doesn't our great difference amount to this:—

That you regard things, situations, objects, as literally "given," and therefore "found" by the investigating mind, just as they are, just as they lie: so that the mind aforesaid may bring to bear upon them whatever methods of research it regards as profitable for theory or practice;

whereas I (so to say) run the "objects" and the "investigating mind" together, in such wise that for me nothing is literally given and nothing therefore is nakedly found; but in every case the object dealt with is a function of the method which deals with it?

You then can treat all sorts of things "biologically" because you can "apply" biological methods wherever you think anything interesting will come of such application; and you have no logical limits; you would allow another man to treat just those same things physically, if he wanted to, or anthropologically, or common-sensibly. Whereas I cannot thus divorce the "things" from the "method of treatment": I think that the application of biological methods is possible only with a correlated biological subject-matter, and that if you try to apply physical methods to the same mass of data you inevitably transform those data and so get in reality a different mass or set.

So your /first/ question is: Here are such-and-such data; how can I best treat them? And my /first/ question is: Here are such-and-such data; how must they already have been treated to appear such-and-such?

Where you, for instance, find naked facts, waiting to be treated, I may find (as has happened in our correspondence) very-much-worked-over affairs bearing all the ear-marks of common- sense interpretation upon them, — nothing naked at all, but something very definitely clothed.

So you would start out with

GIVEN OBJECTS = FACTS	waiting to be dealt with by SCIENTIFIC METHODS,
while I start out with WORKED-OVER OBJECTS	waiting to be variously transformed (stripped, unclothed, shown in their various naked aspects) by SCIENTIFIC METHOD as applied from VARIOUS POINTS OF VIEW

If this is true, I can understand how your use of FACT should differ so immensely from mine. You find FACTS as things given; I get them only by a long process of excavating (so to say), and so regard them as the very antipodes of things given.

Yours sincerely,
E. B. Titchener

37 M [M 13]

May 29, 1918

My dear Titchener,

There is no doubt about the importance of the different way we look at the data to be investigated. I cannot help feeling mystified by any efforts to throw suspicion on our capacity to find "the facts as they are" sufficiently well to avoid errors and false identifications. Whether I would call the facts naked facts is of course a question: I should rather speak of facts open to as much investigation as anybody wants to apply to them, and instead of suspecting at the outset any common-sense interpretation that may be involved, I would take exactly the reverse attitude, namely, that of confidence until the contrary is proved. Therefore the given objects are facts awaiting to be dealt with by scientific methods, first by being formulated with a denominator which the facts share with the scientific methods in question. I believe that this formulation is not essentially different from what you call more drastically, "transformed, stripped, unclothed, shown in their various naked aspects." I am perfectly willing to speak of "crude facts," but I cannot look upon them as necessarily viciously worked over. They may be worked over in a way that makes them unfit for work, /but/ to get them /"fit"/ I have to formulate them or, to use another expression, to get out of the crude material those points and principles which are workable.

Your running the objects and the investigating mind together is in keeping with strong tendencies such as the one represented by Avenarius and by certain philosophizing physicists and by those who shrink from materialism and want to pay their due respects to idealism without transcending the two. The result has been the production of /a/ philosophy that doesn't quite want to face itself. It turns, after all, on epistemological assumptions and the only thing to do is to face them squarely and I do it by using critical common sense as the best starting point at our disposal.

Don't you think that your attitude concerning epistemology and philosophy is born of the dissatisfaction with the various existing efforts and a pragmatic determination to let the philosophic problem be solved by the experience with your life work /(just as I do with my interests in biology, neurology, phys. & psychol.)/ rather than the other way around? /Why the fear of the reality of the outside world?/

It may be that this leads us again to old difficulties, but it seems to me that the only thing to do is to meet them squarely where we find them.

In reading over your first chapter in the Beginner's Psychology with Mrs. Meyer, I found her as a rule sympathetic with your critical remarks about common sense but in the end at sea with regard to the actual position to be assumed. My own attitude, on the other hand, is the conviction of common sense and the feeling that unless that is understood we had best be resigned to blundering along, which evidently my own constitution does not allow me to do.

I dictated these remarks rather hastily on the receipt of your letter because it may help in the further discussion of my last letter.

Believe me

Very truly yours,
Adolf Meyer

38 T [T 11]

June 2, 1918

Dear Meyer,

It was very good of Mrs. Meyer to serve as Versuchsperson,[1] — and good of you too to be sufficiently interested to make her interested. I think that the result of the little experiment is all that I could wish. You say that (1) she sympathises with some of my remarks on common sense. That is first-rate; for I have waked her up to the realisation that common sense is not necessarily the last word upon things. You say (2) that she is after all at sea as regards the position I want assumed. Well, is not that result foreseen and accounted for in {S} 8?[2] Given a set of attitudes and beliefs that have persisted unchallenged into middle life: and given now a sharp affirmation that that set of attitudes and beliefs is not final: what more can one expect than that the reader, recognising that there is justice in the affirmation, shall be all at sea as regards the new set of attitudes and beliefs that are to be superimposed upon, and in part substituted for, the old? If Mrs. Meyer (for the book is a text-book) would now read the introduction and the following chapters with such repetition and seriousness as should enable her to pass a college examination in them: and if she should concomitantly answer the questions appended to the chapters in such wise as to obtain again a college passing-mark upon them: isn't there a probability that she would get some sort of grip upon the new position? Not so easily, of course, as the beginner; because the beginner is malleable, and comes to a class expecting to be taught and to accept what he is taught; but still with the effort made I see no reason why the grip should not be taken. So I think I may be satisfied! — though I need not say that we should neither of us accept as final the result of such a single test upon a single individual.

So that part of your letter doesn't bother me. But another part does, because in it you seem to me to slip right back into the very first stage of our discussion. You pencil in the sentence: "why the fear of the reality of the outside world?" Such a remark, at this stage, is somewhat astonishing. For

(1) I have no fear of the reality of anything.

(2) If you are talking philosophy, I have said that any systematic philosophy, idealism or realism, is able (and welcome) to swallow me whole.

(3) If you are talking science, I have said over and over that the three typical sciences, one and all alike, deal with existence; and I don't know of anything more real than that.

I don't want to give up; but it seems to me that we are not making headway. There is hardly a sentence in your last brief letter that I can admit as touching my position. Thus, as regards the "discovery" of facts, I should have thought that the whole history of civilisation is with me. If facts are lying round for common sense to pick up, why did science develop so slowly? Why did Aristotle, the incarnation of common sense, not inaugurate what we know as science? Why did we have to wait until the "modern" period for physics, and chemistry, and physiology? Common sense was as strong and active B.C. as it has ever been since; and yet the sciences are modern developments. My position is that it was only when common sense saw its own weakness, and was willing to have recourse to experiment in the control of observation, that science became possible. — Moreover, if facts are so obvious and detached and accessible, why are they so much debated and disputed in current science? If you can get all the facts you want for the mere taking of them, why do all the universities, and all the leading men of science, lay so much stress on the cultivating of powers of observation? Why do we need to train our students to make observations? — Suppose you found a flint, chipped in the shape of an arrow head. Your attitude is to say: This is a natural specimen, until somebody can prove to me that human hands have touched it! My attitude is that the shape is a positive presumption in favor of human workmanship. And in the case of ideas, the evidence of past workmanship is far more obvious and far less escapeable than it is in the case of flints. Your position, if strictly carried through, negates the witness of history and especially the witness of the history of language. But all this is old ground between us. — You make me say "viciously worked over." I have never used that adverb. Common sense has done good service in the struggle for existence, and I have also admitted that positivism is a respectable philosophical position. I have said that c.s. is different from science; that c.s. deals with meanings and science with facts; but I have never said that c.s. did anything viciously. Even where I differ from a c.s.-philosophy (as in the case of Aristotle markedly) I have in the same breath admitted the service of that philosophy to civilisation. — You try to explain me by assuming that I am producing a philosophy that doesn't quite want to face itself. That thought may be comforting to you; but it can hardly touch me, since I have repeatedly said that my aim is to demarcate science, and to do this in such a way that any of the large philosophies can accept my demarcation. If you can prove that my position is incompatible with any one of the typical philosophies, well and good: then I should have to consider whether I should (a) accept the compatible philosophy or (b) alter my position. But meantime the mere statement doesn't touch me, because I know of no arguments for it and have a great deal of evidence against.

I have given you my position, in detail, in several phrasings, in tables. You have never given me yours. When I asked you to define "integration," you threw back the task on me. When I have asked for definitions of "critical" and "common sense," I haven't got them. I have made various attempts to characterise your position for you: I have suggested a fundamental positivism, a scientific-technological blend that preferred not to define rigorously, a classification by objects, an assumed independence of fact from method, and so forth. In reply, you attack these proposals of mine as if I were making them on my behalf. What I have done, is to do my best to get a formulation of your position — a formulation which you, I think, owe me, but which you have never given. For myself, I am not a positivist in science, I do not believe in mixing science and technology. I do not classify by objects, I do not regard fact as independent of method. In attributing these positions, one after another, to you, I have been trying to grope my way towards understanding you; your denial of them I of course accept; but why you should deny them, when your writing suggests them, I still don't know! If "crude fact" (your phrase, and never mine) isn't positivistic, I don't know what is! I had as soon talk of a virtuous carpet.

I come back therefore to a position already stated. You have every right in the world to work as you please, with what terms you please, in whatever universe you please. But if you challenge discussion, then you must define your terms, and delimit your universe. Otherwise the discussion is fruitless. What is your criterion of "critical?" How do you know that a given statement is critically justified and another not? What are your standards of test? — What do you mean by common sense? Is it an interpretative or a descriptive system or both? In any case what are its methods and canons? — And so on. All these questions you have left me to answer for you!

Yours sincerely,
E. B. Titchener

1. Versuchsperson = experimental subject.
2. Titchener, *Beginner's Psychology*, 34–36.

39 M

June 6, 1918

My dear Titchener,

I am sorry that my last letter should have side-tracked the discussion from the questions of my letter of May 23 [35M]. I therefore want to take up directly your questions on pp. 3 and 4 of your last letter and formulate the definitions you want.

Critical common-sense accepts the medium of human thought and verbal formulation as a system of symbols or rather as systems of symbols in which we can formulate in shorthand the carefully selected fundamental facts and happenings of the existential world, in terms of the fundamental "experiments of nature." Critical common sense subordinates the logic of words and symbols to the most economically chosen systems of facts, carefully and critically chosen, controlled by experiment, and tried by modifications for a maximal consistency of the facts and the terms accepted in the formulation.

In distinction from your viewpoint, critical common sense, as I said in M12 (May 23) [35M] p.2, (4), maintains one consistent objective viewpoint, even for the mentally or consciously integrated psychobiological functions; without excluding the facts the individual can make objectively observable in himself; and it has but one existential universe and recognizes in it facts integrated in systems of functions of things. What I mean by things and functions is stated at the foot of p. 3 and on p. 4. We find them and formulate them by methods, but the facts are there even without our methods; they occur sometimes practically in pure culture; but the clever observer is the one who can give the facts a setting in which they are as economically presented as possible and as clearly as possible in pure culture.

It was common sense that took the step from Aristotle to the Baconian and present-day attitude concerning the relation of the logic of words and the logic or system of facts and thereby it became critical common sense.

My definitions are /or aim to be/ rigorous but not necessarily /absolutely/ limiting.

My classifications are by objects and functional topics; "independence of fact from method" is not a specific demand, but clear in the sense stated above. This should suffice to make unnecessary the claim that "we can get all the facts we want for the mere taking of them," or a negation of the witness of history and of the history of language.

Now the concept of integration. It takes the place of your universes, and makes them objective instead of pseudo-subjective. The one existential universe presents systems of integration irrespective of the onlooker (See p. 1 (1) of my letter of May 23, — M12 [35M]), and it does justice to wholes and to parts, to correlations of facts entering into various systems, to classification of objects, functions, facts and methods, capable of rigorous definition.

For my formulation, I have referred to my reprint on Objective Psychology, my refutation of Moebius's Hopelessness of All Psychology (Psychological Bulletin, 1907) and my review of the Specht Journal in 1912.

If I denied the positions you attribute to me, it is because you take them over into your system, or you use them in the light of your multiple viewpoints without translating them and without accepting the essential starting points — one viewpoint, one universe and various systems of differently integrated facts.

The question is whether with this simple formulation we can do justice to the world as it is and as we find it, and that without creating a whole science dealing with facts outside of the pale of causal relationships. Unlike Watson, I have all due respect for the results of your special working scheme. I can translate them easily into my field as far as they go; but I refuse to accept the classification as technology for many facts and problems which you are forced to treat as such. The continual reference to "sets" and other neurologizing inferences are replaced by me in terms of reaction-tendencies, just as you speak of association-tendencies; and I am convinced that they cannot be reached neurologically but require correlations of studies of what I term full-fledged activity rather than studies of correlation in terms of neurologizing tautologies.

I hope that with the articles referred to and with this very brief formulation, my standpoint may be clearer.

Your viewpoint obviously construes a very different philosophy. Mine deviates less from the common sense of the average man working in science; it appears to me simpler and as far as I can see, it is clear without having to exclude or pass on from science to science conscientiously collected experience of dynamic functions of psychobiological character; and without the rather confusing stigmatizing of "meaning" and "explanation."

The last questions of your letter might very succinctly be answered as follows:

How do I know that a given statement is critically justified and another not? Essentially on ground of strictly obligatory experimental or experiential test.

Common sense is the unitary conception of the world as opposed to the building up of as many universes as there may be different conceptions or sciences. It is primarily and fundamentally descriptive, but includes in the description and experimental formulation situations which the human being legitimately looks for when in need of interpretation and explanation and formulation of "nature's experiments."

The methods and canons? Observation, analysis, modification and reproduction of the experiments.

Don't you feel after all, — in all seriousness — that these discussions have not been fruitless? I do not want to be lazy in the work entailed. I really am anxious to do my share, and I hope I come nearer your demands in this letter.

Very truly yours,
Adolf Meyer

40 T

June 19, 1918

[Postcard]
I have been busy with special work, and have had no time for writing. Next week I hope to send a response to your last!

E. B. T.

41 T

October 28, 1918

Dear Meyer,

I owe you an explanation, if not an apology, for this long silence. My memory is that I sent you a card in the early summer, to say that I was just entering on a special bit of work that would probably occupy me entirely for a couple of weeks. It took longer, as is usual. Then I had family occupations and preoccupations which kept me away from work altogether for a while. After that period I had yet another bit of special work, which absorbed yet more weeks. And when that was done the troubles of preparation for term — a most anxious and time-taking job under present conditions — were upon me.[1] Since term opened I have hardly been able to call my soul (if I have one) my own.

I do not see much spare time ahead till after Christmas, and I want to give to my book all the spare time possible. Whether we should gain anything by resumption of our technical correspondence I don't know; but I am very willing to make a new start in the winter, if you think it worth while. I have the general impression that we have got about as far as we can, until I have published my views in full and you have furnished your promised definitions: and it is very likely that my book will give you the impulse either to formulate these definitions by way of antagonism, or to state in definite form the points at which your vision diverges from mine. So far we have, I think been arguing largely alongside of each other and not point to point.

Yours sincerely,
E. B. Titchener

1. During the war Titchener—like Meyer—lost most of his graduate students and junior faculty to the war effort and had to take a heavier teaching load.

42 M

October 31, 1918

My dear Titchener,

I appreciate your note of October 28 [41T]. I saw Sanford this summer and he told me of your being very busy. I fully understand that you might well wish to formulate your standpoint fully in connection with your book. On the other hand, I had hoped that possibly our discussion might mature to the point where our respective points of view could receive a discussion prior to the final formulation of the book which could bring us and the student of these problems just one step further along. It seems to me that the two methods of procedure have enough in common with each other when one comes to actual work and it is a pity that there should be appearances of antagonism where there are mainly divergences of the line of attack. The difference is one of a difference of philosophical point of view and one of scope of the problems that one actually wants to draw within one's research. You put a strong emphasis on correlations with neurological facts and /I/, just because I am working personally in the neurological field, consider the structural application very premature and prefer to fall back upon the physiological-biological data and come over to a ground such as Woodworth works on in his Dynamic Psychology.[1]

Somehow I seem to be constitutionally averse to thinking in terms of antagonisms and hungry for common ground, and that undoubtedly will be in work more readily than in the philosophical or systematic deductions.

We also are under great pressure, but at last it looks as if there were a let-up in sight and as if a degree of happiness and peace of mind could return to us.

Believe me

Very sincerely yours,
Adolf Meyer

1. Robert Sessions Woodworth (1869–1962), American psychologist, after studying psychology with James at Harvard University and with Cattell at Columbia University, was professor of psychology at Columbia University from 1903 to 1942. In his *Dynamic Psychology* (New York, 1918), Woodworth adopted a functional approach in psychology in opposition to Titchener's structuralism and Watson's behaviorism.

43 T

November 2, 1918

Dear Meyer,

Your patience and friendliness invite strongly to continuation. I wish I could feel it would be any good. But in proportion as you find me strict and pedantic do I find you elusive and intangible. I do not see any positive outcome.

I read your letter with assent till I came to the sentence: "The difference is one of a difference of philosophical point of view . . . ." Then I had a sharp negative reaction. "It is not! I have told him several times that my attitude to science is compatible with <u>any</u> philosophy — idealism, pragmatism, realism, positivism, or whatever isms there may be." But then I thought: "Yes, — but then he doesn't use the term 'philosophy' as I do. He means by philosophy any largish attitude to any general subject — to science, to religion, to art, to the war, and so on." And then I thought again: "But if I say that to him, he will reply that that isn't quite what he meant by the term. But I shall not be able to get any clear formulation of what exactly he did mean by it."

I have written that out because I think it is typical of the course of our arguments so far. I insist that Ideas must be razor-sharp. I don't at all mind being wrong, provided only I am clear. To be <u>clearly</u> wrong is about the biggest service the individual may render to the cause of Thought at large. You insist that Ideas must be flexible, loose-edged, geared with a lot of play in the gearing. You hope, if only you are thus empirically flexible, that somewhere in the loose running of your Ideas you will strike what is right. To be right, even in the midst of muddle, is (I take it) your notion of the biggest service an individual may render to the same cause. If I interpret you aright (and I am always doubtful about that), our aims and ideals will never square.

And even at this date you can refer me to Woodworth's "Dynamic Psychology," as if you didn't know that for me "dynamic" and "psychology" are impossible of joining! Woodworth himself gives away his case on p. 35: his point of view is that of present-day common sense and of the British theorists of knowledge!![1] But please-God we have now a Science that is neither common-sense nor epistemological; and please-God we have also the power to follow the method of this science in dealing with Psychology. In so far as Woodworth is true to his acknowledged principles, Psychology drops out of sight altogether, and we are left with the views of common sense and of empirical epistemologists. What would there be of Physics, if we followed the same course, — if we took the views of the man in the street and of philosophers who wrote some centuries before a scientific physics had arisen!?

The exasperation of this question is due to my being as willing as possible to meet you half-way, and to my having a countervailing conviction that we shall never by this means get anywhere. I wish to goodness I saw a way out, but I don't. Only don't attribute any antagonism to me. I feel not the least antagonism to Woodworth or anybody; I read them with interest and try to understand them; and if I find them muddled, I classify them with other representatives of like muddle, as nearly as I can, and always dispassionately. They do the best they can, and I do the best I can; and I don't feel the least bit of antagonism against a man because I heartily disagree with him. Dodge[2] once staggered me by saying that science is about as personal a thing as there is in life to a man; and I can account for that utterance only on the ground that the American is unused to criticism and so, when it comes, takes it personally. That is certainly not our way. A recent English cyclopedia-article on psychology devotes a good deal of its space to pulverising me; and I was so naively pleased at the author's attention that I sent the offprint across to my Mother, — feeling that the old lady would like to see her son made so much of!! It never occurred to me to regard the writer as a personal antagonist.

I fear that we had better await the book. Then you will have something coherent as well as positive before you. Meantime, if you will reread Woodworth and ask for definitions of all his terms as you proceed, you will probably be less ready to endorse him!

Yours,
E. B. Titchener

1. On p. 35 of his *Dynamic Psychology*, Woodworth identifies his "dynamic" psychology with the commonsense point of view "but also the point of view that is most in evidence in the history of psychology." As examples he cites John Locke, George Berkeley, and David Hume, whom Titchener refers to above as "the British theorists of knowledge."

2. Raymond Dodge (1871–1942), American psychologist first at Wesleyan and later at Yale, was the first to criticize Titchener publicly for the "exclusiveness" of his system.

44 M

November 5, 1918

Dear Titchener,

All right — let it be so. Putting your statement into my terms, you mean to assure me that you have the conception of science; that you can afford to disown all responsibility for what must be classed as philosophical frame, as long as your own "Science itself" is neither common-sense nor epistemological. For the rest I may give you credit, then, when we come to the broader settings, for being "clearly wrong," and I may find your picture of my "open definitions" a muddle, because you refuse to pay attention to the epistemological and philosophical moorings. I suppose the attempt to go half-way instead of taking each position on its own ground, accounts for the failure of clearness in your eyes. I frankly admit that you have so trimmed the world of fact that it is easier to maintain an artificial clearness; and if you wish to use the term muddle for the broader formulation, I suppose I have to accept the fact as an expression of your own personal blur due to constriction of the field of vision.

In the meantime let us work on the respective books and formulation.

I see that Krueger[1] has become Wundt's successor. The passing of Wundt marks an interesting epoch. Will the next epoch be biological psychology or a new edition of exclusive salvation of the Geisteswissenschaften[2] with a new camouflage of parallelism? I personally trust the problems of a biological psychology as one of the "natural sciences" with replacement of the parallelism and its substitutes by the concept of integrative levels. I call it critical common-sense (not merely the views of the man in the street) with a philosophical frame very different from that of the systems to which you devoted the five years of philosophical study to which you once referred.

Woodworth may lay himself open to many criticisms and does not reach the ideal (and that because the Cattell school, as I put it in my review of Well's "Mental Adjustments" in Science,[3] has never had the courage to formulate its philosophy); but the little book is rather refreshing. The emphasis rests on what he quotes from Cattell on p.30,[4] and what he quotes on p.35 need not cause any muddle.

I am very much delighted over the great progress made in Europe. Our ranks may soon be repopulated with workers and there may be more time again for vigorous construction.

With my best wishes,

Yours sincerely,
Adolf Meyer

1. Felix Krüger (1874–1948), German psychologist, succeeded Wilhelm Wundt at Leipzig in 1917. He established the Leipzig Gestalt school of psychology, a holistic psychology, influenced by *Geisteswissenschaft*, which became a significant school of psychology in Germany after the First World War.

2. Geisteswissenschaften = human sciences or human studies.

3. Adolf Meyer, review of Frederick Lyman Wells, *Mental Adjustments* (1917), *Science* 46, n.s. (1917): 587–88.

4. On p. 30, Woodworth quoted Cattell as stating in 1904: "'I am convinced that psychology should be limited to the study of consciousness as such . . . . There is no conflict between introspective analysis and objective experiment—on the contrary, they should and do continually cooperate. But the rather widespread notion that there is no psychology apart from introspection is refuted by the brute argument of accomplished fact. It seems to me that most of the research work that has been done by me or in my laboratory is nearly as independent of introspection as work in physics and zoology'" (*Dynamic Psychology*, 30).

45 T

November 7, 1918

Dear Meyer,

You have been so patient and so earnest in this correspondence that I shall be very heartily sorry if it ends on a note of acrimony. I have always had a high respect for your work, and felt personally drawn to you even at our first meeting at Worcester. It is true that I propose now to interrupt the correspondence for a time. It needed a little "moral courage," as they say, to take this step, and I am sorry to take it. But it is my sincere belief that we have got as far as we can for the present, and so I say — Let us stop for a while. If my book urges you to further expression, or if you meanwhile publish something that gives me a definite hand-hold, well and good: we can, if you are willing, try again.

But I do not want to end on this personal note. I will once more recite my Credo in brief form.

(1) I think that Science deals with existential experience from the three methodologically different points of view of physics, biology, psychology. The Fact, a matter of direct acquaintance-with, I regard as scientifically ultimate. The System of science I take to be built of nothing more than facts and logic. Hence I consider science to be independent of Philosophy. Any philosophical system, on the other hand, must, if it is to satisfy, take account in equal measure of the three scientific systems. Hence Philosophy is not independent of Science.

(2) Outside of science I find that men recognise Values. Apparently these values are taken by these men to be no less ultimate for axiological systems than facts are for science; and apparently there are different classes of values (as in science there are three classes of facts) which appear from methodologically different points of view. I am ready to accept these conclusions, and the resulting systems of values. I regard all such value-systems as independent of Philosophy. Any satisfactory philosophy, however, must take account, in equal measure, of the various value-disciplines. Hence philosophy is not independent of Axiology.

(3) Beside Science and Axiology I find mixed aggregates of knowledge and precept, held together by a Purpose, which I call collectively Technologies. There seem to be technologies roughly correlated with value-disciplines, as there certainly are technologies roughly correlated with sciences. I am concerned primarily with those that correlate with sciences. The interrelations are extremely complex. Common to all such technologies, however, — for the obvious reason that they aim to "get things done," — is an ultimate recourse to physical energies. The physical technologies work directly with energy; the "biological" technologies work at one logical remove, and the "psychological" technologies work at two logical removes, from physical energetics. Misunderstanding on this point is, I believe, responsible for the controversy of mechanism vs. vital-

ism in biology, and of parallelism vs. interactionism in psychology. I can thus understand how those controversies arose, and why they survive. Personally, I regard them as transcended.

(4) Philosophy begins, I think, as the great universal technology of Common Sense, the Art of Living. I regard the Aristotelian system as typical; it is at once a cyclopedia and a sublimation of Common Sense. Facts and Values were at first undifferentiated within this vast technology. As they have become differentiated, the various philosophical systems have naturally tried to cover and include them. But a satisfactory philosophy must take account of all the sciences, of all the value-disciplines, and of all the technologies: not in detail, but nevertheless adequately, so that there is no loose end left over. It must both legitimate distinctions and transcend them.

I cannot assure myself that this task has as yet been satisfactorily performed, or even that the existing systems promise its satisfactory performance. Hence I cannot as yet commit myself to any existing philosophical system.

(5) All this scaffolding I have worked out in the interest of my scientific work within Psychology. When I began to "profess" psychology, I found that I did not know what a science was, or in what sense psychology was a science, or how a science was related to its "applications." The greatest obstacle to my thinking on these and cognate questions has been (in myself and in others) what I have called "muddle," — a lack of strict usage following on strict definition, and the presence of vague fringes of implication never made explicit. I am not sure that the clearest thinking will ever be adequate to the universe; but I am very sure that muddy thinking cannot be. And sad experience has taught me that my own training and that of many of my contemporaries did not insist on clear thinking. So I am trying to be so far clear as that those who read me later on will be able to accept or reject with full understanding of what it is they are accepting or rejecting. No doubt, the attempt is aimed too high: let us call it rather an ideal.

(6) I hope, as I suppose we all do, that something of my constructive work will stand the test of time; and when a man crosses my field I am very happy to match logics with him and to test my own ideas by his. But I have changed so much that I can't feel antagonistic to a difference of opinion, and I certainly have never tried to proselytise. The synthesis that I look forward to will take, I believe, some centuries to accomplish, and meantime I would let every man go his own way, checked only by the logic of his critics.

If you care to send me a similar confession of faith, please do, — and if not, let us end at this point amicably. Our remote grandchildren will be better equipped for agreement than two men of this generation can possibly be!

Yours sincerely,
E. B. Titchener

Just as I was ending up a friend telephoned that the Germans have accepted the terms of our armistice. May it be true news! I have suffered too much by this war (what English family hasn't?) to want to talk about it. But we have come through better than many. My son was all right, except for a slight gassing, on Oct. 1; and my mother has pulled through without bodily injury, though she has been in the air-raid zone all along. I hope we make peace either in Brussels or in Berlin.

46 M[1]

November 12, 1918

My dear Titchener,

You may rest assured that there is no feeling of acrimony about the evidently more or less urgent suspense of discussion, and in the somewhat drastic response of my last letter.

The Credo of your letter of November 7, '18 [45T], is a helpful summary and in part a further development of part of our discussions. I shall try to formulate my standpoint in a similar program.

1. As a worker in neuropsychiatry and in my comparative work, I have had to face the question whether there is a sharp line of demarcation between the strict fundamental "sciences" and their application and between the sciences and trained critical common sense. I have come to a standpoint which sees no absolute contrasts.

It is not the point of view, but the material of investigation and the way it behaves and presents itself to the worker and the problems it brings up that constitute any special domain of science.

There is but one realm of natural science /including everything of any dynamic nature/ —sets and combinations of facts (things and functions and relations) which could stand out distinctly even if the last scientist were wiped out. /Each/ set has its common links with every other set, so that their correlation and comparison does not call for a /fundamental/ change of point of view of the observer, but only for the recognition and acceptance of special objective conditions and functional relations. /The reduction of the facts to the simplest types & the demonstration of their principles of relations/ is a matter of objective work, not of viewpoint. In other words, the viewpoint theory is more psychologizing than is called for by the facts and therefore apt to be a personal variation rather than a generally desirable type of science.

The strict sciences are systematized presentations of the principles presented by bodies of facts (objects and their functions and relations with due logical consideration of the relations between these facts and the verbal or symbolic formulations), chosen /for/ maximal /clearness/ economy and simplicity /& studied for their interrelations/. They are not different in principle from the less economically than practically chosen facts and problems of applied science.

There is an option between starting from objective material such as exists irrespective of the personal observer, and from the data which the personal observer finds in himself /such as Mach's objectivizing type of scientific formulations/. I choose the objective attitude, with the assumption that the Berkeleyan evasion of this objective world has no fundamental weight, and that the common-sense attitude is safer as long as we insist on experimental formulation and demonstration as the essential feature /and obligatory test /of our procedure.

Therefore, while Science is organized experience, I am not so much concerned with the "experience" as with the facts experienced. The experience and its symbolic formulation is a help in the process of systemization; but the substance of the Sciences is the aggregate of concrete experiments and their best formulation is the demonstration of the /types of/ interrelations irrespective of the "state of mind" of the investigator. The substantial part is the concrete experiment and its relation to the fundamental experiments of the same and other groups of facts.

The types and principles of fundamental experiments determine the existence of more or less contrasting "sciences." Of these, the principle of economy of thinking and working has led us to recognize a variable number, according to whether we include only the fundamental detachable types of experiments and facts, or give groups of non-detachable facts independent positions. I am thinking, e.g. of such a field as the special type of facts spoken of as contents and data of consciousness /as experienced by introspection/, or to [*sic*, of?] such problems as that of fluidity, etc. — which of course may command our attention but which may be of subordinate and not fundamental interest. The question is whether in the arrangement of fundamental experiments we do not after all start with necessity from units better handled and worked over with a more generally accessible common denominator /—such as the psychobiologically integrated organism in action./

The types of fact presenting themselves and the methods of study involved in working with the facts determine the type and number of our sciences. It is the common principle or denominator / and the special set/ of the objective facts and events that appear to me /to determine/ the best criterion of independent sciences.

There is but one world of existential facts and relations, and many groups /of integrations worth keeping apart/. It is the kind of objective criteria of the groupings that marks off the sciences; it is not the "point of view" of the observer that is used. There is no dominant and fundamental call for a detailed consideration in terms of physics and biology and psychology of every fact and relation of the existential world, such as is suggested by your three viewpoints of existential experience.

There is one /existential/ world and one type of /scientific/ experience worth opposing logically. What constitutes physics, biology or psychology is determined as much by the type of thing, fact and relation as by the mode of accessibility in experience, and science is established when the experience is so formulated that it is the potential experience of any one sufficiently trained and critical. I should not study the physics of circles and the psychology of sulphur. Physics consists of a certain range of methods applicable in a certain range of combinations /or interrelations/ of objects. Only a limited number of such combinations form a topic of biological study and still a smaller one of psychological study. On the other hand, logical study embraces the symbolic data covering any type of fact, etc.

I doubt whether I should make a study of values a fundamental discipline. And I doubt whether the existence of a potential purpose in a system of fact (such as a temporally serial system or sequence of cause and effect) would necessarily establish a new category calling for the term technology. The mechanism vs. vitalism and parallelism vs. interaction controversies are transcended in my viewpoint. Philosophy may be viewed as a technology; to my mind it is largely the theory of systematization.

If now I come to psychology, I may remain uncertain as to what you mean by the term. There is undoubtedly an interesting fact to be noted; namely, that it deals with facts part of which are essential for all science, — for science or experience is a function of our psychobiological capacities, — and part of which is formed by the data of introspection as contrasted with the data of direct objective accessibility to any one sufficiently trained. These two facts for a period led to the psychologizing even of non-psychological science in the sense of Mach and others. But the attitude of a practical realism is certainly reasserting itself vigorously and it is, I believe, quite conceivable that as the Ptolemaic view of the world yielded to the Copernican view, so the anthropomorphic conception of science with its subjectivism is yielding more radically to the objectivism sketched above. To this end, it is not necessary "to spill the child with the bath" as was done by materialism and lately by Watson. It is, I am convinced, perfectly compatible with objectivism to include self-observation as far as it can gain objective corroboration.

As far as "muddle" is concerned, I feel free from it, but see it arise when my presentations are considered with the astigmatic distortions of the outspoken or disguised parallelist and the dualistic interactionist, or by the methodological trinitarian I see in you. To obviate the incompatibility of the structural, the physiological and the psychobiological series of facts, and the implications of a spiritualistic and animistic common sense, I urge a consistent and elastic integrationism. Like every other view, it has got to be experienced and assimilated in one's ordinary and critical thought-habits. It has many interesting philosophical and logical implications, the most important of which is that it is freely open to dynamic conceptions, indeed that it favors an essential dynamic (energetic) point of view, akin to voluntarism but really better described as actualism or activism.

Any one who is afraid of a frank consideration of integration will consider my views "muddled." To me <u>your</u> system has merely an artificial clearness and it lacks the fundamental tenability and applicability that a sensible observer of the facts as they are has a right to ask for.

Your psychology may "teach" well; but I doubt whether it is heuristically fertile beyond what it has done in the last 30 years.

For a critique of your position I should have to attack a number of points such as your view of philosophy, your view of the essential character of axiology, your trinitarian division of science, etc. When your book is out, I may feel tempted to do it so as to explain the contrast of our positions.

I certainly appreciate your patience as well. I feel I can get a clearer view of your structure than you can of mine. Mine presupposes a wider experience and willingness to be concerned with many matters categorically excluded by you from your restricted fields of vision. Time will judge whether I shall get my viewpoint "across" with a growing number of workers or not. Whatever may happen, I shall, I hope, not cease to have an interest in the views and ventures of others.

With my warm appreciation, I remain,

Yours sincerely,
Adolf Meyer

1. This letter was not sent (see 47M).

47 M

December 22, 1918

My dear Titchener,

A slight hesitation about sending you a good long letter Nov. 12 [46M], because Mrs. Meyer said it was a repetition of criticisms and not a simple credo such as you asked for — that is what has apparently put a temporary /end/ to our discussion. Perfectionism! I finally concluded to or rather was forced to /wait, but I hope I may get back to the topic again and do what you ask for.

In the meantime I want to send you my wishes of the season and my thanks for your discussions. I am trying now to reach some friendly opponents to get them to bombard me with point-blank questions /(for information and definitions)/ about my view-point. To make it profitable it naturally must be done taking for the time the attitude of wanting to accept my stand-point and then pointing to the difficulties. Your antifunctional attitude nips the discussion in the bud. It might be that a discussion limited to the reasons why a functional attitude should be discarded would draw out the crucial points. I maintain the obligation of a functional conception for anything that has any /claim to obligatory/ dynamic actuality and practicality & that the fact of ultradynamic or extradynamic (logical) features does not take the psychobiological reactions out of the dynamic or potentially dynamic class. As long as they are studied as activities and attitudes of living organisms they are functional problems.

I hope you will be in Baltimore for the meeting.[1] I shall certainly hope to see you.

Very sincerely yours,
Adolf Meyer

1. Apparently the annual meeting of the American Psychological Association.

Appendix: Tabulation of Letters

T = Titchener Papers
M = Meyer Papers
O = Original
C = Carbon
Draft = Handwritten draft

Number	Original		Carbon	Typed	Xerox		Draft
	T	M			O	C	
1 M	x			x	x		
2 T				x	x		
3 M	x			x	x		
4 T				x	x		
5 M				x		x	
6 T				x	x		
7 M			x			x	
8 M						x	
9 T				x	x		
10 T				x	x		
11 T				x	x		
12 M				x		x	
13 T				x	x		
14 M	x			x	x		
15 M	x			x	x		
16 T				x	x		
17 M				x		x	
18 T				x	x		
19 M	x		x		x		x
20 T		x			x		
21 M	x		x		x		

(*continued*)

Number	Original		Carbon	Typed	Xerox		Draft
	T	M			O	C	
22 T		x			x		
23 M	x		x		x		
24 T		x			x		
25 M	x		x		x		
26 M	x		x		x		
27 T		x			x		
28 M	x		x		x		
29 T		x			x		
30 M	x		x		x		x
31 M	x		x		x		x
32 T		x			x		
33 M	x		x		x		
34 T		x			x		
35 M	x		x		x		
36 T		x			x		
37 M	x		x		x		
38 T		x			x		
39 M	x		x		x		
40 T		x			x		
41 T		x			x		
42 M	x		x		x		
43 T		x			x		
44 M	x		x		x		x
45 T		x			x		
46 M			x		x		
47 M	x				x		x

Index

Designed by Martha Farlow

Composed by The Composing Room of Michigan, Inc., in Bookman
and Stempel Schadow Bold Italic

Printed by Thomson-Shore, Inc., on 50-lb Glatfelter B-16 and bound
in Joanna Kennett

LIBRARY OF CONGRESS CATALOGING-IN-PUBLICATION DATA

Meyer, Adolf, 1866–1950.

Defining American psychology : the correspondence between Adolf Meyer and Edward Bradford Titchener / edited by Ruth Leys and Rand B. Evans.

p. cm.

Bibliography: p.

Includes index.

ISBN 0-8018-3865-7 (alk. paper)

1. Meyer, Adolf, 1866–1950—Correspondence. 2. Titchener, Edward Bradford, 1867–1927—Correspondence. 3. Psychologists—United States—Correspondence. 4. Psychology—Philosophy. 5. Psychology—Methodology. I. Titchener, Edward Bradford, 1867–1927. II. Leys, Ruth. III. Evans, Rand B. IV. Title.

BF109.M49H4 1990

150′.973—dc20 89-33535 CIP